NEPALESE
TEXTILES

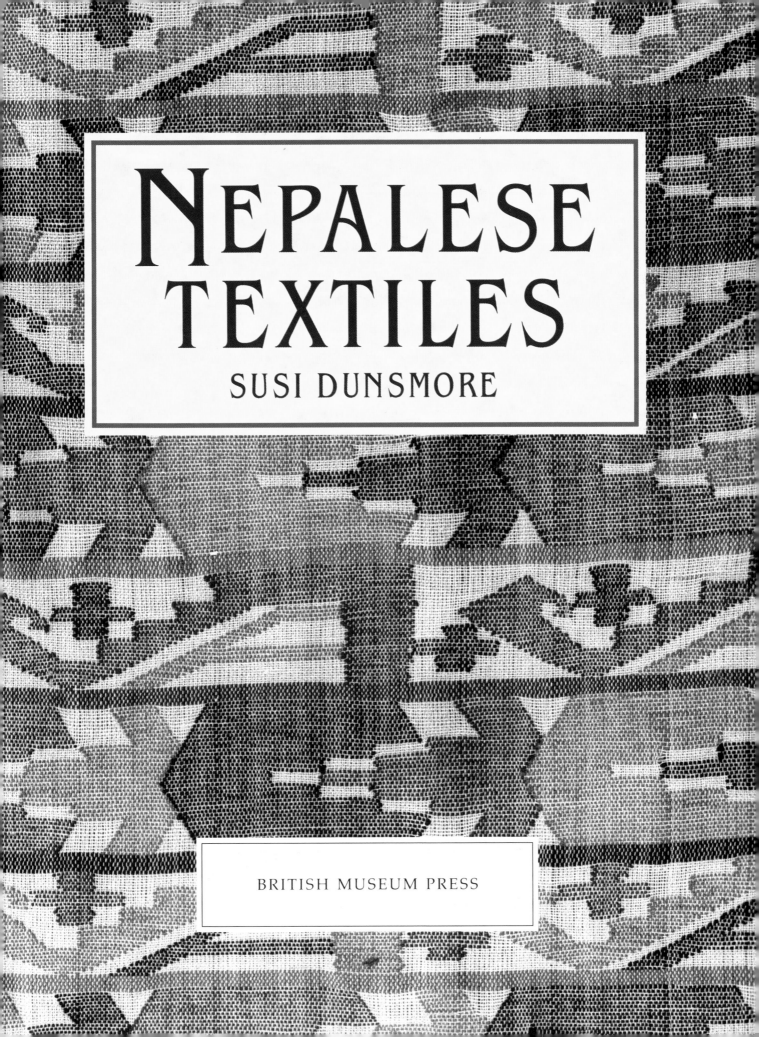

NEPALESE TEXTILES

SUSI DUNSMORE

BRITISH MUSEUM PRESS

© 1993 Susi Dunsmore
Published by British Museum Press
A division of British Museum Publications Ltd
46 Bloomsbury Street
London WC1B 3QQ

ISBN 0-7141-2510-5

British Library Cataloguing-in-Publication data
A catalogue record for this book is available
from the British Library

Designed by Harry Green
Set in Palatino and printed in Italy by
New Interlitho SpA, Milan

Cover Detail of a shawl with a multitude of patterns in eighteen different colours, woven in handspun cotton, silk and pashmina supplementary weft yarns.

Page 1 A Limbu weaver at her loom weaving the pattern illustrated on the front cover

Page 2–3 A traditional textile design showing the temple pattern alternating with the elephant trunk motif. (See also illustration on p. 104)

PHOTOGRAPHIC ACKNOWLEDGEMENTS

Royal Anthropological Institute Photographic Collection p. 154; Archaeological Department, HM Government of Nepal for permission to take photographs on pp. 22, 26, 27, 38; Oriental and India Collection, British Library pp. 14, 41, 42, 48, 172; Trustees of the British Museum pp. 9, 20, 29 top, 31, 36, 37, 58, 121 top right, 124, 146, 147, 152, 169; British Museum Press pp. 18–19, 82–3, 107, 116, front cover; Syndics of the Cambridge University Library pp. 24 top, 34 top, 49; Jane Clark pp. 183 bottom, 184; Sean Conlin p. 49; Gyanendra Das pp. 133, 136; John Dunsmore pp. 12, 67; Royal Geographical Society, London p. 40; Trustees of the Hunterian Collection, Royal College of Surgeons of England p. 50; Nigel Herring p. 170; Ruth Hurle p. 183 top; Corneille Jest pp. 50 bottom, 138, 151, 162–7, 176; Mani Lama pp. 25, 135, 141 top, 148; Tim Martineau pp. 71, 112 left; Alan Macfarlane p. 139; Natural Resources Institute p. 60 right; Pratapaditya Pal p. 30; Liz van Rensburg pp. 62, 64; Colin Rosser p. 134; Board of Trustees of the Royal Botanic Gardens, Kew pp. 43, 60, 68 left; David Russell p. 122–3; Ang Diku Sherpa p. 69; Amar Simha pp. 23, 26, 34 bottom, 93; Board of Trustees of the Victoria and Albert Museum pp. 32, 55; Fiona Welford pp. 113, 143.

CONTENTS

◈

ACKNOWLEDGEMENTS

I would like to express my deep gratitude to the many weavers and basketmakers of Nepal who so generously shared their knowledge and often their homes with me, and to Ang Diku Sherpa, who inspired and supported the weavers in many remote areas, and untiringly helped me to gather information on all aspects of textiles.

I wish to thank the Staff of the Koshi Hill Area Rural Development Programme (KHARDEP) and particularly Shiva P. Acharya for his support and encouragement, Dick Jenkin, Usha Nepal, Major G. V. Gurung, Mahesh Sharma, Amar Simha, Rajendra Neupane, Surendra Shahi and the Staff of the British and German Embassies. I am grateful also for the assistance of HM Government Departments and entrepreneurs, particularly the Department of Cottage and Village Industries (DCVI), the Mahaguthi shop, Himalayan Leather Handicraft Industries and the Association of Craft Producers. I appreciated the opportunity given to me by the Director and Staff to examine and photograph items in the Collection of the National Museum, Kathmandu.

I am greatly indebted to Dr Brian Durrans, Museum of Mankind, who has been a source of encouragement and advice for over a decade; Dr Corneille Jest, for his kind counsel and great generosity in making available material from his research in the High Mountain areas; Marianne Straub RDI, for her stimulating practical guidance; Peter Collingwood for illuminating some complicated techniques; Ruth Hurle, who helped particularly with the chapter on jute, John Makin and Ken Teague, for providing much source material, and members of the London Guild of Weavers, especially Melanie Venes, Nancy Lee Child, Ann Hecht and Erna Lenel, for their support and advice.

Working in a number of museums and libraries has been both rewarding and a pleasure thanks to the kindness and help of the staff of the Oriental and India Office Collections, British Library; the Museum of Mankind (Library and Student Room); the Oriental Antiquities Section, British Museum; the Victoria and Albert Museum; the Horniman Museum; the Royal Anthropological Institute; the Royal Geographical Society; the Royal Botanic Gardens, Kew; the Pitt Rivers Museum, Oxford; the Bankfield Museum, Halifax; the University Library and University Museum of Archaeology and Anthropology, Cambridge.

For their help in connection with Nepalese textiles in various ways over the years, I am indebted also to many other people. I would specifically like to mention Michael Allen, Professor L. Bangdel, Richard Blurton, Richard and Ann Burges Watson, David Field, Sylvia Fitzgerald, Dr Hans Gsanger, John and Anjuli Henley, Sue Holmes, Dr Caroline Humphrey, Dr Michael Hutt, Pat Kattenhorn, Imogen Laing, Eileen Lodge, Dr Alan Macfarlane, Tom Mackillop, Sarah Posey, Colin Powe, Liz van Rensburg, Anthony J. Smyth and, particularly, my sister Gisela Horsnell.

My deepest gratitude is to my husband without whose support, suggestions and word-processing I would not have been able to write the book.

Shawl, *pachaura*, with traditional
colours and patterns
from Pokhara in west Nepal

PREFACE

❖

Traditional shawl pattern from east Nepal in a variety of new colours using silk as well as cotton.

One of the elaborately carved bamboo spindles used by Rai women of Sankhuwasabha District to spin nettle yarn. British Museum As 1992 01.1.

The natural beauty of Nepal and the art treasures, architecture, sculptures and paintings of the Kathmandu Valley have gained admiration throughout the world. Overshadowed by such perfection, domestic crafts were hardly noticed or mentioned: yet the remarkable range of such crafts, especially textiles, which reflect the diversity and ingenuity of the people throughout the whole of Nepal, achieved equal perfection. Strong sacks and bags made from nettle fibre or yak hair, woollen blankets, bamboo baskets or an exquisite inlay-patterned cotton shawl or cap, *topi*, all bear witness to an independent achievement of the Bauhaus principle of combining beauty with utility. No king, or other patron of art, inspired the people in the almost inaccessible mountain areas, yet their skill in carving – although it might be only a spindle or a flute – equals that of any craftsman in the Kathmandu Valley, and the sophisticated weaving and basketry methods developed on isolated, self-sufficient farms evoke admiration from any professional weaver. This book was written in the hope of bringing recognition to the little-known, beautiful and unusual textiles and textile structures, particularly of the remote areas of Nepal.

After a brief account of the country and its people, I have attempted to trace the history of some textiles through sculptures, paintings, manuscripts, legends and travellers' stories. Following this, the wide variety of textile raw materials employed in Nepal today, amongst them the hair of the yak and the little-known fibre of the Himalayan Giant Nettle, are described. This leads on to the main part of the book which examines how the textiles are made and how they are used for clothing and as protection against the elements, as

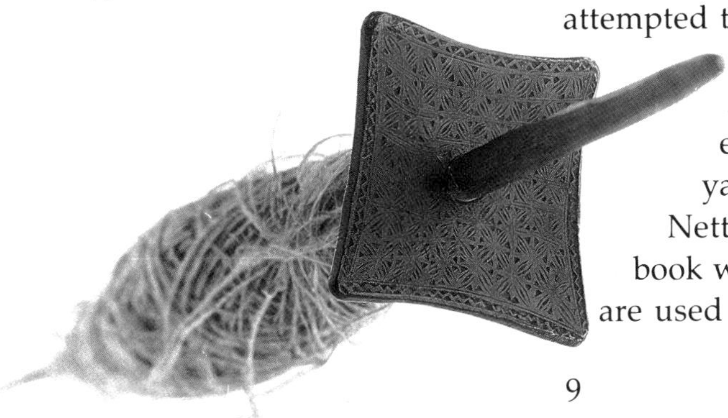

9

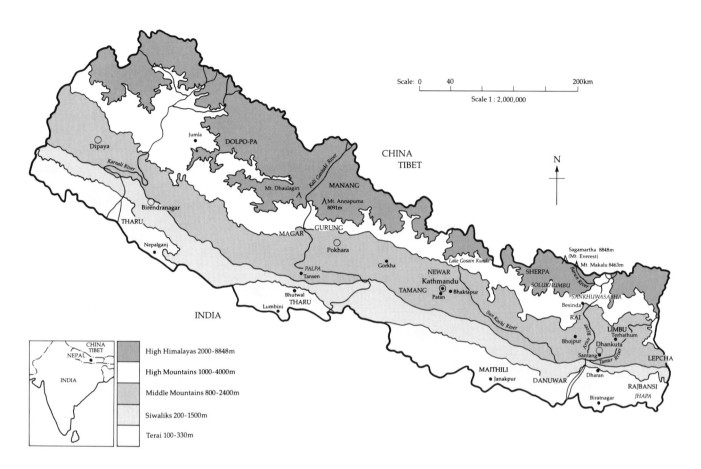

Map of Nepal showing the greatest concentration of peoples mentioned in the text, although some have migrated across the country, resulting in an exchange of cultural influences.

well as for decoration and a means of identification with a particular group. Other textiles are made for festivals or ceremonies, but the main emphasis is on the manufacture and use of textiles in daily life, illustrated with pattern diagrams of traditional costumes and unusual or so far unrecorded warping and weaving methods. The tradition of women weaving all the clothing for the family has changed rapidly with the ready availability of factory-made materials and clothing. Special mention is made, therefore, of methods which, as a result, may fall into decline. Happily, a number of textiles associated with the Nepalese national dress and with certain ethnic groups continue to be made, and new outlets are being developed by groups of handweavers thus further enhancing the general high regard for the skilled weaver.

It would be presumptuous to try to cover the whole wealth of Nepalese textiles and the diversity of weaving techniques, which are rooted in the different origins and cultural backgrounds of the people of Nepal, the availability of raw materials and people's varying requirements for textiles resulting from the range of climates from the subtropical south to the arctic north. I have tried to record those textiles which are representative of the main regions of Nepal, especially those made by the Rais, Limbus, Newars and Gurungs of the Middle Mountains, the Sherpas and people of Dolpo and Manang in the north and including short notes on those of the Tharu and Rajbansi of the subtropical southern plains. By showing how the weavers and basketmakers of Nepal work, often in most difficult conditions, with material they find and equipment they make, and how they respond to opportunities opened up by new markets, I hope to evoke in the reader the same feeling of joy and admiration I felt when I had the privilege of learning from and working with some of the weavers and basket-makers, particularly in east Nepal. At the same time, I believe it will also become evident that the rich profusion of textiles can rank with Nepal's other outstanding achievements in art. The ways in which HM Government of Nepal and some Aid Agencies are trying to revive traditional skills and thus bring essential supplementary income to the weavers and basketmakers is also considered, together with the environmental and social issues linked to this, and potential developments for the future.

Many of the textiles illustrated in this book form part of the British Museum collection. Beginning with a small exhibition, 'Himalayan Rainbow', in 1983–5 the Museum has acquired over the years an increasing number of textiles which document tradition as well as contemporary change and draw attention to the rich variety and beauty of Nepal's material culture – a dynamic organism on which each generation builds. 'The culture of Nepal, as a living organism, subject to adaptation and growth, will continue to imbibe the best from the different cultures . . . yet maintain a distinct and separate individuality' (Bhattaraya 1962, 45).

INTRODUCTION

❖

Pilgrims of ancient times, like travellers in Nepal today, stood in awe and wonder at the sight of the majestic splendour of the Himalayas, including the highest mountain in the world, Sagarmatha (Everest), and the beauty of the country. The fascination with the distant magnificence of the Himalayas was vividly expressed by the nineteenth-century British botanist and plant collector Sir Joseph Hooker (1854, 191), who was enthralled by the most impressive and magical scenes he ever beheld, and by the historian Daniel Wright (1877, 74) who wrote 'as for the country of Nepal, it would take the pen of a Ruskin and the pencil of a Turner or Claude to do justice to its beauties'. A beauty with a changing face, Nepal lies in one of the most geologically active of all major mountain systems. For over 25 million years, the land surface of the country had been formed by the effects of the underlying 'collision of the continents' – the Eurasian and Indo-Australian plates – which resulted in the formation of the Himalayas, together with massive folding, compression and metamorphosis. As a consequence, within a land area of 147,181 km² (CBS 1988, 1), roughly the same as that of England, altitude above mean sea-level varies from 70 m in the south (part of the Gangetic Plain) to 8,848 m, the summit of Sagarmatha (Everest). Even over short distances, there can be considerable altitudinal and climatic variation. One reason for this is that the major rivers of the country

A farming landscape in the Middle Mountains of
east Nepal. In the background is the road from
the *terai* and the district town, Dhankuta.

The centre of Lalitpur with Krishna Dewal Mandir, a watercolour by H. A. Oldfield, *c*.1855. Sylvian Levi, in 1905, described Durbar Square as 'a marvel which defies description', a statement as true today as 100 years ago. In the centre is the Krishna Mandir temple. A detail from the intricate carving on the temple appears on p. 23.

rise to the north, in Tibet, and predate the uplift of the Himalayas. As the mountain range slowly rose, and they are still rising by about 1 cm per year, the rivers cut their passage through it. Thus, for example, the Arun river in eastern Nepal, has eroded an 8,000 m-thick rock sequence through the Great Himalayan Range (Shrestha 1989, XIV), and the Kali Gandaki river basin, central Nepal, has become the deepest valley in the world. Where it flows between Dhaulagiri and Annapurna, the river bed is six vertical kilometres below the mountain peaks (Attenborough 1984, 9). In the warm, humid south of the basin, the forests are as luxuriant as tropical jungle, and rhinoceros and tiger roam. At 3,000 m, amongst rocks and sparse vegetation, is the home of the snow leopard. The highest point of all above the valley, the peak of Dhaulagiri, stands at 8,167 m.

Within this setting, the kings of the Kathmandu Valley created cities with indescribable marvels – Kathmandu, Bhaktapur (Bhadgaon) and Patan (Lalitpur), the 'beautiful city'. At an altitude of some 1,300 m, surrounded by good farming land, Kathmandu and its sister towns have for centuries been administrative and cultural capitals, and an important centre of international trade between India, Tibet and China. Pokhara, some 125 km due west of Kathmandu, is rather similarly situated in a valley, though at a lower altitude (950 m). The nearby lakes and its position at the foot of the Annapurna massif have made it a popular tourist resort.

Other urban centres in the hill/mountain areas are much smaller, the major industrial and urban development occurring in the southern plains or *terai*. Over the centuries, the indigenous population was augmented by waves of immigrants and by invasions of Indo-Mediterranean people from the south and others of Tibetan origin from the north. The 1991 Census recorded a population of 19.6 million. Each of some fifty groups, with their sub-divisions and classes, has its own cultural background and language. The table below outlines a general guide to the major groups and the environmental variations of the country, though, as Professor K. P. Malla (1977, iii) points out, 'neither the ethnic nor the geographic distribution of social groups in Nepal is along any hard and fast lines'. The same may be said of the major religions, Hinduism and Buddhism, which have greatly influenced one another and pervaded everyday life: the beliefs of the peoples of the middle mountains are frequently found to represent an amalgam of these and other religious beliefs.

Characteristics of the physiographic regions of Nepal: the inhabited areas

Feature	Terai	Siwaliks	Middle Mountains	High Mountains	High Himalayas
elevation (m)	100–330	200–1,500	800–2,400	1,000–4,000	2,000–5,000
climate	tropical	tropical/ subtropical	subtropical/ cool temperate	warm–cool temperate/ alpine	alpine–arctic
major natural vegetation	sal and mixed hardwoods	sal and mixed hardwoods, pine	pine and mixed hardwoods, oak	fir, pine, birch, rhododendron	open meadow, tundra
major crops	rice, maize, wheat, mustard, sugar-cane, tropical fruits	rice, maize, wheat, millet, radish, mango	rice, maize, wheat, millet barley, pulses, potato, cardamom	oats, barley, wheat, potato, buckwheat, yam, medicinal herbs	grazing (June–Sept.)
livestock	cattle, buffalo	cattle	cattle, sheep, buffalo, pigs	cattle and crosses, sheep, goats	yak and crosses, sheep, goats
textile materials	jute, straw, grass	bamboo	nettle, hemp, bamboo, agave, cotton, sheep's wool	nettle, bamboo, sheep's wool, yak and goat hair	sheep's wool, yak and goat hair
ethnic groups	Tharu, Indo-Aryan groups, migrants, Rajbansi, Musalman	Tharu, migrants from the middle mountains	Gurung, Magar Tamang, Newar, Rai, Limbu, Indo-Aryans	Thakali, Sherpa, Tamang, Khas, Chhetri, Tibetan, Gurung	Sherpa, Tibetan (seasonal)

Each group – indigenous or immigrant – also had its own domestic skills: these have been preserved within the household for generations. An individual group might settle in an isolated area where rugged mountains, torrential rivers or dense forest formed physical limitations to outside contacts. Locally available sources had to meet their needs for food, shelter, utensils, medicines and dyes, as well as raw material for textiles. The great diversity of climate, topography and soils provided an astonishing range of flora and fauna, which were exploited with great ingenuity. Fibres from many different types of plants are still extracted, spun and woven today. In the cold northern areas, where plant resources are more limited, people use wool from sheep and hair from goats and yaks, and also hides and skins. The wide variety of looms and equipment for weaving, built from local wood and bamboo, were designed to suit the specific raw material and the purpose of the textile. The result of this ethnic and geographic diversity has been that even quite small groups retain a distinctive culture, with its own identifiable type of textile.

If one thinks of the word textiles as originating from the Latin word *texere*, meaning to plait and braid as well as weave (Smith 1864), one could say that there are some kinds of textiles made, or in daily use, in every rural household in Nepal, even today when fewer farms are so isolated that self-sufficiency is a necessity. A single photograph, taken on a small farm in the middle mountains, may illustrate this. The wall for the house and the fencing were woven from bamboo: the oblique interlaced (braided) bamboo mat is used for sitting on and for drying maize. There are also two carrying baskets, *dhoko*, combining plain with hexagonal interlacing, a folded woven straw mat on the weaver's seat and a plain weave, inlay patterned cotton textile in the process of being woven on a home-made loom: this is going to be used for a colourful cap, topi, such as the little boy is wearing. The patterned headscarf of the mother was woven on the same loom: her wraparound skirt was block-printed. The major economic activity in Nepal is agriculture, based on small-scale farming being undertaken over this great range of ecological conditions. In the subtropical southern plains, where irrigation is possible, mixed farming (crops and livestock) is practised, with two to three crops grown per year. In the cultivated areas of the middle hills, the climate varies from hot, dry subtropical in the valley bottoms to cold, moist temperate at the higher altitudes (2,800–4,000 m) and households farm small, often fragmented, areas on steep hillsides. At the higher elevations, rice, maize and finger millet give way to barley, wheat, buckwheat and potato. Higher still, in the High Himal (up to 5,000 m) agricultural activity may be limited to the summer grazing of livestock (yaks, sheep, goats). On most mountain farms, where the arable area totals less than one hectare, survival depends on a supplementary source of income. One major source for generations has been the barter trade with Tibet and also India: this includes textiles and also textile raw materials.

A Limbu farm in the Middle Mountains. Weaving is still part of the domestic scene here.

Until 1951, Nepal had little contact with the outside world, except in areas close to its borders or near corridors of ancient trade routes between India and China. Such contacts might have influenced weaving techniques and domestic skills, but, even then, these retained their individual character. 'A capacity to absorb and transform seems to characterize Nepalese society' (Malla 1977, ii). Sadly, no textiles from ancient times have yet been found, even in the Kathmandu Valley, although the excavations being undertaken by the Government Department of Archaeology might yet reveal some fragments of cloth or a spindle or part of a loom. They might also bring to light information on the arts from areas outside the Kathmandu Valley on which, so far, few records are available. However, the magnificent sculptures and paintings in the valley give some indication of the mode of dressing over the centuries, particularly from the style shown in representations of the donors, who commissioned the work, but also, to a lesser extent, in that of the deities. For, although the iconography of most deities was described in detail in books of meditation or visualisation, *dhyan*, thereby providing the basic schema of the image, the artist was still free to follow the fashions and modes prevalent in his country (Pal 1985, 35) and reveal some of the textile tradition through history. This is explored in the following chapter.

17

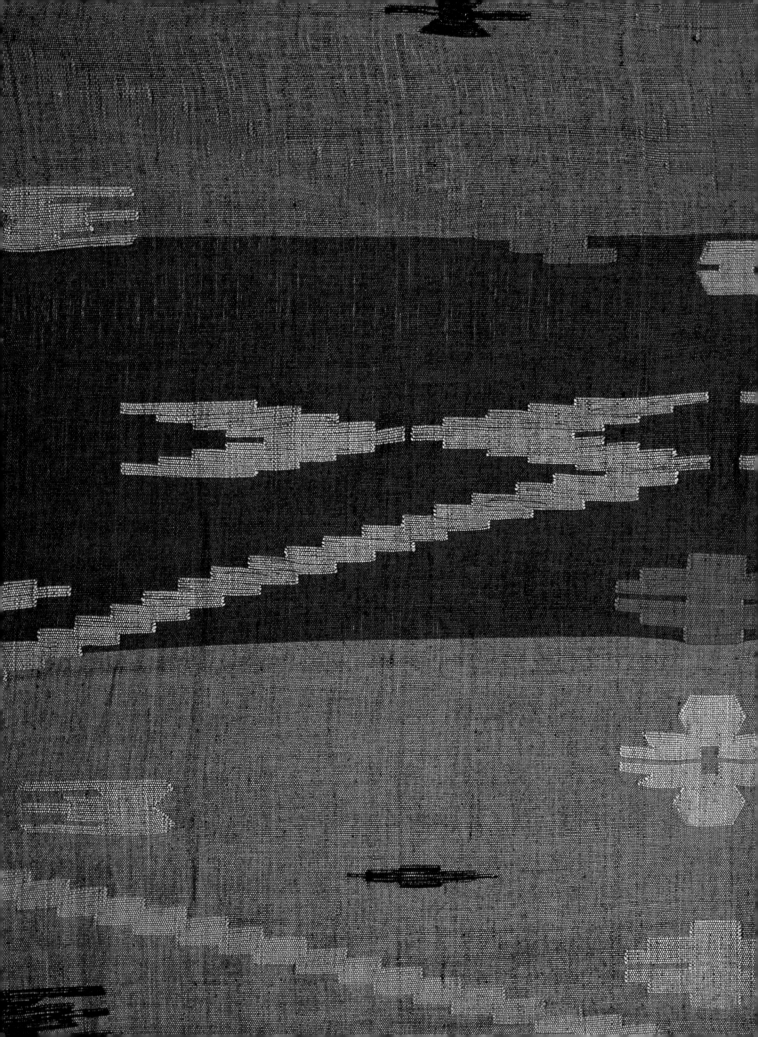

PART ONE

❖

TRADITION,

INNOVATION

AND

NATURE'S

RESOURCES

1

HISTORY, LEGEND AND TEXTILES

◈

Left This regal gilt bronze of Vajrasattva with *vajra* and *ghanta* follows an old Nepalese style of representing Bodhisattvas. 15th century, H. 44.5 cm. British Museum OA 1932 2–11.4.

Previous page Cotton shawl woven by Sita Subba, a Limbu weaver from east Nepal. Many of the traditional weaving patterns resemble those on ancient sculptures, such as the floral diamond design incised on the garment of Vajrasattva (left).

Little is known about the early history of Nepal, although it has been proved that the Kathmandu and other valleys of Nepal were settled by neolithic man. Many kinds of stone tools of the period have been discovered (Amatya 1991, 54). In the old texts, *Puranas*, collections of myth, legend and chronicles, the dividing line between myth and fact becomes imperceptible. Uhlig (1987, 11) suggests that this tendency to link worldly reality with trance and dream experience is one of the fundamental differences between the way of thinking of East and West – the factual consciousness of the Occident in contrast with the imaginative consciousness of the Orient. One of the legends states – and geological evidence supports it – that the Kathmandu Valley was once a lake surrounded by snow-capped mountains. A beautiful lotus bloomed in the centre of the lake and contained a sacred flame from which the primordial Buddha, Swayambhu, revealed himself. Pilgrims from many lands came to meditate on the shores of the lake. When Manjusri Bodhisattva came from the Tibetan mountains to worship, he wished to see the flame more closely, so he drained the lake by cutting a passage through the rock Chobhar. The water flowed out through the gorge and formed the Bagmati river, leaving behind a fertile valley for people to live in. The lotus settled on the valley floor at the place where the stupa of Swayambunath now stands.

The Kathmandu Valley became politically and culturally the most important area of Nepal: in remote parts of the country until recently the valley was still referred to as Nepal proper. In considering the history it must be remembered that the present geographical borders of Nepal were established as late as the nineteenth century. Who

21

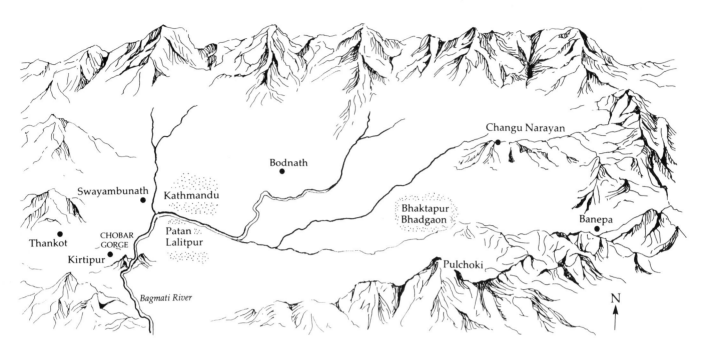

Relief map of the
Kathmandu Valley.

were the first settlers in the valley? Since early times, several millennia ago, waves of human migrants from different directions must have been attracted there. Kramrisch (1964, 16) mentions 'a substratum of a race of Pre-Dravidians and Dravidians, who were in Nepal even before the Newars, who formed the majority of the ancient inhabitants of the valley of Kathmandu'. Levi (1905, Introd.) suggests that there was an early migration from the north followed by others from India, but that local tribes had previously occupied the valley or land nearby. Doherty (1978, 444) states that 'a major ancestral portion of the Newari people seems to derive from the southeastern Tibetan sphere, at an early but uncertain date'. Regmi pondered on the point that the Kiratas were the occupants of the valley for a long time, and the same is said of the Newars, whose contention is supported by ethnic and anthropological findings. However, while the Kiratas' claims are supported by the evidence of chronicles and further confirmed by the *Puranas*, the Newars are not mentioned in these treatises. Curiously, though, it is the Newars who have been closely associated with all Nepal has stood for in the past – its name, fame and grandeur (Regmi 1969, 19).

Wright (1877, 106), in an English translation of the *Vamsavalis* (chronicles compiled by Gubhaju of Patan in the fourteenth century AD), states that 'the Kiratas came into Nepal at the 15,000th year of the Dwapar Yuga and they ruled over the country for 10,000 years' and were associated with the very dawn of history. Little is known about the life of the Kiratas during the period of their rule, which is now generally accepted to have run for some hundreds of years in the first millennium BC. There are several references to the Kiratas in the ancient Hindu epic *Mahabharata*. This great epic, which inspired writers, painters and sculptors alike, describes the adventures of Krishna, his brother Balarama and Arjuna, the noble warrior. The events are believed to have taken place in India and Nepal between the eleventh and eighth centuries BC. Arjuna is reported to have gone to Nepal to gain the powerful weapon Pashupatashtra.

Scenes of the Maharbaratha are carved in stone on the Krishna Mandir temple (AD 1635) at Durbar Square, Patan. Draped garments adorn the women. The warriors appear to wear flowing skirts with decorated sashes and coats of armour at the top.

The birth of Buddha. Blue-grey polished limestone, 9th century AD, H. 84 cm. National Museum, Kathmandu.

There he met Kirateswar – Shiva in the guise of a hunter – who challenged him to a trial of strength before bestowing the weapon upon him. The whole story of the *Mahabharata* is depicted with much vivacity on a stone frieze around the first level of the seventeenth-century Krishna Mandir temple at Patan. The exquisite carvings probably reflect the mode of dress of the artist's time rather than that of the earlier period of the events themselves, although they may not have been substantially dissimilar.

During the time the Kiratas ruled in central and eastern Nepal other cultural centres developed in the southern plains of the country, now known as the *terai*. It was there, at Lumbini, in 543 BC that Prince Siddhartha Gautama was born. The son of the local ruler, King Suddhodana, of the Sakya clan of Kapilvastu, the prince became Buddha, the Enlightened One. The National Museum in Kathmandu houses a beautiful ninth-century AD stone relief representation of the Buddha's nativity. The graceful figure of Maya Devi, his mother, is clad in a striped *lungi*-type cloth, delicately draped around the body and held below the waist with a decorative three-line bead-patterned waistband. With her finely formed hands she holds the flowers of the tree branch which is bending down to support her. The baby, decorated with an aureole, has water and lotus petals showered on him by two angels. According to the records collected by Hiuen Tsiang (AD 629), the new prince was wrapped in a cotton vestment. 'When Bodhisattva was born, from the right side of his mother, the four kings wrapped him in a golden coloured cotton vestment and placing him on a golden slab (bench) and bringing him to his mother, they said ''The queen may rejoice indeed at having given birth to such a fortunate child. If the Devas

23

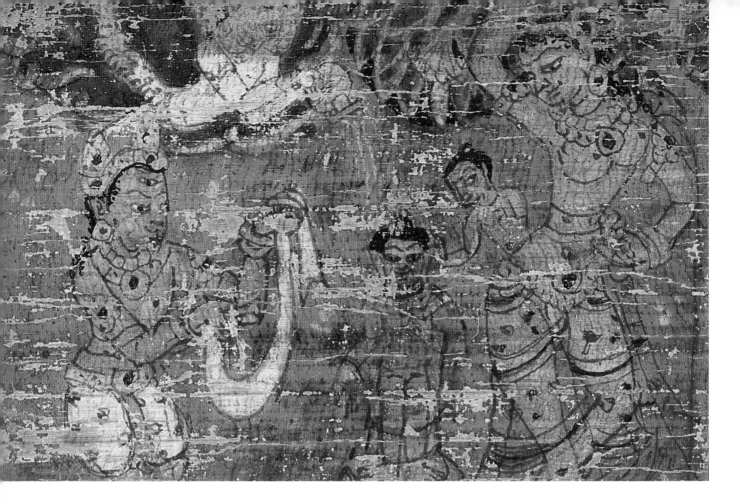

A Nepalese palm-leaf manuscript, *Astasahasrika Prajnaparamita*, dated AD 1015, showing the birth of Buddha. Queen Maya Devi, wearing a striped patterned lower garment, is grasping the flowering branch of a tree. The infant Buddha is offered a white cloth as a wrapping. This may reflect the Buddhist custom of offering a white shawl to show honour and respect. Cambridge University Library Add. 1643.

A woollen blanket or rari. British Museum As 1984 27.40.

rejoiced at the event how much more should man''' (Beal 1906, vol. II, book VI, 25). Could the golden-coloured cotton be the same variety of cotton, *kogati*, still grown and woven today?

During the third century BC the Emperor Asoka of Magadha (273–236 BC), a follower and promoter of Buddha's teachings, is said to have gone to Lumbini and erected a commemorative pillar in 249 BC to mark the birthplace of Buddha. From Lumbini the emperor is reputed to have gone to Patan where he set up four stupas at the cardinal points of the compass. It is said that these are the stupas that stand to this day and that the emperor's daughter, Charumati, who was married to a Kshatriya of Nepal, founded the monastery Chabahil, a name which resembles her own.

The first written evidence of Nepalese textile production is found in Indian sources of the Asoka period. Kautilya's *Arthasastra* ('The Science of Politics') refers, in the rules for the superintendent of the treasury, to Nepalese blankets as items of trade. 'That (blanket) which is made up of eight pieces and black in colour, is called Bhingisi used as rainproof; likewise is Apasāraka – both are products of Nepal (Naipàlakam)' (Shamasastry 1908, part 1, 95). Reference is made also to a Nepali woollen blanket being sold in Pataliputra (now Patna).

It is quite probable that the blankets referred to are the *rari*, woollen blankets, which are still manufactured and in demand today as protection against cold and rain. Large blankets are made up usually from several pieces, as the backstrap method of weaving allows only

Gurung wearing rainproof woollen blankets. These are folded in half and the selvages are stitched up at one side to form a hood, (a *bokhu* or *ghum rari*), which gives the impression of an all-enveloping garment. This is worn in various ways – over the head, one shoulder or the back – and is also used as a mat.

a limited width. The black colour referred to would be the natural wool colour of the local Baruwal sheep or the yak. The rainproof quality – achieved by felting the woven cloth – is still appreciated today. A *ghum* rari can provide more shelter and warmth than an umbrella. As trade with India was already established in the third century BC, it may be presumed both that production of woollen textiles had flourished for some time before then and that indigenous arts were established before the Indian influence reached Nepal through trade, pilgrimage and, eventually, settlers. It is not known exactly when the Kiratas left the valley and settled in the eastern part of Nepal, where they are considered to be the forebears of today's Rais and Limbus. It is apparent, though, from inscriptions that the Indo-Aryan Licchavis of Vaiasali had established themselves by the fifth century AD and begun to extend their rule beyond the valley. Ancient sculptures show that not only the worship of mother goddess, solar deities and folk divinities but also Shiva and Vaishnava cults flourished side by side. It can be assumed that beliefs in the power of natural and supernatural forces and of ancestors are even more ancient than Buddhism and Hinduism. Indeed they still play a vital part in the life of many people, especially in the hills; tribal and immigrant cultures influenced present beliefs, contributing to and synthesising their development. Some of these ancient sculptures can provide the first indication of the nature of early textiles, but details will remain speculative unless one day cloth or fibre fragments are found during excavations, such as those now being undertaken by the Government Department of Archaeology in several parts of Nepal.

The garment on a torso of Yaksha Bodhisattva from the first century AD suggests that some lightweight thin cloth might have been woven at that time. The fine drapery over the shoulder could be cotton cloth. The sash or belt has an incised check pattern which shows clearly on the back of the torso. A powerful statue from the third century AD is believed to be a Kirata king: square-shouldered and upright, he holds a robe or cloak of heavier material with pleated drapes alongside his legs. A sash or belt with line patterns is fastened just below the waist.

Terracotta figures from the fourth century AD, excavated at Dhumbarahi, include a figure of one man wearing a knee-length cloak and trousers. Another man, wearing only a loincloth, is carrying over his shoulders two baskets which are tied to a pole. This type of carrier, called *khamu*, is still used by the Newars today to carry goods, especially vegetables, and occasionally children.

The earliest sculpture of a confirmed date is the image of Visnu of the three strides or Visnu Trivikrama. The relief stele depicts Visnu taking three giant strides to outwit the powerful Bali. Incarnated as a dwarf, Visnu had gained a promise from Bali that he would receive as much land as he could cover in three steps. As soon as the request was granted Visnu grew into a giant and with three steps encompassed the whole universe. He wears a striped cloth with a broad decorative border around the lower part of his body covering both his legs, which are stretched out in an elegant stride. This border could be either embroidered or woven. The sculpture was installed in AD 467 by the Licchavi King Mandeva, who is considered to be the founder of the distinctive classical art of Nepal, for, 'although Licchavi art is closely related to Indian

Statue of a king carved in grey limestone from the 3rd century AD. H. 40 cm. National Museum, Kathmandu.

Parvati in penance as 'Asparna', 'the one who eats not, even leaves' (Banerjee 1968). Parvati, in a life of fasting and penance in the mountains, is trying to regain Shiva as her lord and husband. With a gentle gesture, she is refusing the food offered by her attendant. Her penance is rewarded when Shiva, in disguise, tests her loyalty and then reveals himself, and is united once again with his wife. 5th–6th century AD. W. 40 cm. National Museum, Kathmandu.

A stone relief depicting Visnu Vrikanta from AD 467. The finely incised border on Vishnu's garment suggests a highly developed textile technique. National Museum, Kathmandu.

Gupta influences, in terms of form and content, a Nepali style is clearly recognizable' (Pal 1985, 36).

The beautiful stone relief panels depicting the legend of Kumaras-amhavan from the fifth to sixth centuries AD can help to shed more light on the textiles of the Licchavi period. Some sculptures of that time show strong Gupta influence, but these domestic scenes, with their mountainous background and figures with distinctive Nepal-ese features and mode of dressing, bear witness to the original interpretations of Nepalese artists. In the relief of Parvati in penance the tenderness and lyrical charm are expressed in the gentle lines of the composition, the graceful form of the two figures and the expressive movements of the hands. Although the relief is badly damaged, one can recognise the delicate patterns of the garments. Could there be a link with the inlay weaving patterns seen on the traditional *chaubandi cholo* blouse of today? The upper garment suggests a cross-over fastening, although the right breast seems to be uncovered. Both figures wear belts around the lower waist or sashes over what appear to be patterned skirts or wraparound lengths of cloth. The sash or belt bears a resemblance to the *patuka* of today – a strip of cloth (approximately 40 × 400 cm) which is wrapped tightly around the waist to form four or more layers or folds that give support and serve as pockets for small items.

There is no doubt that the arts must have flourished during Licchavi rule. Chinese pilgrims, followers of Buddha who went to Nepal and India, reported to Hiuen Tsiang (AD 629) that the

Nepalese 'are skilful in the arts' (Beal 1906, 11, 80): it may be presumed that these included textile arts. They also reported that in Nepal Buddhist monasteries and Hindu temples stood side by side, marking, even at that time, a coexistence of the two major religions.

The beauty and grandeur of the palace and the splendour of the attire of King Na-ling ti-po (Navendra Deva) are described in the Chinese T'ang annals, based on the account of the Chinese envoy Wang Hsuan Ts'e (Levi 1905, I, 164). However, there is little information about the actual garments worn by the king and, indeed, they may have been brought from India even at that time. It was recorded, though, that the king 'adorns himself with real pearls, rock crystal, mother of pearl, coral and amber; he has in his ears rings of gold and pendants of jade, and amulets at his belt ornamented with a Foutou (Buddha). He takes a seat on a throne of lions'. It is probable that Kailasakatu, the palace referred to in the Chinese account, was in Patan or Deopatan. It was also recorded that while merchants, both travelling and resident, were numerous there were few farmers. The ordinary people appear to have dressed themselves with a single piece of material which enveloped the body. This suggests a woven length of cloth, probably draped around the body and held by a belt, one shoulder left free, or the kind of cloak worn by some Sherpas. Alternatively, it may have been two lengths of cloth, stitched together at the selvage part of the way to form the back of the garment: no cutting would have been necessary and there would have been no wastage. A similar approach may be found in the jacket that is worn today.

By this period, also, contact had been established with Tibet through pilgrimage, trade and marriage bonds. Indeed, from the evidence of the T'ang chronicles of China it seems that in the seventh and eighth centuries Nepal was already commercially very active, enjoying a monopoly of trade, especially transit trade, between Tibet and India. The seventh-century ruler of Nepal, King Amshuvarman, is said to have given his daughter, Bhrkuti, in marriage to the Tibetan Emperor Srong-tsan-gampo (AD 620–49). The Nepalese princess carried with her a statue of Tara and a begging-bowl made from lapis lazuli, which had belonged to Lord Buddha. It was said that she, together with the emperor's Chinese wife, Princess Won-cheng, brought Buddhism to Tibet. Both are venerated as incarnations of the Tara, Princess Bhrkuti as the green Tara, bringing the gods and treasures to Tibet, and Princess Won-cheng as the white Tara. The contact with Tibet continued through the ages and was strengthened further when in 1260 the architect, bronze caster and painter Arniko, heading a group of eighty Nepalese artists, went to Tibet at the request of the Abbot of the Sasky monastery to create a golden stupa. Later Arniko entered the service

A scene from a 14th-century palm-leaf manuscript. The graceful goddess, the manuscript's protector, is wearing a semi-transparent, draped lower garment with a cross pattern, outlined in blue and red. The cross motif occurs throughout the centuries in weaving, printing tie-dye and carpet designs. 5 × 55 cm. British Museum 1959 2–14 02.

Bodhisattva Padmapani, a sculpture from the 7th-century Chaitya of Dhoka Bahal, Kathmandu. The Bodhisattva is holding the stalk of a lotus flower in his left hand while his right, above the small kneeling figure, is opened in a gesture of welcome. The finely incised geometric patterns on his lower garment, a kind of wraparound cloth with cascading folds at the centre, suggest a textile with inlay weaving patterns.

of Kublai Khan and eventually was appointed controller of the imperial studios. The Nepalese influence on Tibetan art is evident in manuscripts, *thankas* and mandalas.

An impressive seventh-century AD stone relief of the four-armed goddess Sarasvati gives a further indication of the type of textiles which might have been woven at that time. (Sarasvati is the patron of the arts and of learning and to this day during the annual festival of spring, Basanta Panchami, the shrines of the goddess are visited by students and artists, who make their offerings, including cotton puffs from weavers, in the hope that Sarasvati will make them skilful in their work.) In the seventh-century stele Sarasvati is standing upright holding a string of beads in her right hand and a manuscript in her left hand, two of her usual attributes. The two other arms and the vertical curved background, which is framed by a line of beads and a garland of rays (flames), are badly damaged. Her long skirt, with an arrangement of pleats in the centre, has a line and cross pattern. It is draped in the way a skirt is worn today, the pleats in front allowing for easy movement of the legs. The cross-pattern is of particular interest: the angular lines strongly suggest an inlay weaving pattern with its characteristic angles. Many of the garments of statues from the Licchavi period and the following centuries are decorated with patterns which are still woven by the Limbu and

A stone sculpture of a boy wearing a cross sling which stands by a wayside shrine in Kathmandu. *c*.8th century.

Opposite Mandala of Vasudhara, the six-armed goddess of abundance, dated 1504. The mandala, a painting to inspire meditation, shows the goddess wearing an elaborate crown and a full, flowing, patterned skirt. Outside the circle enclosing the sacred area are bodhisattvas and auspicious symbols. Framing the painting are secular scenes which, with lively charm, give much information on the drapes, folds and colours of garments. The saddle cloth or carpet on the bottom panel indicates a knowledge of carpet making in this period. Painting on cloth, 115 × 86 cm. British Museum OA 1933 7–22.01.

Rai weavers of east Nepal. One of their traditional patterns is clearly recognisable on the beautiful Bodhisattva sculpture.

A stone sculpture in Kathmandu of a boy, with distinct mongoloid features (Pal 1985, fig. 54), probably dating from the eighth century, is presumed to be a representation of Krishna or his brother Balarama and could also form an interesting link with the present. The boy is wearing an outfit which could well be the type of cross-sling still worn in central and western Nepal today. This carrying-sling, *renga*, is part of the traditional garment of the Gurungs in west Nepal (see p. 140). Licchavi rule ended during the eighth century AD and was succeeded by the Thakuri. Little historic evidence is available from four centuries of their rule, although confirmation of cotton cloth weaving and the earliest surviving Nepalese manuscript, with an indication of a variety of textiles, come from that period. Evidence of cotton cloth weaving is available from two sources. To protect them from insects and extreme temperatures manuscripts were wrapped up in large, square pieces of cloth. 'Fine quality manuscripts would have their own individual cloths and the richer the manuscript the more elaborate the cloth, which could be of silk stitched over a tougher coarser cotton as in Nepal' (Losty 1982, 13). In addition from the tenth century AD onwards handspun and woven cotton formed the basis of early Nepalese *thanka* religious paintings inspired by Buddhism. Zwalf (1981, 100) sees the widespread use of cotton reflected also in two Tibetan words used for *thanka* – *ras-bris* and *ras-ri-mo* (*ras* meaning 'cotton'). The cloth for each religious painting had to be woven to the size required and was specially commissioned. 'She who is to spin the thread and weave the canvas should also be of our tradition and united in its sacramental powers' (Snellgrove 1959, 114). Weaving a considerable width exactly to size from single, handspun cotton requires great skill. The cloth could be neither joined nor cut. This raises the question as to whether it required some special frame loom rather than a backstrap loom.

The Malla dynasty was established in the thirteenth century and lasted for over 400 years: during this period Nepalese culture rose to a new height. By the fifteenth century metalwork, woodcarving and terracotta art flourished. King Yaksha Malla (1428–82), who had extended his authority far beyond the valley, is said to have divided his kingdom between his four children with the respective capitals at Patan, Kathmandu, Bhaktapur and Banepa, the last two soon becoming one. Although this division led eventually to the dynasty's downfall in the eighteenth century, the period in between was marked by constructive rivalries, each ruler, a patron of the arts, embellishing his city with beautiful temples and palaces, sculptures and paintings, transforming the valley into a living museum, where art treasures became part of life, to be lived in, to worship

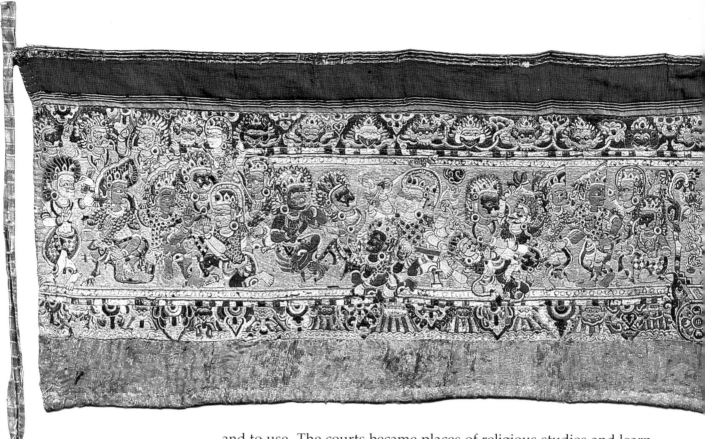

and to use. The courts became places of religious studies and learning, and offered home and shelter to artists and scholars from neighbouring Indian states overrun by the Moguls. Religious festivals, ritual dances and plays based on Buddhist and Hindu mythology became established during the Malla period. It can be presumed that costumes for the dances were made locally.

Artists throughout the ages have found inspiration in the ancient epic of the *Ramayana*, and such work gives some information on contemporary dress. The epic tells the story of Rama, an avatar of the Hindu god Visnu, and his wife Sita, the daughter of the Nepalese hero Janak, the ruler of Maithili. The reputed birthplace of Sita, Janakpur, lies in Nepal, and since images of Sita and Rama were discovered there in the sixteenth century AD, it has become a place of pilgrimage. The legend tells of the banishment to the forest of Rama and Sita through the intrigue of Rama's stepmother, who wanted her own son to succeed to the throne. While Rama and Sita were living in the forest they wore skin and bark clothing.

> Hermit's garments clothe her person, braided is her
>   raven hair,
> Matted bark of trees of forest drape her neck and
>   bosom fair

DUTT 1910, REPR. 1969

Could the hermit's garment have been made from some form of nettle fibres? According to Watt (1890, vol. 1, 472) mention of nettle cloth is made in the *Ramayana* where it is praised for its beauty and fineness, attributes which can be applied to the nettle cloth of Nepal woven today (page 123).

Nepalese embroidery panel showing scenes from the *Ramayana*, 1450–1600. The theme is the defeat of the ten-headed, twenty-armed demon king Ravanna (centre) by Rama, an avatar or incarnation of Visnu. Rama's wife Sita had been abducted by the demon king. Victoria & Albert Museum, 1M24–1936.

When the demon king Ravana kidnapped Sita from the forest, Rama, assisted by his loyal brother Lakshmana and Hanuman, the leader of the monkeys, fought against the demon and after hard battles rescued his wife. After fourteen years in the forest the couple returned to Kosala, and at long last Rama was installed as the rightful king. This victory of Rama over the demon is commemorated in the most important festival in Nepal, Dasain, a ten-day celebration (*das* meaning ten) of the victory of good over evil.

Some of the most beautiful and unusual scenes from the *Ramayana* are rendered in embroidery, possibly from as early as AD 1450 to 1600, on a panel in the collection of the Victoria and Albert Museum, London. Other embroidered fragments, made into pillar decorations blending scenes of Buddhism, Vaishnavite and Shaivite iconography, are embroidered similarly with delicate chain-, brick- and satin-stitches, interspersed with cross stitches. These have been radiocarbon-dated to as early as the thirteenth century. 'Nepalese textile history has been assumed to start around 1700 AD and to be an offshoot of the Sino-Tibetan tradition. The early embroideries show that a distinctive and highly sophisticated Nepali style flourished considerably earlier than that' (Crill 1989, 30). It is of interest that Wright (1877, 26) especially mentions Newars as being skilful embroiderers.

One representation of the *Ramayana* is found in a sixteenth-century AD manuscript now housed in the Cambridge University Library. The manuscript is a *kalapustaka*, where only short descriptions of the event are given with illustrations forming the major part of the folio. The story thus unfolds with graphic detail, vibrating with lines, colour and ornament. Although the artist may have fol-

A scene from the *Ramayana Kalapustaka, c.*1600. The colourful mountain pattern is echoed in the carpet on p. 176. A stripe and dot patterned cloth similar to that worn by Sita is printed and worn in eastern Nepal (see p. 77). Cambridge University Library Add. 864 fol. 4.

Detail from a relief carving by the pool on the palace at Patan, *c.*16th–17th century. The people wear clothes and what appear to be straw shoes similar to those made and worn today.

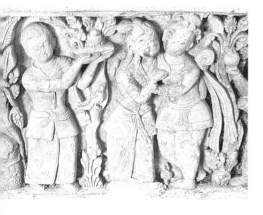

lowed certain conventions in portraying the figures, one can assume that he also incorporated the modes of dress of his time.

In 1722 Father Ippolito Desideri visited Nepal and reported that the people 'wear a woollen or cotton jacket reaching to the knees and long trousers down to their ankles, a red cap on their head, and slippers on their feet; when it rains men and women go barefoot' (De Fileppi 1931, 312). Slippers of straw, *paral*, and of jute, *nalu*, are still made by the Newar farmers, Jyapu, of the Kathmandu Valley. The intricate method of weaving these slippers points to development over successive generations. Father Desideri also mentioned horse-rugs, which were used instead of saddles, and one wonders whether these might have been pile rugs brought by traders from northern Nepal or Tibet.

During the rule of the Malla dynasty in the Kathmandu Valley other kingdoms existed or were established elsewhere in Nepal, including a number under Hindu rulers who had left northern India following its conquest by the Moguls in the early thirteenth century. At various times several larger regimes were built up, such as the Malla kingdom of Jumla and the Sen kingdom of Palpa, but there was a tendency to fragmentation and at one time some eighty principalities existed simultaneously (Stiller 1973, 34–5). Few records are available at present of the arts of these principalities, although some fine sculpture fragments have been found – for example, that of a god or Bodhisattva from about the fourteenth century, discovered at Dullu, western Nepal. The figure wears finely draped lower garments and a wide belt (Tucci 1956, 44, fig. 50). Eventually, in the

34

Nepalese hill porters carrying bamboo *dhokos*, in 1793 the sole means of transport. Because of their perfect shape and lightness combined with strength, the *dhoko* has remained unchanged for hundreds of years. Most mountain villagers use these baskets daily for carrying food, water, fuel and, when necessary, the elderly or sick.

eighteenth century, Prithvi Narayan Shah, the ruler of Gorkha, one of the kingdoms, launched a campaign, which was to last for a decade, to take over the Kathmandu Valley. This he achieved in 1768 and thus ended the 550-year rule of the Mallas. Following the conquest of the valley other petty principalities to the south, east and west were unified into a new realm, which had its capital at Kathmandu, the foundation of the present kingdom of Nepal.

The established cultural tradition continued under the Shah rulers in spite of some political unrest, clashes with China/Tibet and with the British East India Company over boundaries and trade rights. Although the borders of Nepal were closed to most foreigners, from the late eighteenth century onwards more detailed information became available on textiles from writers who were able to visit the country. The British emissary Colonel William Kirkpatrick wrote (1811) 'an account of the kingdom of Nepaul being the substance of observations made during a mission to that country in the year 1793'. Unfortunately, though perhaps not surprisingly, as he was a military man, he recorded very little about textiles. Nevertheless, he does mention cotton cloth made by Newars mainly for home use (p. 209), the fabrication of coarse linen and sackcloth from hemp (p. 143), and the export of rugs and blankets (p. 205). The accompanying engravings reveal more. The hill porter, carrying the traditional basket, *dhoko*, with a headband, is wearing a cross-over, long jacket and a wide sash/cummerbund around his waist, with the kukri, the traditional Nepalese knife, tucked in at the front. His head is covered with a turban-like cloth. One of the sitting porters appears to be wearing the kind of slippers described on p. 137. Another engraving shows details of the *dhoko* and a hammock made up of one sturdy pole and a length of check patterned cloth, presumably handwoven cotton.

References to cotton cloth weaving become numerous in the nineteenth century. The large painting of a *Pilgrimage to Gosainthan* on cotton cloth (125 cm wide) serves as visual evidence. Sadly, there is no record of how such considerable width was woven, but it is clear from the depictions of a backstrap weaver and a spinner that the artist must have witnessed the spinning and weaving. Lake Gosainkund (top left in the painting) lies 4,380 m above sea-level to the north of Kathmandu and has been a place of pilgrimage for Hindus and Buddhists for generations. Within the lake there is said to be a natural stone figure with a human shape. According to Hindu legend, the god Shiva, in his battle with demons, had to drink poison which gave him such a scalding sensation in the throat that he fled to the Himalayas to plunge into the icy water of Gosainkund. Tibetans consider the image to be not Shiva but Arya Avalokiteswara (Gurung 1980, 269–70).

From Hamilton (1819, part 11, 232) we learn that 'two kinds of

Left and above Pilgrimage to
Gosainthan, *a large topographical
scene painted on cloth in the early
19th century. The whole story of
daily life, rituals and the long
pilgrimage to Gosainthan is
unfolded. A weaver and spinner
(*detail, above*) form part of the scene
on the lower right, and Lake
Gosainkund appears in the upper
left-hand corner. 179 × 125 cm.
British Museum IF 19287–7/1.*

cotton cloth, called *khadi* and *chana*, are woven by the Newar women
of all ranks, and by men of the Parbatiya [hill] caste, called Magar.
The cotton grows in the hilly parts of the kingdom and is sufficient
for the consumption; but none is exported from Nepal Proper'.
These cloths constituted the dress of the lower and middle classes,
but we also learn that the entire dress of the higher ranks in Nepal
was imported – mainly silks and shawls from China and muslins
and calicoes of 'the low country', presumably India. The military
wore European broad cloth. Hamilton (p. 76) also gives an appraisal
of the fine-quality cloth woven in the hills outside the Kathmandu
Valley area, where all the women were weavers and seem to have
enjoyed great privileges. The Gurung and Limbu tribes were
shepherds and possessed numerous flocks. 'The sheep are called
Barwal and their wool is said to be fine. It is woven into a cloth
which is finer than that of Bhotan.' Hamilton also mentions (p. 27)
that the chief wealth of the Gurungs consisted in sheep, that 'the
men also employed themselves in weaving blankets', and that Jumla
traded a woollen cloth called *pheruwa* down to India around the year
1815, thus continuing the long tradition of trade established from
at least the third century BC.

B. H. Hodgson, who was British Resident in Kathmandu from
1833 to 1844, wrote a substantial number of reports and papers on
the country. In his papers relating to the colonisation, commerce
and physical geography of the Himalayan mountains and Nepal
(1857) he stated that 'there are no craftsmen generally speaking to
these tribes, located among them for ages untold, being their smiths,
carpenters, potters etc. and the women of each tribe being its domestic weaver' (p. 131). One wonders, though, whether Hodgson,
like the other foreign male visitors of the period, failed to appreciate
the ingenuity and artistic skills of these domestic weavers. Nevertheless, elsewhere Hodgson (p. 33) stated that the Nepalese manufactured cotton stuffs as fine as *kharwa*. He also gives an indication
of the great physical difficulties that must always have been involved
in trading between Kathmandu and Peking. In a detailed account of
the route as traversed by the Nepalese ambassador Kaji Dalbhanjan
Pande in 1822–3 he lists 102 mountain ridges and 652 rivers to be
crossed. The travellers set off on 7 June and arrived in Peking on
12 January (p. 101). In another report (1874) he mentions 'blankets
of good wool but very coarse and heavy, save the *chourput*, which
is light and finer. It is made of the inner coat of the chowree ox or
yak. The others, of sheep's wool, the *kachar* blankets, sell well as
they are warmer and more durable than Indian blankets. Some of
the former are felted not woven' (p. 43). Woollen textiles are mentioned also by Boeck (1891, 8), who wrote of 'garments made of
brown and white sheep's wool'.

Wright (1877) and Oldfield (1880) reviewed the situation regarding castes at this time. Wright (1877, 182–7) noted that early in the Malla dynasty King Jayasthiti Malla (1382–1429) had overseen the revision of the laws affecting houses, lands and caste for the people of the Kathmandu Valley and such other areas as lay under Malla authority. The population, other than brahmins and Kshatris, was divided into sixty-four sub-castes of the Vaisya and Sudra castes, according to their occupations, and were assigned a particular place in society. Rules were laid down on the dwellings, dress and ornaments of the low castes: thus Kasais were not allowed to have sleeves on their coats and Podhyas were not permitted caps, coats, shoes or gold ornaments. Wright, however, found (p. 186) that by the nineteenth century many of these castes were unknown. Oldfield (1880), surgeon at the British Residency in Kathmandu from 1850 to 1863, described Newar, Hindu and Buddhist castes at that time: these included a number of craft-related castes. Of these Oldfield includes Tatti, who made dresses for idols and also the caste thread, *janeo*, the sacred plied thread worn over the left shoulder by brahmins and Chhetris. A lower caste of weavers, Tatee, wove *ponga*, a kind of cotton cloth to put on the dead, as well as the cloth with which certain servants of Machendranath, venerated as the divine provider of rain and thus a good harvest, covered themselves when performing their services. It was also worn when a Newar embraced Buddhism or a Sati immolated herself on her husband's funeral pyre. The Bikhu Bandya or Bikhu Burraj caste made vestments of deities. In addition to these weavers, who ranked in the middle class, women would have spun and woven cloth for their own families. Oldfield mentions two castes of dyers: the Bhat were dyers of red colour for all sorts of hair or woollen cloths but not linen. This limitation would suggest that a kind of linen from hemp, ramie or flax was produced. Chippah dyed all types of cloth blue. Pihi were makers of wickerwork baskets, *dhoko* (measures holding ten handfuls of corn), *karmos* and wicker *chattahs* (umbrellas). There was also a special caste who made *charkas* (spinning-wheels) but which did not do general carpentry; other carpenters would not make spinning equipment.

The Buddhist priestly caste, Banhra, continued to wear the Newari national costume of a close-fitting jacket, *jivara*, and a long shirt, *nivasa*, pleated at the waist and reaching to the ankles. The two garments joined at the waist round which was worn a cummerbund or thick-rolled waistband. The majority of the Newars, though, wore 'the costume of the Gorkhas', that is, 'regular trousers with a short coat or blouse reaching a little below the hips and fastened round the waist by a scarf or cummerbund' (Oldfield 1880, 140–1).

During the nineteenth century detailed information on the nature of textiles becomes available. One of the most comprehensive

An early example of the skill of the spinning-wheel maker, this elaborately carved 17th-century Salwood wheel probably formed part of the dowry of a Newar bride. Images of Garuda, Visnu and Buddha embellish the base and the handle support, showing how Hinduism and Buddhism blend and coexist in Nepal and remain part of everyday life. National Museum, Kathmandu 23/137 457.

reports was written by Campbell (1836). It was he who recorded (p. 220) that most Newar women wove the cotton cloth required by their family. For this they bought seed-cotton which was grown in abundance in the hill valleys east of Kathmandu, especially in Timal, to the east of Dhulikhel/Sun Kosi, and the southern plains (*terai*). Campbell also noted (p. 221) that every father was expected to present his newly-married daughter with a seed-cotton separating 'machine', *keko*, and a spinning-wheel, *yeau*, in addition to her dowry. Campbell listed the seventeen principal cotton piece goods manufactured in 'Nepal proper' (1836, 224 *et seq.*).

Based on Campbell 1836, 224 *et seq.*

Changa. Produced in almost all Newari homes and also widely in the hills. Coarse, hard and thin in texture. Pieces usually 10–14 yds × 18 in (9.1–12.8 m × 46 cm).

Kadi. Produced in considerable quantity in the valley of Nuwakot, as well as the Kathmandu Valley and throughout the hills. Widely worn by cultivators, both Parbatiyas (hill people) and Newar. Pieces usually 6.5 yds × 16–18 in (5.9 m × 40–6 cm).

Purabi chint. An imitation of Indian chintz, produced at Dhankuta and elsewhere in the eastern hills. Generally black and red in a small striped pattern. Coarse and heavy. Much worn by poorer people. Pieces sold in Kathmandu 5 yds × less than 2 ft (4.6 m × 61 cm).

Mumi chint. Similar to *purabi chint* and also produced in Dhankuta and other eastern areas. Worn by Parbatiya and Newar women as bodices and saris. Pieces 6 yds × 18 in (5.5 m × 46 cm).

Banarasi chint. An imitation of Indian chintz, hence the name. Produced in Bhaktapur. Various colours and patterns. Less coarse and heavy than other cloths; used for lining jackets and for women's dresses. Pieces 6 yds × 18 in (5.5 m × 46 cm).

Kalu chint. Produced chiefly in the hills west of Kathmandu. Coarse, heavy and 'very rudely dyed and printed'. Widest of the Nepalese textiles', a piece being 8 yds × 2.5 ft (7.3 m × 76 cm).

Durkeah chint. Produced principally at Pokhara and Bhutwal. Very coarse and heavy but with a greater width than the valley chintzes. Used for jacket linings and women's dresses. Pieces 6 yds × 2 ft (5.5 m × 61 cm).

Butedar chint. So called because of its spotted pattern. One of the preferred Bhaktapur chintzes. Pieces 5.5 yds × 18 in (5 m × 46 cm).

Hara chint. Produced almost exclusively in Banepa 32 km east of Kathmandu. Quality similar to the others.

Purabi kadi. Produced in the eastern hills. Broader and rather finer than the Nuwakot *kadi* recorded above. 'A good deal' exported to 'Bhote'. Piece 14 yds × 2.5 ft (12.8 m × 76 cm).

Much of the cloth mentioned by Alan Campbell in his 1836 account could have been woven on a loom such as the one in this 1894 photograph. If the photograph was actually taken in Nepal, the clothing, absence of nose jewellery, the topography and the faint outline of temples suggest the weavers are from the Jyapu, a Newar farming community in the Kathmandu Valley. Photo: Johnston and Hoffman, Royal Geographical Society.

Kassa. Nepalese form of the Indian *mulmul* or common gauze, made in large quantities in Bhaktapur and by Newars generally throughout the valley. Used for making turbans, a piece 8 yds × 6 in (7.3 m × 15 cm) being sufficient for a *pagri*, worn by the poorer Parbatiyas and some Newars, though the latter generally wore a small conical skull-cap.

*Bhangara.** Coarse but strong sackcloth or canvas, made from the inner bark of trees, possibly several species, by the hill people. Much used in the Kathmandu Valley for grain-bags and sacks for transporting merchandise. The poorer hill people, who subsist by collecting and carrying firewood, produce the cloth for their own wear. The cloth is very strong and durable and will stand long periods of dampness without rotting or loss of texture. Pieces are 5 yds × 12 in (4.6 m × 30.5 cm).

Rhari. A coarse woollen blanket, of thick and heavy texture, pro-

* Campbell presumably refers to cloth made either of nettle, *Girardinia diversifolia*, or hemp, *Cannabis sativa*.

duced by 'Bhoteahs' in the hills and worn by them almost exclusively. Admirably suited for the rainy season. Pieces 7.5 yds × 14 in (6.9 m × 35.5 cm).

Bhote. So-called after the name of the people who make and wear it, in the hill areas north of Nuwakot and the Kathmandu Valley up to the snow-line. Thick and soft woollen stuff, half-blanket, half-felt, warmer and lighter than the *rhari* but less effective as protection against rain. Pieces 7–8 yds × 18 in (6.4–7.3 m × 46 cm).

Putassi. Produced exclusively by Newar women for domestic purposes. Strong and coarse, generally blue and white check, sometimes red and white; also striped. Pieces 5.5 yds × 2.5 ft (5 m × 76 cm).

Punika. Produced by Newars, principally in the larger towns of the Kathmandu Valley. An imitation of the Dinapur 'bird's-eye' tablecloth. Three or four sorts, all but one coarse and heavy. This one is worn by higher-class Newars and, occasionally, by Parbatiya soldiers. Pieces 6 yds × 2 ft (5.5 m × 61 cm).

Bhim poga. Although of ancient origin, in the 1830s the cloth was worn only by a class of outcasts and was difficult to obtain. Its only other use was to 'roll the corpses of religious persons in previous to being burned'. The warp was coarse cotton thread, the weft a soft spun woollen yarn: in addition some fine wool 'is amalgamated with the web in weaving it'. The texture of the cloth was very soft and would keep the wearer warm indoors but was too fleecy to keep out the rain. Pieces were 4 × 2 ft (1.2 × 0.6 m).

Oldfield, the British Residency surgeon, was an understanding observer who used his paintbrush as well as his pen to bring the

Temple of Mahadeo, 1650, with a corner of a temple of Harreeshunker, Bhatgaon (Bhaktapur), a watercolour painting by H. A. Oldfield, 1853. 23.5 × 33 cm. British Library WD 2837.

Street scene, Kathmandu, a watercolour painting by H. A. Oldfield, 1850. In the foreground on the left traders from the north, perhaps Sherpa, in their traditional garments with their laden sheep, negotiate some transactions with a Kathmandu merchant. 37.5 × 54.5 cm. British Library WD 3284.

nineteenth-century Kathmandu Valley to life – magnificent temples, dwelling places and the ordinary people at their daily tasks. In the painting of Bhaktapur, where the population would have been predominantly Newar, the women's outfit consists mainly of a full skirt reaching to just above the ankle. The skirt appears to be a length of cloth wrapped round and folded so as to allow for leg movement. The endpiece is either tucked in or draped over the shoulder, like a sari. Some women wear shawls. A wide wrap-around waistband is worn by most women as well as men. The men are wearing either long white tunics or nearly knee-length jackets with tight-fitting trousers underneath or bare legs, as is the case with the basket carrier. All the men wear headgear, either turbans or caps. In a painting of 'Sambhunath' temple one of the men is wearing the type of cross-sling which is worn to this day by Gurungs and Tamangs. (This Buddhist temple is still visited by people from all parts of Nepal, especially at Buddha Jayanti, the birthday of Buddha, and the Tibetan New Year.) Spinning must have been one of the major occupations of women. Hand-turned spinning-wheels appear on several of Oldfield's paintings.

One of Oldfield's paintings of Kathmandu shows a group of

traders from northern Nepal in the foreground. These could have been Sherpas, who maintained regular contact with the merchants of the Kathmandu Valley. The animals are laden with bags which might have contained salt from Tibet or might have carried 'Nipal blankets'. These strong bags, usually with stripe patterns which make it easy to identify the owner, are woven from yak hair or wool. Oldfield describes how rock-salt, brought down from the north, was packed in bags holding 15 lb (6.8 kg) each, fastened upon the back of sheep: 'whole flocks of sheep thus laden may be frequently met with outside the valley of Nipal by the road from Nagacot [Nagarkot]

Wallanchoon [Walungchung] *10,000 feet above the sea*, by W. H. Fitch after a sketch by J. D. Hooker, made between 1849 and 1851. Royal Botanic Gardens, Kew.

and Kerang' (Oldfield 1880, vol. 2, p. 11). In the painting the men are wearing cross-over, calf-length coats, the traditional garment worn by people in northern Nepal (see p. 153).

Sir Joseph Hooker, who traversed the slopes of Nepal and Sikkim from 1847 to 1851, made numerous sketches showing flora, fauna and the magic scenes he witnessed. Some of the sketches include people and, as a keen observer of all that went on around him, he carefully noted their way of dressing. On his visit to Walungchung (Hooker 1854, vol. I, 209, 211–12) he observed 'wooden houses ornamented with hundreds of long poles and vertical flags'. Hooker presumably refers here to the prayer-flags which are so evident

43

outside Buddhist homes throughout Nepal. The narrow woven cotton strips have prayers printed or painted on them – prayers believed to be carried to heaven as the flags flutter in the wind high up on bamboo poles. Houses 'were built of upright strong pine-planks, the interstices of which were filled with yak-dung; and they sometimes rest on a low foundation wall.' The low pitched roofs were covered with shingles kept down by stones. 'Many herds of fine yaks were grazing about Wallanchoon . . . The base and sides of the flanking mountains are covered with luxuriant, dense bushes of rhododendron, rose, berberry and juniper.' Hooker also remarked that both men and women seemed fond of decorating their hair with wreaths of lichen (*Usnea*), which they dyed yellow with the leaves of *Simplocos*.

In 1846, following a period of ferment and uncertainty, an army general, Jung Bahadur Rana, was installed as Prime Minister and commander-in-chief of the army. He subsequently seized full power, with the king's authority becoming purely nominal. The Rana family was to rule Nepal for over 100 years. The court textiles during that period, of which samples are preserved in the National Museum, Kathmandu, and elsewhere, including the Victoria and Albert Museum, London, are mainly of Indian and Western origin. Wright (1877) includes a lithograph of 'a Rani or Nepalese lady of high rank' in his book and comments: 'the ladies of the higher classes like their muslin to be 60 or 80 yards [55–73 m] in length. Of course, they cannot walk much with such a bundle round them'. He also states that 'the lower orders infinitely prefer their home-made cloth, both cotton and woollen, which is far more lasting than that which is imported' (Wright, p. 69). It speaks well for the quality of locally woven cloth that it could find a market in spite of the pressures of traders with foreign textiles, although the price may well have been a major factor.

During the 1880s, when cameras became more portable and easier to handle, the first photographs from Nepal appeared. They were mainly of people connected with the court wearing garments made from Indian and European fabrics, although some of the fine embroidery on the garments might have been worked in Nepal. In 1899 L. A. Waddell used photographs of 'types of Nepal', taken by Johnston and Hoffman, to illustrate his *Journey among the Himalayas*. These posed portraits of people from eastern Nepal were probably taken in a studio in Darjeeling, a place where a great variety of people gathered for the market. Waddell's own photographs were taken actually in Nepal. The garment of a Lepcha he describes thus: he 'is clad in a long plaid of blue and white striped cloth of home-spun nettle-fibre or cotton, which is wound round his body and descends to the knee . . . His waist is girdled by a red or blue band, from which is suspended his long, formidable-looking, straight,

'A Rani or Nepalese lady of high rank' from Daniel Wright's *History of Nepal* of 1877.

one-edged knife'. The Lepcha woman's dress consists of a long, loose, wrapper-like, white cotton gown with long, wide sleeves turned up in Tibetan fashion at the cuffs to show red lining . . . 'many of them as they walk busily twirl a distaff' (Waddell 1899, 296). Shuttle and spinning-staff were of such importance that they were included in the sad Lepcha maiden's love lament which was recorded by Waddell.

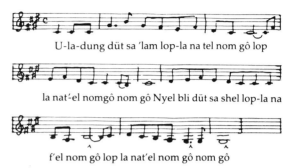

U-la-dung düt sa 'lam lop-la na tel nom gô lop

la nat'-el nomgô nom gô Nyel bli düt sa shel lop-la na

f'el nom gô lop la nat'el nom gô nom gô

I [am] a maiden like an unopened bud,
like a pretty supple shuttle,
like a whirling staff.
I am a maiden standing like a twirling spinning thread
like a bright golden tassel standing forlorn behind.
I am a maiden like a tender coiled bud
sung like a sorrowing bird,
loudly lamenting like the tak-mok bird,
I feel sad, very sad.

Lepchas love lament *U-La Dung Dut*
from L. A. Waddell, *Among the Himalayas*

In 1951 the Rana regime was overthrown and the authority of the king was re-established. The doors of the country were opened again revealing to the world a land of undescribable scenic beauty, of art treasures and, perhaps not so immediately apparent, a rich variety of unusual textiles. These were yet further enriched by the Tibetan refugees in the 1960s, who brought with them the skills of carpet weaving. But it was also a country of hardship and poverty, especially in the remote mountain areas. Since 1951, successively under King Tribhuvan, King Mahendra and King Birendra, much has been done to try to relieve poverty, to abolish the caste system with its attendant prejudices and inequalities, and to improve education and communications throughout the kingdom. King Birendra, the present monarch, declared Nepal a Zone Of Peace and introduced the objective of meeting the basic needs of all citizens by the year 2000. In 1990 multi-party democracy was reintroduced followed by national general elections in 1991. Nepal remains the only Hindu kingdom in the world, but individual freedom of religion for Buddhists, Christians, Muslims and others is a right enshrined in the Constitution.

45

2

RAW
MATERIALS

❖

Harvesting *allo*: stripping off the
outer bark. The leaves in the
background give an indication of the
size of the plant.

The nature of a textile depends to a large extent on the type of raw material used. Nepal, with her contrasting climates and altitudes, provides a wealth of materials from which fibres have for centuries been assessed, extracted, spun, twisted into a continuous yarn and made into textiles suitable for their specific purposes. Local raw materials for textiles are obtained from both animals and plants. Animal sources include sheep's wool, yak hair, and both the rough outer hair and the luxurious cashmere-like inner hair from goats, and, more recently, silk from the *Bombyx* moth larva. Fibres from plants are extracted from many different species. The main sources are the seed fibres from cotton, the stem fibres from nettle, jute, hemp and bamboo, and leaf fibres from the sisal family. Imported yarns, particularly cotton, and locally produced acrylic wool have found their way into Nepalese textile production since the 1960s, but mainly as a supplement rather than a substitute for local resources.

Yak hair

The noble, massive, long-haired yak, *Bos gruniens*, and the female *bri* (Tibetan) or *nak* (Sherpa) is invaluable in the cold, northern mountainous areas above 3,000 m. It provides milk, butter, cheese and meat for food, dung for fuel, two types of hair for making shelters, ropes and clothing, skin for shoes, saddle-bags and straps, and a tail as a precious trade good. It also affords transport for carrying loads (60–80 kg) and even people over high passes through snow and ice, which no other large animal could tolerate. The horns of yaks are placed as an offering on shrines, *laptse*, on high mountain passes (Kihara 1957, 147).

47

The even more impressive undomesticated yak is rare now: in ancient times it was considered a demon and was hunted, in spite of the danger involved. For this reason 'mythology, before it became mellowed by Buddhism, told of the great deeds of heroes, who overcame tremendous and malevolent deities in the form of this animal' (Tucci 1962, 29). It is unclear whether the yak mentioned in the seventh century by the Chinese Hiuen Tsiang (Beal 1906, 80) in the statement 'the country Ni-po-la produces red copper, the yak

William Moorcroft, an official of the East India Company, and his partner Hyder Jung Hearsey (who painted this picture) in Tibet in 1812. Both Europeans are depicted riding yaks, which were probably more comfortable, sure-footed and warmer than horses. British Library WD 350.

and the ming-ming bird (jivanjiva)' was wild or tame. Hooker (1854, vol. I, 213) describes the domesticated animal as a handsome, true bison having 'large and beautiful eyes, spreading horns, long silky, black hair, and grand bushy tails: black is their prevailing colour, but red, dun, parti-coloured, and white are common'. According to Waddell (1899, 168) 'the tail ends in a great bushy tuft, which serves the same purpose as the bushy tail of the hybernating [sic] squirrel, curling over its owner's feet and nose when asleep, like a rug, and thus affording protection against the intense cold of the Himalayan nights'.

The yak tail is one of the oldest and most precious trade goods:

A Nepalese palm-leaf manuscript, *Astasahasrika Prajnaparamita*, dated AD 1015, showing an attendant of Buddha carrying a yak-tail whisk. Cambridge University Library Add. 1643.

Spinning yak hair from an arm-ring with a spike spindle. A similar spindle is now in the British Museum (As 1992, 10.14).

it was much in demand by Indian princes for use as a fan to drive away flies and also as a royal emblem. According to Captain Samuel Turner of the East India Company Army (1800, 188) yak tails 'are esteemed throughout the East as far as luxury or parade have any influence on the manners of the people. . . . They are also employed as ornamental furniture upon horses and elephants'. Several sculptures in Kathmandu depict dependents of deities waving yak-tail fans. The palm-leaf manuscript of AD 1015 shows an attendant of Buddha carrying such a whisk. On a twelfth-century wooden manuscript cover in the Victoria and Albert Museum, London, flywhisks are painted between the gods as insignia of royalty and symbolising compassion. The tail hair has the highest commercial value of all yak hair, especially if it is white, the preferred colour for flywhisks. Tibetans and Mongols sought it for their banners (Jest 1992, personal communication). It can also be dyed easily. The tail hair is cut every two to three years only, so as not to deprive the animal of its protection.

From the body the outer hair, which grows to a length of 20 cm on the lower parts of the flank, is cut once a year, at the onset of the milder weather from the second week in May to the second week in June. Neither shears nor scissors are used: the usual method is to take a bundle of hair in one hand and a sharp two-edged knife in the other and cut the hair above the soft, down-like inner layer. This fine, inner hair, *kulu*, is just plucked when the yak naturally loses its winter coat, at which time the soft layer comes away easily. Although it is almost as soft as cashmere, *kulu* is not valued as highly as the harder but stronger outer hair. Humphrey (1980, 47) estimated that one shearing can yield about one *dharni* (2,400 g) of yak hair.

George Stubbs's 1791 painting of the yak does full justice to the thick coat of the animal, although the even length of the hair suggests some use of artistic licence. John Hunter, FRS (1728–93), a renowned surgeon and eminent scientist, commissioned Stubbs, the anatomist and artist, to paint the yak from life: a yak in England must have indeed been a rare sight. Captain Samuel Turner (1800, 188), who had travelled in Tibet and Bhutan, wrote that 'I had the satisfaction to send two of this species to Mr Hastings after he left India and to hear that one reached England alive. This, which was a bull, remained for some time after he landed, in a torpid languid state, till his constitution had in some degree assimilated with the climate, when he recovered at once both his health and vigour. He afterwards became the father of many calves'.

Yak hair is never washed prior to spinning. It is sorted into different colours and qualities, and then fluffed up either in the same way as sheep's wool with a bow or beaten with two sticks, to give the hair the right texture for spinning, and also to get rid of dust and other foreign matter. The spinning of yak hair is usually done by men using spike spindles of various forms and weights. Some consist of three parts – a wood or bamboo shaft which is set into two wooden cross-sticks, *kariog*. Another spindle, used by Sherpas in the north-east of Nepal, has a bamboo shaft (24.5 cm long), which fits into the centre hole of a smooth, curved, tapered piece of wood measuring 19 cm across. The yarn on this spindle is spun from an arm-ring: this is formed by winding strands of yak hair around a stick, approximately 36 cm long. They are then slid off the stick and the twisted strands, a half to three-quarters of a centimetre thick, are put round the hand two or three times. The ring is secured by forming crochet-type loops all round with the remaining part of the strand. The ring is put over the left wrist, and the spindle, with some previously spun yarn attached to it, is given a twirl. The strand, which is easily released from the ring, can now be opened

Above Contemporary Nepalese five-rupee banknote, depicting yaks with coats even longer than that in Stubbs' painting.

Right George Stubbs representation of a yak. Oil on canvas, 1791, 57 × 73 cm. Hunterian collection, Royal College of Surgeons.

Below Spinning in Tarap, one of the most northerly regions of Nepal.

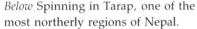

up with both hands and the required amount of fibres is drafted into the spun yarn on the freely rotating spindle.

Women in the Dolpo area mainly use a tapered stick spindle, *phan*, without a whorl. A strand of fibres is fixed with spittle to the spindle, which is turned, usually on a small bowl, with the right hand, whilst the left hand, holding a *rolag*, or bunch of fibres, controls the tension and the thickness of the strand. When the spindle is full, the spun yarn is wound off into a ball (Jest 1975, 192).

Following the death of a yak – killing is not compatible with Buddhism – the hide is used for a variety of purposes including tents, the soles of boots and backstraps for weavers. It is not tanned, like the skins of sheep and goats, but simply dried.

Sheep's wool

Sheep's wool has been an important textile fibre in Nepal for millennia, both for home use and for trade. More than 2,000 years ago rainproof Nepalese woollen blankets were mentioned as trade items in India (see p. 24). Locally woven woollen clothing, blankets and rugs are still in widespread use in the mountain areas. The most common breed of sheep in the country is the Baruwal. The majority are raised in the mountain areas where the flocks move with the seasons between the middle mountains and the high-altitude alpine pastures. The wool of this small, hardy sheep is very suitable for felting, a characteristic it must share with the wool used for the blankets of 2,000 years ago to make them waterproof. The short fleece, with little crimp, is springy, strong and easy to spin. The breed thrives in both the mild climate of the middle mountains and the cold of the high altitudes. Its short fleece may be helpful in tolerating heat and avoiding the dangerous chilling that might arise with a longer, soft fleece in the harsh mountain conditions where driving rain or hail is common. A long fleece would also soon get entangled in the thorny shrubs. A number of cross-breeds have been introduced, particularly Polwarth crosses, but their benefit has yet to be demonstrated. Some Gurung shepherds have expressed their preference for the pure Baruwal because of its hardiness and the suitability of the wool for felting: this is required for rari/rug weaving (see p. 145). The sheep is also strong enough to be used as a pack animal, carrying up to 12 kg or more. Sheep caravans can still be met with in the middle mountains of Nepal, each sheep laden with a handwoven double bag or a sack of grain or salt. In the more northern Dolpo area the Tibetan sheep breed *byang-lug* is more common. Valued for its wool and suitability as a pack animal, its soft wool has been traded from Tibet into Nepal for centuries and is particularly suitable for clothing.

Sheep may be sheared twice a year, in March and September, before and at the end of the warm monsoon season: the yield is usually less than 1 kg per shearing (Oli and Morel 1985, 7). Traditionally the fleece, or rather bundles of wool, are cut with a 30 cm-long knife. Scissors are never used: a Gurung shepherd thought that this would make the sheep sick. Hand shears have been introduced in recent years and are used in some areas. The cut bunches of wool are then sorted according to colour, which varies from white to beige-brown and black. Sometimes the wool is gently rinsed in water and spread out on mats to dry. Otherwise the following process of bowing would also free the wool from dirt. The bow in the British Museum collection is made of two pieces of split bamboo – the curved bow (105 cm long and 2.3 cm wide), to each notched end of which the bow strand (97 cm long and 0.4 cm wide) is joined with bark string. The flexibility of the split bamboo

Baruwal sheep, a hardy mountain breed.

51

Opposite Woollen front apron worn by Sherpa women made up from three 2/2 twill weft-faced *c*.19 cm-wide panels. The fine single weft yarn is hand spun and coloured with natural dyes.

Below A spinning wheel carved by the husband of a Gurung weaver from east Nepal. Shown before and after assembly. British Museum As 1992 18.1a–q.

holds the bow strand under tension. Crouching on the floor, the weaver holds the bow in one hand whilst flicking the bow strand with the other, just above or through the tangled bunches of wool. The vibration loosens the wool and fluffs it up. In the 1980s carders, imported from India, became increasingly used in preference to the bow.

The wool, shaped into loose rolls (rolags), is spun on a hand spindle or a hand-turned spinning-wheel (*charka*). The hand spindles vary in length, the average being about 30 cm, and also in weight, which varies with the type of yarn to be spun. The finest thread is spun on the lightest-weight spindle. The shaft is usually made of bamboo and the whorl is carved from wood, horn or a buffalo hoof. The whorl can be a stone or even, as the sample of a Manang Gurung spindle in the British Museum shows, a piece of a discarded rubber slipper. The *charka* is often handmade. The British Museum example, carved in east Nepal, consists of twenty parts including a bamboo cord, 213 cm long. All parts are slotted together without any nail or screw. The wooden base consists of three parts joined in an H shape. One arm of the H supports two uprights with the spindle holder and the metal spindle in its bamboo casing. The other arm of the H supports two uprights which hold the axle with the wheel spikes between them and a crank handle attached to the axle on one side. Three slightly curved spikes are mounted on top of each other on both sides of the axle, the axle shaft going through the centre hole of each spike. The two sets of six-armed star-shaped spikes are placed on either side of the axle with the spikes of one set lying at the midway point of an opposite pair: they are then connected by winding a length of split bamboo across from

one side to the other, around the notched ends of each spike. This split bamboo is 0.4 cm wide and, as it is difficult to get a strip of smooth bamboo 213 cm long, there are two joins. The length of bamboo acts as a kind of rim around the wheel. The driving band, a two-ply string, is laid tightly over this rim and the bamboo casing of the spindle. When the handle is turned, the motion is transferred to the wheel with the driving-band, which will set the spindle in motion.

The spinning process is similar to that described by Campbell (1836, 219): a length of twisted yarn is attached to the spindle tip; the rest of the bunch of fibres, or rolag, is held by the spinner in one hand, whilst she turns the handle with the other. As she moves her hand with the fibres away from the spindle and releases fibres, these are twisted by the rotations: this newly spun yarn is then wound on to the spindle as the spinner reverses the wheel just a little. She thus continues to draw out and wind on the fibres controlling the twist by the number of turns she gives to the wheel and the direction of the twist (s or z) by turning the wheel either to the right or the left: the more common is the z twist.

Cashmere, pashmina

The warmest and most luxurious of all the animal fibres, finer even than the best merino wool, comes principally from a Central Asian species of the mountain goat, the cashmere or shawl goat, *Capra hircus*. The name is misleading for although the cashmere shawls which made the name famous were woven in Kashmir the fibre came from goats in Tibet and Central Asia. In Nepal the shawls woven from cashmere hair are referred to as pashmina shawls, *pashm* being the Persian word for 'wool'. Persian goat fibres, although much coarser than the true cashmere, are sometimes marketed as cashmere; they are, however, not used for Nepalese shawls.

As the pashmina shawls have become a major trade item in the Kathmandu Valley, where the fibres are processed and woven, some details of this intriguing industry may be justified. Also a number of cashmere goats are found in some of the northernmost parts of Nepal, for example Mustang. In some areas these cashmere goats have crossed with the local breed. This has increased their milk yield but unfortunately has adversely affected their fibre production: even the pure-bred goat will provide little more than 115 g (4 oz) per year of the soft white, grey or buff-coloured down, which is found under the long, coarse outer hair. This down is combed out during the spring. It may also be shed naturally at this time and be rubbed off by the animal against rocks and shrubs, from where it can be collected.

Cashmere down has been a valuable trade item between Tibet and

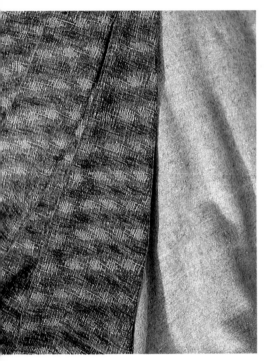

The soft, natural-coloured, pashmina shawls on the right are woven on 4-shaft frame looms in Kathmandu, usually with a cotton warp and pashmina weft in a 2/2 twill weave. The shawl on the left is the first trial (in 1992) by a dhaka weaver from east Nepal using pashmina weft on a black cotton warp with natural colour silk and black cotton inlay patterns.

A watercolour painting of a shawl goat inscribed in Persian with the name of the artist, Zayn al Din, a native of Patna, Calcutta, 1778. Victoria & Albert Museum IS 51–1963.

Kashmir for centuries and the monopoly of the trade was fiercely guarded. From Kashmir woven and embroidered shawls were exported to many parts of the world and gained the reputation that some were so fine they could be pulled through a finger ring. In Europe, where they became high fashion in the eighteenth century, they stimulated the search for this luxurious material. Turner (1800, 356), who considered the shawl goats the most beautiful species of the whole goat family, discovered to his dismay that 'upon removing them to the hot atmosphere of Bengal, they quickly lost their beautiful clothing'. Moorcroft, who was employed by the East India Company as superintendent of a stud for cavalry horses, went trekking at considerable trouble and danger from India through Nepal to Tibet in search of both horses and shawl goats. Some of the goats were sent to Scotland but the venture failed. Nevertheless, his trials with Tibetan shawl wool played a large part in establishing the shawl industry in Britain. Moorcroft's handwritten letters, now held in the British Library's India Office Collection (MSS Eur F38/-G30/45) contain particularly interesting information on the preparation of the fine goat hair. In one letter dated 18 July 1820 he gives a detailed description of how rice flour was prepared and then mixed with the hair to clean it:

1 The husked rice is soaked in water for twenty-four hours.
2 The water is changed and the rice is soaked again until it is soft enough to be squeezed into a flour.
3 The water is poured off and the rice is 'reduced to flour by being bruised and rubbed with a smooth clean hard stone in a wooden dish of a circular form'.

'The picked wool is laid on the rice flour in the dish and lightly prefused into it with the hand then turned upside down and again flattened and squeezed; upon this the flour is sprinkled and patted into it. The wool is next pulled to pieces and again lightly beaten in the flour and turned until the whole of it has been well mixed.'

The cleaned wool is opened up with the fingers so that no knots or lumps remain and then formed into 'thin loose flats about three inches long, two broad and three quarters of an inch thick'. These are stored in a covered earthen dish until ready for spinning. If,

Preparing pashmina fibres. The woman on the right (wearing a pashmina shawl) is cutting the tufts of down and hair from the skin. The woman on the left is pulling out the long hair through a comb. Fluffs of down are on the tray on the left and the hard long hair and one comb are on the floor.

however, the wool is not spun within fifteen days, the old flour is 'lightly dusted out and fresh flour added by which the wool is rendered still whiter . . . The flour that hangs loosely in the flats flies out in spinning and loose hairs that are left here and there in the wool are detached at the same time of themselves'. One wonders to what extent this was wishful thinking as the total separation of the hair from the wool seems to cause difficulties until the present day. But this process, according to Moorcroft, had the added advantage of improving the colour of the wool and 'keeping the fibres individually apart . . . in a loose open state favourable for spinning . . . while washing with soap and water would render the shawl wool harsh, knotty and difficult to spin'.

At the present time the processing of pashmina in Kathmandu involves first of all the cutting of the down and hair from the skin. A few cashmere goats are brought down to Kathmandu during festival times including Dasain, when goat meat is much in demand. However, most of the pashmina used for weaving shawls comes from the skins which are traded in from Tibet/China. After cutting, the tufts comprising down and long hair are carefully put over a bamboo comb, near the point where the long hair joins the down, and the hard hair is pulled and combed out leaving the soft down on the other side of the comb. Much patience and skill is required to ensure that none of the long hair remains with the down – an almost impossible task. The down is separated into colours, the white being the most valuable. The down is then lightly teased out, carded and spun on the *charka*. The hard outer hair is used mainly for ropes and rugs.

Pashmina goat cross-breeds in Dolpo provide milk and textile raw material (rough outer and a little soft inner hair). They are also used as pack animals (Jest 1993, personal communication). Other goat breeds, including Sindal, are kept mainly for meat and manure, rarely as a source of textile raw material (Oli and Morel 1985, 2). In some northern parts they are used as pack animals.

Silk

Silk is generally perceived to be the most precious of the natural fibres, fine, lustrous and strong, and producing more cloth, weight for weight, than any other (Seagrott 1975, 15). The fibre is produced by the larvae of a number of species of moth, and quality is affected by their feed. There are two main types of silk fibre in Nepal – the high-quality silk from mulberry in the hills and *eri* silk from castor, mainly in the southern plains, *terai*. The best-quality silk is that from *Bombyx mori*. This moth lays thousands of eggs of which one gram will contain some 1,400 eggs. When the larva hatches, it eats voraciously and grows rapidly, so much so that it periodically has to pause from eating to grow a new and larger skin before casting its old one and starting to eat again. This happens four times before the larva is fully grown some six weeks after its emergence; by this time it will be about 7.5 cm long. It then ceases to feed, becomes restless, its skin changing to a semi-transparent pink, and seeks a place in which to change into the chrysalis or pupa form. Silk farmers prepare frames for this purpose which are often most interesting constructions of bamboo or straw: flexible split bamboo strands are looped or coiled in various ways into a loose woven bamboo mat. Some farmers simply incorporate lengths of straw in

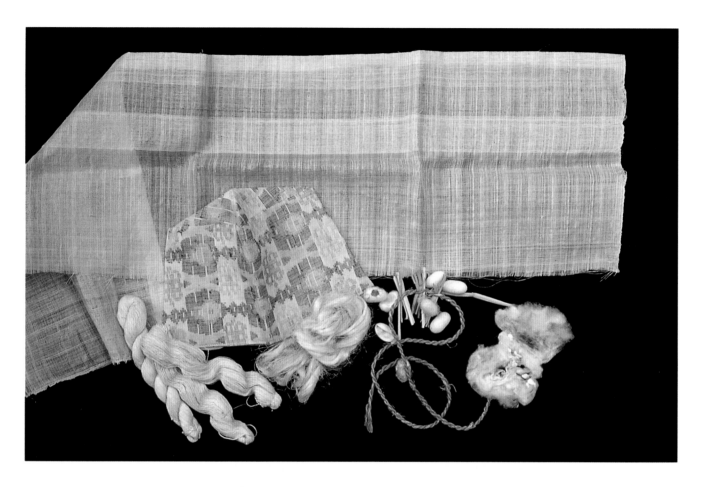

From right to left 2-ply, split breeding straw; cocoons from which the moths have emerged; degummed and teased out cocoons; treadle-wheel-spun silk yarn; hand-woven silk cloth and an inlay-patterned topi from a farm at Ruptse, west Nepal. British Museum 1992 10.40–42 a, b, c.

between the twist of a two-ply straw cord. When the worm has selected its loop or straw corner, it begins to spin its cocoon. Such a cocoon will contain a thread that may vary from 500 to 1,300 m long. After about ten days a moth will break out of this cocoon and in so doing will damage the coils of silk fibre. Such cocoons are placed in boiling water to degum the fibre. They are then opened up, teased out and handspun. This type of yarn, with its lively texture, has been used by dhaka-cloth weavers with much success. The more commercial method of reeling off the silk, which has to start before the moth emerges in order to obtain a continuous silk thread, is also practised. The cocoons are put into nearly-boiling water for five minutes. This softens the gum and releases the silk filament. The cocoons are then stirred with a bamboo fork in order to pick up the ends from about ten cocoons: these are reeled off together on to a rotating frame.

The Industrial Entomology Project at Kopasi, in the Kathmandu Valley, has been working on the production of mulberry silk since the 1970s and has become a centre for assisting farmers to establish mulberry and rear silkworms. Mulberry trees (*Morus* spp.) have been planted by farmers for many years in certain parts of Nepal, mainly as fruit and fodder trees. They are found usually between

700 and 1,750 m. Mulberry can be raised from seed or cuttings and coppices and pollards well. In India mulberry is used for silkworm production on very short coppice or pollard rotations. In addition to guidance on mastering the method of managing mulberry for feeding silkworms, farmers have also been given assistance with the annual supply in spring of silkworm eggs of *Bombyx mori* to overcome the problems of over-wintering and, for a number, the purchase of cocoons so that the farmer is spared the task of reeling off the silk. The project established a fairly wide geographical spread of participants in the 1980s, but the quantity of silk yarn available to weavers so far remains relatively limited.

The other food for silkworms that is widely available in the sub-tropical parts of Nepal is castor, *Ricinus communis*. The silk produced from larvae fed on castor is less lustrous but is soft and comfortable to wear. The plant is easy to cultivate and leaves can be picked within months of sowing the plant. There is a market also for castor-oil seeds. It has been recorded that the silkworm *Attacus ricini*, which is native to north-east Bihar, is capable of producing four to five broods a year under the climatic conditions of the *terai*: periods of very hot dry weather or cold and humid conditions which are sometimes experienced in certain parts are unsuitable (Berry *et al.* 1974, 201). Small projects on rearing silkworms on castor have been initiated by the Japha Training Centre, and there is much interest in expanding this type of silk production. The worms also provide an extra source of protein for some people who roast and eat them.

Stem or bark fibres

Himalayan giant nettle, *allo* **(*Girardinia diversifolia* (Link) Friis)**
Fibres from this nettle have been extracted for generations in the Himalayan region. Watt (1890, 472) states that nettle cloth was mentioned even in the Hindu epic *Ramayana* where it was praised for its beauty and firmness. It might not have been used for the garment of the saint and poet Mila Repa, who is reputed to have visited Nepal; however, nettles were the food on which he 'had lived while he endured the rigours of solitary meditation' (Snellgrove 1989, 74). The utilisation of the fibre has continued up to the present time. In the northern middle mountains of east Nepal Rai weavers speak of its use for ropes, sacks, mats, cast nets and clothing for as long as anyone can remember.

Hooker (1854, vol. 1, 182) described these gigantic nettles, which he named as *Urtica heterophylla*, and stressed that 'their long, white stings look most formidable, but though they sting virulently, the pain only lasts half-an-hour or so'. One specimen of this plant which Hooker collected in the 1850s together with a roll of plain-weave nettle cloth from Sikkim are held in the Economic Plant and Conservation Section of the Royal Botanic Gardens, Kew, England. Watt

Scanning electron micrograph, ×
165, showing a sectional view of
Girardinia diversifolia, allo, with the
fibre cells within the layer of bast
between the outer bark and the
inner wood and pith. Natural
Resources Institute, Chatham.

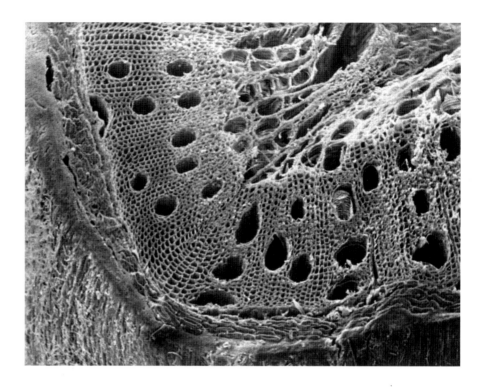

Allo plant collected by Sir Joseph
Hooker on his travels through Nepal
and Sikkim in the 1850s for the Royal
Botanic Gardens, Kew. Sir William
Hooker, his father, had established
a Museum of Economic Botany
there in 1847 'showing plant
products that were either eminently
curious or in any way serviceable to
mankind.'

(1890, 499) lists 'Ullo, Nepal' under '*Girardinia*, Gaud., a genus of
annual or perennial herbs, belonging to the Natural Order Urticaceae' and the Nilghiri Nettle. The specific naming of the species has
recently been clarified by Kew which classified the *allo* plant as
Girardinia diversifolia. (The Kew *Bulletin*, vol. 36 (1), presents a synop-
sis of the genus *Girardinia* (*Urticaceae*) and gives a detailed, botanical
description of *Girardinia diversifolia* and related species including *G.
palmata* or *heterophylla*.) From now on the plant will be referred to
by its most widely used local name – *allo*.

The *allo* plant occurs in most northern parts of Nepal at altitudes
between 1,200 and 3,000 m, flourishing under the shade of mixed
deciduous forests, comprised mainly of various species of oak,
maple, alder and cherries, in moist, sandy soils, especially ravines.
It can also be found on shrubland and on the edges of cultivated
land, where it can help to consolidate bunds on terraced land. Growing to a height of 3 m, the 'thorn'-covered stem, which contains the
fibres, can measure up to 4 cm in diameter at the base. A mature
stem has about thirty alternate leaves, which can be up to 50 cm
wide. The leaves, with three major nerves from the base, are lobed,
coarsely dentate and covered with fine down but also thorn-like
stinging hairs. Each of these, about 0.4–0.9 cm long, arises from a
swollen base which contains the venom. About a hundred of these
grow from the main veins on the back of a mature leaf and fifty on
the upper surface, where they sprout from anywhere. Small green
flowers, which hang in clusters up to 30 cm long and are covered
with stinging hairs, appear around December. The seeds are shed

freely and begin to grow with the onset of the monsoon rains between April and June, varying with the location. At the same time the plant throws out fresh shoots from the perennial roots and the basal stem. Sheep and cattle, which like to eat the young shoots, are kept out of the area at that time, although the areas are browsed during winter which has the advantage that the seed is dispersed in the fleece of the sheep (Gurung 1988, 4).

The following account of *allo* harvesting and spinning is based principally on fieldwork in Bala, Sankhuwasabha, east Nepal, undertaken in the 1980s for the Koshi Hill Area Rural Development Programme. Although there are variations in different areas of Nepal, the basic methods are similar. Harvesting begins towards the end of the monsoon season, August/September, and continues until the plants begin to flower, around December. The best-quality fibre comes from the early harvests. *Allo* weavers also state that *allo* growing under shade yields the finest and whitest fibres: those of plants more exposed to the sun are brownish in colour. Fibres from plants growing at high altitudes are the most valued for weaving. Most villages have special areas available to them. Both men and women are involved in harvesting. In some parts of Nepal, where *allo*-growing areas are several hours' walk away from the villages, harvesting becomes a group activity, often a cheerful occasion, aided by millet wine, *roxi*, when men, women and children walk to the *allo* areas where they may stay for several days. During this time young *allo* leaves, cooked like spinach or as a soup, are an important part of the diet.

Only mature, thick stems are harvested; others are left to seed. The stems are cut about 15 cm from the ground in order to leave sufficient stem for new shoots to sprout. Men use the kukri, which they carry, sheathed, held in front in the waistband. Women use sickles, *hasia*, which are tucked into the waistband at the back. The stinging thorns on both stems and leaves make the cutting of the stems hazardous: the situation is exacerbated by the presence of leeches in large numbers during the wet season. The harvesters protect their hands with a bundle of cloth while cutting the stems and stripping off the leaves and thorns. In the Dhading District, where *allo* areas are close to home, it was observed that the stems were left for a few days before fibre extraction began, in order to reduce the potency of the stinging hairs. After the cutting and stripping, bundles of about five stems are held at the butt end and an incision is made with the teeth in each stem in order to separate the outer bark and fibre layer from the inner stem: about 30 cm of the bark are pulled loose and left hanging. Then, with the bark ends held in one hand and the inner stems in the other, the harvester separates the two with her foot (see p 46). The inner stems are left to rot. One maund, 37.5 kg, of bark, a porter's basket load, can be

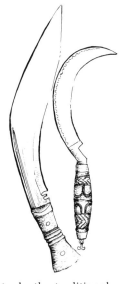

Harvesting tools: the traditional Nepalese knife, kukri, *c.*40 cm long, and the sickle, *hansiya* (30 cm).

harvested in one day. This would comprise the bark of about 370 stems. The fresh bark of one *allo* stem can weigh up to 100 g and yield a maximum of 5 g of dry fibre.

The barks are either processed while still lush or dried and stored in bundles: the dried bark will be soaked in water before fibre extraction. The bark, fresh or soaked, is processed by boiling for two to three hours, usually on the evening cooking fire, in water to which wood ash (from any species of firewood) has been added. In some areas the procedure is to coat the bark with the wood ash in a bowl before putting it into a pot of cold water, the remaining ash from the bowl then being added. Elsewhere the water for boiling the bark is filtered through a basket, *dhoko*, containing wood ash, as a way of obtaining an alkaline solution (Pokharel 1989, 4). It is then generally left to simmer overnight, on the dying fire, although this period may be reduced by previously beating the dried bark with a mallet, thus helping the process of separating out the fibre from the crushed bark. In all cases in the morning the exposed fibres are beaten or rubbed between finger and thumb to remove any remaining plant matter, and rinsed in water. The wet fibres are then coated with a white micaceous clay soil, *kamero mato*, also used for whitewashing houses (Pokharel 1989, 4), to lubricate the fibres and make their separation and spinning easier. Mica can be collected in rock form and crushed into powder: this is mixed with a little water to a porridge-like consistency and the *allo* fibres soaked in it. Finally the strands of fibre are hung up and sun-dried.

The dry bundles of *allo* fibre are prepared for spinning by being shaken to remove the surplus micaceous soil and then opened out: one end of the bundle is wound round and grasped with the toes, while the other end is put under and around the arm. Under tension the fibres are gently pulled apart and separated.

For spinning women use a lightweight hand spindle, about 40 cm long, often elaborately carved by the husband or father of the spinner. The whorl is usually carved from wood or bone, the shaft from bamboo. Spinning by hand spindle might be slower than spinning on a wheel but the spindle has the advantage of weighing very little, being easily carried and used anywhere. *Allo* fibres are taken on most journeys and are spun not only when resting but on even the most difficult walk. The spinner from Yangsema was spinning while crossing the unsteady suspension bridge at Sisuwa Tar. One end of the 3–4-cm-thick, 150-cm-long bundle of fibres is twisted round the waist and tucked in; the other end is held under the left arm. Whilst sitting down, the fibre is sometimes just put over the shoulder and under the arm. With the left hand and the help of teeth bits of fibre are pulled out and twisted on to the spindle which is held between the middle and ring fingers. The spindle is rotated with the thumb and forefinger. During this process the spindle is

Opening up the fibre bundles in preparation for spinning.

moved forward towards the right to arm's length and the twisted yarn is then wound on, bringing the spindle back towards the left hand. The yarn is wound from the bottom of the yarn cone upwards, securing the thread over the little finger of the left hand. Most of the yarn is spun with a z-twist. The s-twist is used mainly for plying two or more z-twist yarns together to produce a very strong yarn, for example, the yarn used for fishing nets. Coarse *allo* tow is used for spinning thick yarn for mats. *Allo*-tip fibres are sometimes separated and spun into fine yarn for stitching or for fine garments.

Allo 'ultimate' (single) fibres are amongst the longest found in plants, up to 53.6 cm, with a diameter of 3.5–342.5 microns. Although not as fine as those of cotton, flax or ramie, their linear density has been estimated to be six to seven times that of ramie and the treated *allo* fibre 'highly lustrous and smooth and very strong' (Canning and Green 1986, 80). Singh and Shrestha (1987) reported a similar fibre length but found the linear density of the fibres they examined to be similar to that of ramie. These variations may be due to differences in the conditions where the plants were grown, their maturity at harvesting or possibly the botanical variety. In response to requests from a group of Sankhuwasabha weavers a major objective of the investigations by Canning and Green was to find an alternative to the long and laborious process of extracting *allo* fibre: several of their proposals were put into practice. To save firewood retting was suggested. It was found that the top and middle fibres softened within a week, whilst the butt ends unfortunately did not separate, even after six weeks. Where a suitable source of water is available further trials on retting have been recommended. Another possibility was processing with sodium hydroxide using a liquor : fibre ratio of 20 : 1 with a maximum of 10 g sodium hydroxide per litre and boiling for less than one hour, followed by thorough rinsing possibly in acetic acid or other neutralising agent. This method proved popular with the weavers who were fully aware of the dangers in using caustic soda. To avoid the use of any chemicals further trials are being undertaken on mechanical means of fibre extraction: these include beating the dry bark or crushing it between rollers (a mangle or a type of cotton gin) using methods similar to those of flax extraction. Hackling or combing the fibre has already been tried and resulted in soft and lustrous fibre but proved to be a long and slow process by hand.

Bleaching fibres or yarn was one of the most welcome recommendations. The white yarn in conjunction with the natural beige/brown colour added an extra design element and also improved the dyeing results. The weavers use the following recipe for 1 kg of fibre, yarn or cloth: add 200 g of bleaching powder to 1 l of water. Stir vigorously. Decant liquid. Repeat procedure twice. Dilute the resultant 3 l to 20 l and add 200 g of sodium carbonate. Soak fibre for two

A spinner from Yangsema, Sankhuwasabha District, spinning *allo* yarn on her way to market.

63

Treadle spinning-wheels were introduced in Sankhuwasabha in the 1980s. The spinner has the bundle of fibres wrapped around her waist and holds one end under her arm, the same method she uses for the handspindle.

hours, stirring occasionally. Both bleaching powder and soda are available locally. Experiments with washing the yarn together with the seeds of the *rhita* tree, *Sapindus mukorossi*, was also shown to lighten the colour a little and soften it at the same time.

With increasing demand for natural fibres shortages might occur. Planting of *allo* has therefore been undertaken in some areas. Nepali (1990, 48) reported that 2 ha were planted by two weavers in Sankhuwasabha and yielded 10 kg of fibre at the end of the second year, and yields were expected to increase subsequently. As the plant grows on areas unsuitable for arable crops, such cultivation would not compete for land with food crops. 'Cultivation of allo could well be encouraged along forest edges and on rocky slopes' (Shrestha 1989, 84). The suggestion has also been made that *allo* could be grown as an under-storey in newly established forest plantations (Pokharel 1989, 22). The recognition of the value of existing stands of *allo* might help the conservation of older forests in which it grows.

Fibres are not the only product from *allo*; it is also a source of stock feed and medicine. Manandhar (1989, 46) states that 'a decoction from the leaf is applied to treat headaches and joint ache. It is considered efficacious against fever'. The Research Centre for

Applied Science and Technology (RECAST) of Tribhuvan University showed that a blue dye can be obtained from the boiling liquid used for fibre extraction, the inner stems left after fibre extraction can be used for making paper, and that *allo* seeds, which can contain 10–12 per cent oil, could be used for soap and other oil-based products.

Common nettle, *sisnu* (*Urtica dioica*)

The common nettle, *sisnu*, is a much smaller plant than *allo* which because of its size is sometimes called *hati sisnu*, 'elephant nettle'. The common nettle grows to a height of up to 2 m and is found throughout the temperate regions of Nepal. Its finely serrated, heart-shaped leaves taper to a point, and the stem (about 0.5–1.0 cm in diameter) is downy and also covered with stinging hairs. The thin stems yield little fibre and they are therefore seldom used except partly processed for rope-making. The young leaves, though, are collected, with bamboo tongs to avoid being stung and made into nourishing and delicious soup. They are also used for pig feed. Manandhar (1989, 92) includes a decoction of the root as a treatment for asthma amongst the plant's medicinal uses. Shrestha (1978, 175) mentions that 'a common punishment is to beat the culprit with nettles'. In Europe 'urtication or flogging' with nettles was an old remedy for chronic rheumatism and loss of muscular power (Grieve 1931).

Weaving with nettle fibres, according to Geijer (1977, 10), must have been known since the early Bronze Age, as a fragment of cloth found in Denmark revealed. Once common in Scotland, Scandinavia and Germany, nettle weaving has almost ceased as the extraction of the fine fibres (2–6 cm long) proved to be too laborious and uneconomic. This could change in the United Kingdom with the introduction of set-aside (natural fallow) areas, which may come to cover considerable areas, and the new interest in natural fibres, even though the yield from six English common nettle stems (140 cm long and 0.5 cm in diameter) is only 1.25 g of fibre, using similar methods to those described for *allo*. However, nettle cloth will probably live on in the fairy tale of Hans Christian Andersen about the princess who wove nettle coats to bring back to human form her eleven brothers who had been bewitched and turned into swans.

Hemp (*Cannabis sativa*)

Hemp is a robust, erect annual herb (1–5 m tall) which can grow in a wide range of altitudes, soils and climates: small stands are found in widely separated parts of Nepal. The plant is probably most widely known as a source of narcotics but in fact it has three main products, each of which may be locally important; they are: a white bast fibre from the stem; oil from the seeds; and narcotics (*bhang* from dried leaves and flowering shoots, *ganja* from dried, unfertilised female inflorescences (a term used also for the whole plant), and *charas*, crude resin, collected by rubbing the tops of the plants).

The various products require different conditions for optimum quality. A mild, humid temperate climate, such as may be found in some hill regions, is best for fibre production. Hemp is usually dioecious, that is, the male and female flowers are borne on separate plants. The male plants produce the best fibre. The seed for oil extraction comes from the female plant, and narcotics are produced from leaves and both male and female flowers.

Two hundred years ago Kirkpatrick identified the medicinal element as the most important. During his visit to the Kathmandu Valley in 1793 he noted (1811, 142) that some cultivated fields were skirted with 'Jeea' that yields the drug 'cherris' (*charas*) 'for which Nepaul is famous'. Kirkpatrick recorded that the 'proper season' for extraction was when the plant was in flower and seeds on the point of maturity. Leaves were rubbed gently between the hands and the juice then scraped off the palm with a knife. When clarified it was known as *momea*, which Kirkpatrick reported (p. 143) as 'a most potent narcotic, possessing it is said very valuable medicinal qualities'. *Ganja* was produced from the flowers and *bhang* from leaves. Kirkpatrick further noted that the Newars made some coarse linens and also a very strong kind of sackcloth from the fibres.

Bhatt (1977, 183) recorded that 'large acreages' were grown in a number of districts of the central, western and far western regions and the banning of its cultivation had caused great hardship to hill people. *Charas* fetched a high price on the Indian market, the seeds were used as food and its oil in soap making, and the strong and durable fibre was used for ropes and twine and to weave a cloth used by poorer people as a toga or *gado*. Bishop (1971, 682) found that the fibre in Humla District made a very serviceable twine and that the oil was used for cooking as a substitute for ghee and as an embrocation.

Ang Diku Sherpa (1992, personal communication) recorded the method of fibre extraction in a Tamang community in Trisuli, Nuwakot District, as follows. The hemp, *nena* in Tamang, is harvested in August. After cutting, the stems are left to dry for three to five days before being retted in either still or running water for one to two days. The fibrous portion is teased out with the teeth, like *allo*, and then twisted and pulled clear. This material is sun-dried for two to three days and then beaten with a long paddle, which would free and soften the fibre. After spinning, the thread is boiled with wood ash and water for half an hour, washed until free of ash and again dried. An interesting development has been started in England in 1993, when some thirty farmers asked the Ministry of Agriculture for permission to grow a non-hallucinogenic variety of cannabis for fibre production to be used for high-grade manuscript paper, cigarette papers as well as teabags.

Jute (*Corchorus* spp.)

Jute goods and raw jute are important export items for Nepal. Two of the country's neighbours, India and Bangladesh, are the world's major producers. In Nepal the crop is grown in the eastern *terai* (southern plains), particularly in the three easternmost districts.

Of the two species of commercial interest *Corchorus capsularis*, white jute, is tolerant of flooded conditions. *Corchorus olitorius*, Tossa jute, is not and will thus do well only on better drained areas. Both are herbaceous annuals that grow to 3–5 m. The area planted in Nepal and the yield per unit area show year to year fluctuations: between 1964/5 and 1984/5 the total annual area varied between 27,000 and 60,000 hectares and the yields between 0.94 and 1.50 tonnes per hectare (HMGN Ministry of Finance Economic Surveys).

The crop is harvested with a hand sickle shortly after flowering; the timing is important in achieving the desired balance between yield and quality. The leaves and side stems are discarded and the main stems, which may have a circumference up to 20 mm, are tied in bundles for retting, often in drainage canals. The bundles are held down with mud and turfs (Gajurel and Vaidya 1984, 198). Retting time varies with water temperature and maturity of the stems and may be twelve to twenty-five days. Correct retting is important in achieving good-quality fibre. After retting, the bark should come away easily from the stems and is then sun-dried for several days before being tied in bundles and sold.

Jute produces a soft, bast fibre which is weaker than hemp. (It is interesting to note that the word jute derives originally from the Sanskrit word *yuta*, meaning fibre (Bally 1955a, 3886).) Bhatt (1977, 183) states that Nepalese jute is of medium quality. The ultimate fibre of jute averages only 2.5 mm, very much shorter than other bast fibres or cotton (Bally 1955b, 3894).

Within Nepal most of the jute is sold to the jute mills in the *terai*, where it is machine spun and made mainly into sackcloth and ropes. However, in the Koshi and Mechi zones fine lustrous jute yarn for bags and mats is still handspun by Rajbansi women using hand spindles turned against the lower leg: the fibres are pulled out from long-stranded jute bundles which have been meticulously sorted and prepared (Hurle 1982, 3). Fine s- and z-twist jute yarn is spun especially to weave porters' headbands, *namlo*. A much coarser yarn for an entirely different purpose is prepared from low-grade jute for weaving soil conservation mats (see p. 183). For this purpose small bundles of the jute fibres are simply pulled from a hank and wound round a stick which gives them enough twist to form a thick yarn.

Seed fibres

Cotton, *kapas* (*Gossypium* spp.)

Textiles from cotton are among the most widely used in Nepal, as they are in most countries of the tropical and subtropical world. The cloth is a good conductor of heat and so is cool to wear in hot weather, is highly absorbent and durable, does not attract dirt and washes easily without harming the fabric.

The fibre (lint) comes from plants of one of the *Gossypium* species and is an outgrowth from the epidermis of the seed. Most of the cotton cultivars grown today are annuals and grow to a height of 1.0–1.5 m. Cotton fabrics have been known in the Indian sub-continent for thousands of years (Hardingham 1978, 40), and although all the particular species and races involved have not been identified (Bhatt 1977, 182) cotton growing has been known in Nepal for some hundreds of years. Kirkpatrick (1811, 209–10), following his visit to the Kathmandu Valley in 1793, records that the Newars produced a cloth from cotton grown in 'Noakote'. Where environmental conditions were suitable it may be assumed that other communities also produced their own cotton. In the 1940s, during World War II, cotton textile production was encouraged to meet a severe shortage of cloth in Nepal, but this activity was largely stifled by the end of the decade as a result of cheap imported cloth (Bhatt 1977, 182). Cotton growing among the hill communities has been severely affected by the rise in population leading to a need to devote the limited amount of arable land to food production. Small plots of cotton can still be found, however. Two types of cotton fibre are recognised, one white and the other naturally brown (*kogati*). A project in the 1980s in the *terai*, near Nepalgunj, demonstrated that high-quality cotton could be grown, but demand by local mills, such as that at Butwal, has not been met yet. Imports of lint, cotton yarn and cloth are readily available.

Where cotton is grown on a small scale the traditional method of separating the lint from the seed with a small, hand-operated gin is still practised. The wooden, hand-carved gin consists of two rollers set into an upright frame. This is made stable by a piece of wood projecting from the base, which is weighed down by the operator partly sitting on it. The lower roller is connected to a handle; when this is turned the motion is transferred by the carved screw to the roller above, which rotates in a counter direction. The space left between the rollers can be adjusted by means of a wooden wedge forced between the horizontal frame bar and the rollers. The seed cotton is fed into the rollers and the fine fibres (lint) are carried through them to the other side while the seeds and impurities, too large to pass through, drop down. The lint is teased apart, spread out and then rolled around a stick to form rolags, *pyuri*, 15–20 cm long (the stick having been withdrawn). Some Newar women store

A cotton plant (*Gossypium* sp.) showing one unripe boll still closed and three which have burst open on ripening. The fibres have a natural twist, making them ideal for spinning. Royal Botanic Gardens, Kew.

Using a cotton gin to separate seeds from fibres. The round seat mat is made from maize trush. A dhaka shawl is draped over the *allo* sack on the right.

these in finely carved wooden caskets. The rolags are subsequently spun into yarn either with a lightweight hand spindle or on a *charka*.

A lightweight cotton hand spindle in the British Museum collection, which was used by Rai women in east Nepal, is 25.6 cm long. The delicate whorl is carved from buffalo hoof. A small (1.2 cm) crossbar inserted through a hole near the top of the bamboo shaft can be used to anchor the thread when the spindle is in use as a drop spindle. The finest cotton yarn, however, is spun by turning the spindle on a smooth supporting surface as the weight of the spindle may otherwise break the fine thread.

A very special cotton thread, the sacred thread worn by high-caste Hindus over the left shoulder and tied under the right arm, is spun and plied six-fold. Once a year at *Janai purne*, during the full moon in August, the thread is replaced by a new one. According to Bhatt (1977, 182) a high-quality sacred thread is made by Thakuri women from home-grown cotton (see also p. 38). The spinning of sacred

Spinning the sacred thread from cotton, a Maithili painting from Janakpur, Southern Nepal. British Museum As 1992 10.68

thread is depicted in a Maithili painting from Janakpur, which is in the British Museum collection.

The spinning of cotton with a spinning-wheel has been practised at least since the eighteenth century. Campbell (1836, 220–1) describes how the spinner sits on the ground 'with one hand turning the wheel by means of a handle, and with the other, drawing out the cotton into thread. An iron rod is attached by means of a string to the wheel and revolves in company with it, on which the thread, as spun, is collected. . . . The spinner turns the wheel from left to right while forming the thread and, to allow the portion spun to be accumulated on the iron rod, gives the wheel a small turn in the opposite direction, at the same time lowering her left hand, so as to permit the winding up of the thread'. Campbell (p. 221) also observes that women and girls of all ages, but not men, employ themselves in this occupation 'when not assisting at sowing or reaping, either in front of their dwellings, in the towns, or at the roadside, as may best suit their convenience'.

The Nepalese *charka* made in the 1980s, in the British Museum collection is described on page 52. In recent times most weavers have bought ready-made yarn, which may have been spun and dyed in Nepal or been imported. Mercerised cotton yarn is also used, particularly for dhaka cloth. This is cotton which has been treated under tension with a caustic alkali to make it more lustrous and improve its dyeing qualities and give it greater strength.

A Rai woman spinning cotton on a *charka*. She draws out the fibres whilst turning the handle so the spindle will rotate and put twist into the fibres.

Bamboos

Bamboos in general are not considered as textile raw materials, yet, as Picton and Mack point out in their interesting introduction to textiles (1989, 18) 'there is no hard and fast distinction between cloth and basketry'. Plain-weave, twill and diamond patterns occur in infinite variety in cloth as well as mats and baskets in Nepal. To leave out bamboo structures altogether would be to omit part of the richness of Nepalese design.

The bamboos are perennial grasses with woody culms (stems) arising from rhizomes. They have innumerable uses and a particular species may be more suitable for one purpose than another. The majority of rural households will therefore exploit several species, some of which will be available on their own land, using the most suitable species for a specific purpose. The culms can be used entire, split into sections, crushed into panels or split and then woven. Products include bridges, roofs, floors, ceilings and walls, mats, trays, water-carriers, filters, sieves and a wide variety of baskets. The leaves are an important source of fodder and the young shoots of some species are commonly used as a vegetable.

71

Right Bamboos are usually found in clumps such as that in the left background. This Rai family has used bamboo to build their house and make baskets, the stem sections for carrying water, rainshields and part of the 4-shaft treadle loom on which the twill-patterned cotton cloth worn by the weaver and the two children is being produced. The little girl's jacket was woven from the local Baruwal sheep wool.

Splitting the bamboo into sections with a kukri.

There remains uncertainty worldwide over the taxonomy of bamboo, but in Nepal twenty species have been recognised; seven are still indeterminate (Shrestha 1989, 85). The three broad categories of bamboo (Stapleton in Jackson 1987, 200) in relation to textiles are:

Bans (typified by *Dendrocalamus hamiltonii*), large-statured species with thin flexible culm walls which are good for weaving but not strong or rigid enough for many construction purposes. The new shoots are edible and the large leaves make good fodder. The different species used for weaving may be found at altitudes between 300 and 2,600 m.

Nigalo (typified by *Drepanostachyum intermedium*), small-statured species with small culms which have no constructional value but are superior to those of the larger genera (*Bans*) for weaving. They are found between 1,200 and 2,400 m and can readily be cultivated.

Malingo includes *Drepanostachyum* spp. and *Arundinaria* spp., small-statured species found at the higher altitudes which produce the highest-quality weaving material. *Arundinaria maling* is the common eastern species and is occasionally found as low as 2,300 m but is widespread above 2,800 m: it is the most highly valued bamboo for basketwork. Because of the altitude at which the *malingo* grows few households would have their own stands and they therefore collect material from the forest.

'Sisal' (*Agave* sp.)

The name *hattibar*, or 'elephant fence', as the plant is called locally, indicates the strength of this plant which is grown in short rows or clumps along the side of trails or on field boundaries. A member of the sisal family, this plant, which stands 1–2 m high, is a perennial with a basal rosette of large, stiff, fleshy, persistent leaves with spiny margins. After a number of years a massive flowering pole is sent up from the centre of the plant which produces buds from which new plants are developed. When the fibre is needed, mature outer leaves are cut and the fibres extracted by retting and beating. They are basically used for ropes but also for porters' headbands.

There are many other plant fibres, some of which have been used only in isolated places and are little known. P. P. Regmi (1984–5, 249) lists twenty-five textile and other soft fibres and thirty plaiting and rough weaving fibres but emphasises that the lists are not complete and, that particularly among wild species, there will be others which could contribute to development in Nepal. Yet, as Manandhar points out in his book on useful plants (1989, v), 'beyond exploitation, there is a continuing need to further the study of nature and the concept of conservation'.

3

DYES AND DYEING TECHNIQUES

Beautiful shades of natural dyes in a woollen apron traditionally worn by Sherpa women. The front apron, (57 × 71 cm) is made up from three weft-faced 2/2 twill weave panels. The warp yarn is 3-ply cotton; the weft yarn is a fine single wool. There are about 26 warp ends and 90 picks per inch (2.5 cm).

Colouring cloth with dyes, to enhance or alter the natural colours of the yarn or cloth, has a long history in Nepal. Throughout the country there are a considerable number of plants that have been used traditionally as a source for a range of colours. A special class of dyers, Chippah, has been recognised amongst the Newars in the Kathmandu Valley since the fourteenth century. In the eighteenth century Kirkpatrick (1811/ 1875, 182) found that there was a 'well known creeper called *Munjheet*' and felt that 'there is a good reason to suppose that the Nepaul territories produce a rich variety of dyeing material'. *Munjheet* (*majitho* or madder) is the dye mentioned most frequently in old records. Both Campbell (1836, 223) and Hooker (1854, 11, 41) refer to it, and Das (1902, 10) described how Limbus exchanged the dye creeper for salt.

Fürer-Haimendorf (1975, 79) found that the Sherpas of Khumbu used many vegetable dyes, particularly madder, up to the 1940s but that even by 1953 chemical dyes were rapidly gaining ground. This situation was probably general throughout the mountain areas with increasing use of purchased chemical dyes or coloured yarn. Yet natural dyes still have an important role and are increasingly used by carpet weavers in response to revived interest in these dyes.

Amongst the substantive natural dyes – those which readily impart their colour on to the material to be dyed in water without any further substance – are those obtained from bark and from unripe walnut husks. Most other dyes – 'adjective dyes' – require an additional substance, a fixative or mordant, often a metallic salt, which has affinity with the dyestuff and the material to be dyed to allow absorption of the colour and to increase its permanence. Some

This dot and line pattern is achieved by an unusual method of block printing and dyeing practised by Newar *Chippah* (dyers' caste) who settled in east Nepal (A. D. Sherpa, pers. comm.). To print five 40 × 80 cm cotton lengths, the *Chippah* firstly prepare a black dye from 200 g of mustard seed powder, 200 g of millet flour and 1000 g of iron dust. These are put into a clay jar, covered with water and stirred once a week for 2 to 3 weeks. A second liquid is prepared by immersing the leaves of *asuro* (*Adhatoda vasica*) in water in a clay jar for a week to become a yellow juice. The cotton cloth is soaked in water, rubbed with crushed myrobalan paste, then dried, folded and beaten. The wood block with the carved out dot/line pattern is printed with the first mixture, giving the black background. The second block, with stripes wide enough to cover the dot pattern, is printed over the dot pattern with a mixture prepared from 1 l of the yellowish *asuro* liquid into which 20 g of mineral salt, *khar*, are mixed. When it starts to effervesce, 2 to 3 drops of mustard oil are added. The printed cloth is dried in the sun before it is submerged in a madder dye (powdered madder plus water) and simmered for 5–10 minutes, resulting in black/brown background, red/brown lines and white dots (which have been prevented from accepting colour by the *asuro* liquid). Today the cloth is worn mostly by the older generation of Limbu and Rai, but enterprising designers in Kathmandu have begun marketing garments and bags made from the cloth (see illustration on p. 77).

of these substances are found as natural deposits in the earth or along rocks, for example, alum in the aluminous earth or rock scrapings, widely used in Nepal. Mordants are present also in fruits or plants, for example, lime or the myrobalan fruit. Some of the other mordants used include beer, salt and *puldok* (natron or sesquicarbonate of soda), which is also used with salt, and in Sherpa butter tea. Commercial mordants available to dyers in Kathmandu include ferrous and copper sulphates.

Some recipes for the most widely used dyes of Nepal are described below, but it should be borne in mind that there are wide variations in the preparations of the dyes, the quantity and type of dye material and mordant used. Recipes are handed on through generations, and some particular recipes are kept understandably just within the family, preserving some of the mysteries of all the various shades of natural dyes.

Madder

The rich variety of shades becomes nowhere more apparent than with the best-known and most widely used of Nepalese dyes – madder (*Rubia cordifolia, majhito*), which yields colours ranging from orange-gold to deep red and light pink. For an exhibition of 'The Tiger Rugs of Tibet' in 1988 at the Hayward Gallery, London, some of the beautiful carpets were analysed for colour: to the surprise of the analyst, Dr Paul Mushak, four visually different colours, pale orange, flaming orange, buff-brown and deep mauve-brown, all derived from madder (J. and B. Ford in Lipton 1988, 162). It was suggested that plants of different ages could have been used and that they might have been selectively extracted or used with different mordants. From observation of madder dyeing in Nepal it seems likely that all of these factors could have contributed, as well as the addition of other dye plants to the madder dye bath (see below).

Madder is a climbing herb with long pointed leaves in whorls of four. It occurs in forests and is often collected during the winter as it is more readily recognisable when the deciduous trees have lost their leaves. Manandhar (1980, 63) mentions that in addition to its commercial use as a dye the plant also has therapeutic properties – the root as a tonic and the stem used as an antidote to scorpion bites. The importance of madder as a home dye and also in trade is indicated by the fact that the Sherpa word for 'dye' in general is *tsoe*, which is also used for 'madder', as '*the* dye', whilst other dyes have their own specific names (Ang Diku Sherpa 1992, personal communication). The importance of madder as a trade item was recognised already by Buchanan Hamilton (1819/1986, 207), who stated that madder, 'munjheet', was in demand by Tibetans and that Nepalis bartered it for borax and rock salt. This trade continues, though mainly on a cash basis and principally to the Indian market.

Madder is collected by people from the middle mountains and carried in *dhokos* to Dharan or other centres, where it is bought for export to India and processing. Investigations are being undertaken by Forest Research scientists in Kathmandu into the possibility of local processing and a better return to the collectors, together with studies on a sustainable level of exploitation.

The madder dye is composed of purpurin and an orange dye, *munjistin* (Burbage 1982, 86). A Kathmandu carpet dyer demonstrated the following method for a small amount (250–500 g) of alum-mordanted wool. After collection the roots and stems are dried and crushed to powder. Two handfuls of this powder are boiled in 4.5 l of water for thirty minutes. The wool to be dyed has previously been treated in a solution of water and alum which was left to simmer for one hour. The yarn is then put into the dye solution and simmered for half an hour, which gives a soft red colour. If the same dye solution is used again, the colour would be pink. Corneille Jest (1992, personal communication) observed in Nub-ri, upper Gandaki, in 1970 that the madder root, extracted in autumn, was crushed and made into a paste in a mortar. This was used to dye lamas' robes and other garments red. Another madder dye recipe for a deep reddish-brown shade suggests the addition of the myrobalan fruit, *Terminalia chebula* (*harro*), which also acts as a mordant. The fruits are boiled in the madder dye bath until they become soft; the skin is then rubbed off and put back into the dye bath, whilst the seeds are discarded. The yarn is placed in the solution which is brought to the boil and left to simmer for two hours. For lighter shades the same dye bath can be used again, as with most of the recipes. (The myrobalan fruit is also used on its own for a yellowish-brown shade.) Schmidt-Thome and Tsering (1975, 176) report the addition of a Sherpa 'sour' plant called *chula* as a fixative for madder. The plant, found in high pastures, has two to six leaves growing near the ground and a 10-cm-tall red stem bearing clusters of small red flowers in summer. The leaves, stem and flowers can be used either fresh or dried and powdered, then boiled together with the madder powder until the red colour appears. The material to be dyed is then added and simmered for one hour, covered and left to cool overnight.

Indigo

Indigo (*Indigofera tinctoria*, Tibetan *ram*) is one of the most ancient dye plants, yielding the famous indigo blue. It has been used in India for at least 2,000 years and possibly as long in China. Indigo is obtained from the leaves of a number of *Indigofera* species by fermentation and subsequent solution in an alkaline medium, which assists the release of the initially colourless indigo which turns blue on oxidation: the solution also acts as a mordant serving to fix the dye colour in the yarn or cloth. Hodgson (1880, 110) recorded indigo dyeing by the Rajbansi using their own indigo, but today most of the dye comes from India. It is sold in a solid cake or ball form. Denwood (1978, 20) describes the Tibetan way of using these as follows. The balls are thoroughly ground in a mortar with a little vegetable oil or water. This is then mixed with rhubarb juice or Tibetan beer and left to ferment for several days. After adding water, the solution is warmed, but not boiled, before yarn is steeped in it. Several immersions are required for a strong blue.

Barberry

Barberry (*Berberis asiatica, chutro*), a common thorny shrub, yields a strong yellow dye from the stem. The outer bark is scraped off with a knife exposing the yellow inner layer. This is chopped into small pieces (or dried and powdered), then boiled with the yarn. Some carpet dyers use an alum mordant.

Walnut

Walnut (*Juglans regia, okhar*), a large deciduous tree, is found in Nepal from 1,200 to 2,500 m. The husks of its nuts yield a substantive dye which is used mainly for dyeing wool, particularly for Gurung blankets and rari/rugs and garments. The colour obtained is a beige-brown. The unripe husks are soaked in water until they begin to rot: they are then dried and pounded into powder in a mortar. Alternatively they are soaked in small pieces and then boiled with the yarn until the right colour is achieved. This method was used for wool by weavers from Hile whose forebears came from Tibet. The bark of the walnut also yields a dye which is used by many wool weavers. It has to be chopped finely and is then boiled for about two hours. The bark is removed from the liquid before the hanks of wool, which are about three times the weight of the bark used, are submerged in the dye and simmered for about half an hour.

Sorrel

Common field sorrel (*Rumex nepalensis, halhale*) is a herb growing up to 1 m. The leaves are used as a remedy for nettle stings, a leaf paste for eczema and a root paste for bone setting. Fresh leaves, picked within the previous two to three days, are required for dyeing, an equal weight of leaves to that of the woollen yarn. The leaves are placed into a copper pot in the proportion of 1 kg of leaves to 25 l of water and boiled into a slimy mass, which takes thirty minutes to an hour. If necessary, additional water may be added during the process. The woollen yarn is then placed in the dye bath and boiled for four to five hours, water being added to maintain the level as necessary. If the required shade has not been obtained, additional

The creeper *Rubia cordifolia*, known as madder or *majito*.

leaf slime is added. When the colour is satisfactory, the yarn is removed, shaken to remove any vestiges of leaf, and washed thoroughly in clean water. Sometimes it may be kneaded by foot to ensure a thorough wash. The richness and depth of the colour – a deep olive – depends on the quality of the leaves, young, fresh leaves giving the best shade. The leaves can be used only once (Mohanty 1987, 166).

Rhubarb

Rhubarb (*Rheum emodi* and other species, *padamchal*) is a perennial herb with a large rhizome and large radicle leaves with succulent petioles: a strong yellow colour is obtained from the roots and a yellowish colour from the leaves. The expressed juice of rhubarb is used as a mordant. The Sherpas use a high-altitude species, which they call *aktsho* (Ang Diku Sherpa 1992, personal communication): it grows about 30 cm high and has 15-cm-long, oval leaves. The red stem, with clusters of small red flowers, can grow up to 1 m. The rhubarb is used together with *puldok* (natron) as follows: the dried and powdered roots are boiled together with the *puldok* for an hour. The material to be dyed is then added and simmered for an hour, with occasional stirring. The dye bath is then taken from the fire and the cloth is left to cool in the bath for one night. In the morning the cloth is washed and dried in the sun. The ochre/yellow colour is worn mainly by lamas (Schmidt-Thome and Tsering 1975, 178). Other colours are obtained from the same dye bath by adding fermented sour beer (*chang*), briefly boiling it and adding a little green Indian dye powder: depending on the amount of dye powder added, the resultant colour will be purple, dark red/brown or black.

Morinda

Morinda, which gives a red dye, is mentioned by Hodgson (1880, 110) when he describes the cotton cloth made by the Rajbansi and is probably referring to the shrub *Morinda citrifolia*. This dye is described by Hitchcock (1991, 47) as follows. The morinda root bark is crushed, mixed with water and then boiled. Mordants made from the powdered leaves of alumina-bearing plants are added, and the yarns are usually pre-treated with oils mixed with ash lye prior to being soaked overnight in the dye solution and then dried during the day. Ten or more immersions are required to obtain the red colour.

Other dyes used include one from the leaves of *Symplocos*. Hooker (1845, II, 41) describes women 'engaged in drying the leaves of a shrub (Symplocos) for the Tibet market, which are used as yellow dye'. He mentions the same dye for the yellow 'wreaths of lichen' (see p. 44). Sherpas are also reported to make a yellow dye from the leaves of the *chungen* tree, which might belong to the same family, possibly *Symplocos Racemosa Roxb*. The leaves are stripped off when they turn yellow in the autumn, dried in the shade and then rubbed into small pieces. These are boiled together with a small, wild rhubarb species, *nyalo*, which acts as a mordant. A lemon yellow colour is released (for a darker yellow *puldok* is added as a mordant). The material to be dyed is then immersed in the bath and simmered for one hour. According to Schmidt-Thome and Tsering (1975, 177), the Khumbu-Sherpa have mastered this technique for generations. Other dyes are obtained from the young cones of larch/pine (*talis patra salla*) and fir, *Abies spectabilis* (*gobse salla*) for blueish shades. To obtain yellow the tubers of turmeric, *Curcuma* sp., are crushed and dissolved in water, but this dye fades easily. The yellow/orange from the petals of safflower, *Carthamus tinctorius*, is rare in Nepal: it was used in Tibet to dye the robes of Buddhist monks. For a light brown colour old tea-leaves are used by some carpet dyers.

Chemical dyes

Indian direct dyes in powder form are available even in small villages in Nepal and are now widely used, sometimes together with natural dyes and mordants. The dye is used mainly with *fitkiri*, an aluminous substance, which can be bought in solid form in village shops. In one such recipe, used by weavers in east Nepal for dyeing *allo* yarn, one teaspoonful of alum, one teaspoonful of mustard oil and the juice of a lime are added to 1½ pints (0.85 l) of hot water. After thorough mixing, two tablespoonfuls of dye powder are dissolved in the dye bath, which is then diluted to about 5 l. The wetted hanks (500 g) of yarn are added and simmered for half an hour. The strength of the shade obtained can be varied by altering the amount of dye powder and water used and the boiling time.

Aniline and other chemical dyes are traded and widely used in many parts of Nepal, but particularly in Kathmandu. Procion MX dyes proved to be especially fast for *allo* (Canning and Green 1986, 82). Although the fastness of these dyes surpasses that of the natural dyes, the beauty and subtlety of the latter can rarely be imitated. It is likely that chemical as well as natural dyes will continue to be used side by side or, in some cases, together.

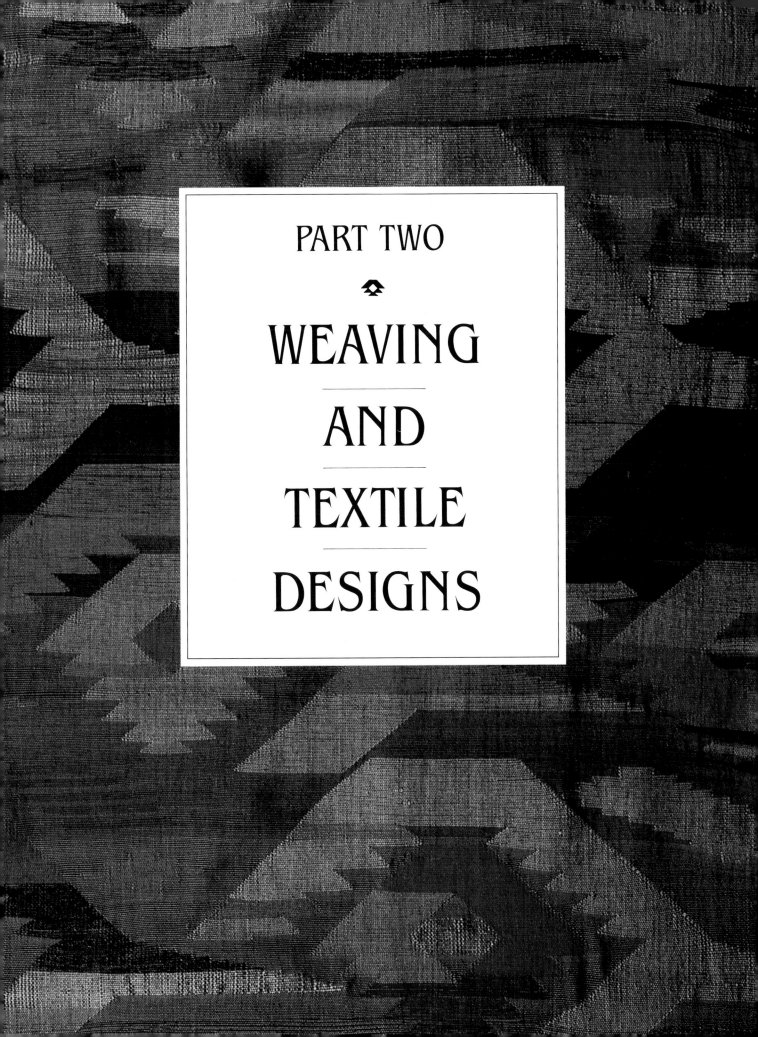

PART TWO

WEAVING
AND
TEXTILE
DESIGNS

Previous page A shawl, *pachaura*, with traditional supplementary-weft patterns, each one different, in variations of twenty basic motifs and a wide range of new colours and yarns, including handspun cotton, silk and pashmina. (Black mercerised cotton warp and various types of cotton and silk weft.)

Plain weave bamboo mats, *chitre*, are made without a loom. Most heavy bamboo work is done by men.

Textiles in Nepal are woven, knitted, crocheted, plaited or braided in many different ways. The main subject of this book, however, is the most widely practised woven textiles. These, according to Emery (1966, 74), are composed of two sets of elements – the longitudinal, passive warp and the active weft, both essentially parallel and interworked, crossing each other at more or less right angles. The variation of a textile structure is effected by the numerical order used for interlacing, the spacing of warp and weft and the type of raw material used. The most simple 'numerical order' is over one under one interworking producing a 'plain weave': each weft passes alternately under and over each successive warp end (one warp thread) in one 'pick' (a single pass of the weft from one side of the warp to the other) and over one, under one in the following pick. All warp ends that lie below the weft in the first pick will lie above in the second pick. Any other numerical order creates floats, either warp or weft thread floating over one or more threads before being interworked. Fences, roofs, walls and, indeed, whole shelters are constructed of bamboo mats of this basic, plain-weave structure. The mats, *chitre*, are made by laying and interlacing on the ground two sets of either split bamboo or small round bamboos crushed flat. Each alternate warp end (bamboo strip) is lifted up by hand whilst the weft strand is pushed into position. As both warp and weft elements are rigid and stay in place once they are interlaced,

Sitting on the completed part of the springy mattress-like straw mat, the Rai weaver interworks the straw weft over and under one pair of the spaced warp strands, and under and over the next pair, reversing the order for the second pick and beating down the weft with the warp spacer. One end of each straw bundle weft is braided in during weaving to form a selvage; the remaining strands are cut when the mat is completed. (A similar mat in the British Museum collection, As 1993.01, is 88 × 44 cm and has eight pairs of jute warp, each pair 5.5 cm apart.

no device or tools are needed to weave such a mat. If, however, the warp elements are soft, some means of keeping the warp under tension, namely a 'loom', has to be used to make it possible for the weft to be interlaced with the warp.

This function of keeping the warp under tension is fulfilled by the simple ground loom, which is used in most rural areas to weave the soft, springy rice, wheat or cardamom straw sitting- and sleeping-mats, *sukul*. The loom consists of just two beams and a length of wood with up to thirteen perforated holes, the warp spacer/beater. The plied jute or grass warp, *babiyo* (*Eulaliopsis binata*), stretched between the two beams, is threaded in pairs through the wooden warp spacer. The weft, overlapping bundles of two to four straw stalks, is laid into the spaced-out warp by hand, the weaver lifting the appropriate warp end with her fingers. For so few warp ends and for this type of raw material the weaver needs no other device to form a 'shed', that is, an opening between warp threads for the passage of the weft. However, other looms used for cloth weaving have such devices, the most basic being a 'shedstick' and a 'heddle'. The shedstick is placed between the alternate warp ends, which have been separated, one from another, during warping. It is either round – for example, a section of a bamboo stem – or flat. With a round shedstick the shed will be visible all the time. With a flat shedstick the shed will show only when it is put on edge. The second or 'countershed', required for the second passage of the weft in a plain weave, is obtained by a heddle. This is made by picking up with a loop over a stick, or 'heddle rod', each second warp end, namely those lying underneath the shedstick. When the heddle rod is lifted, the warp ends caught in the loops are lifted also and the countershed is opened. Shedstick and heddle rod are thus worked alternately to obtain shed and countershed.

This type of shedding device is widely used throughout Nepal on backstrap or body-tension looms. As the name implies, the warp tension is controlled by the weaver's body. Only one of the beams, the back beam, is held in a fixed position: it is tied to a structure, part of the house or a fence post, or held by a stone. The front or breast beam is fitted with a backstrap encircling the weaver's hips or back: by moving her body, and thus the front beam, back or forward the weaver can tighten or release the tension of the warp to manipulate the shedstick and heddle. By leaning back the weaver increases the warp tension and the shed will show in front of the heddle if a round stick is used or a flat stick is put on edge. The length of the loops of the heddle is such as to allow the warp ends to be moved up and down to both the lower and higher positions required by shed and countershed. A shed opener or beater is inserted to clear the passage into which the weft is laid (first pick) and beaten in. For the second pick the weaver leans slightly forward

Opposite Weaving a warp-faced strap for the traditional carrying bag, *jhola*, from *allo* yarn. The Rai weaver uses her body and her big toe to tension the warp, and heddles to lift the alternate warp strands for the shed and countershed. The weaver is wearing traditional clothing. Nose and ear jewellery are worn by most Rai and Limbu women. The glass beads, necklaces and bangles, which are also worn by other ethnic groups, indicate married status.

The working of counter shed and shed. Drawing by Ben Burt.

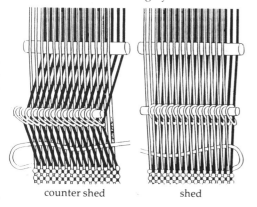

counter shed   shed

and lifts the heddle rod, usually holding a stick behind the loops, to prevent the first shed from showing. Again, the shed opener clears the passage and the weft is inserted (second pick).

An even simpler version, using no beams but two heddles, is sometimes used. The warp, which encircles the weaver, is held under tension between her waist and her big toe. Shed and countershed are obtained by lifting each of two small loop heddles alternately, rather than using a shedstick for the second shed which does not lie securely in a narrow warp. Yet another way of obtaining a shed is by turning or twisting a set of perforated cards or 'tablets' through which the warp ends have been threaded. A shedding device where the weaver need not lift any heddle and has both hands free to manipulate the weft is a pair of heddles operated by treadles: this method is used on a variety of looms which are described in detail in the following chapters.

Although it is tempting to speculate where the different looms originated, the answer is difficult to find. The basic idea of stretching the warp between two beams can be found in every part of Nepal (and other parts of the world) and was probably developed at different times out of the necessity to weave clothing and shelter. Other looms and labour-saving devices might have been invented by weavers independently or, Nepal being on the cross-routes of trade, might have been influenced by weaving techniques from the north and south. If the many different techniques in use in Nepal are taken into account, it is probably a combination of invention and outside influences.

The weaver has put the weft through the counter shed. The shed opener is still on edge to clear the passage for the weft. The coil rod near the back beam is used by some weavers to space the warp and prevent it from becoming entangled. (Every warp end is wound once round this stick). The temple, a flexible split piece of bamboo, is inserted at the selvedges to retain the cloth width during weaving. The temple is moved forward as the weaving progresses.

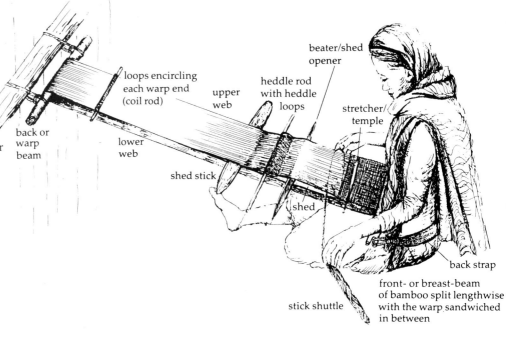

back or warp beam

loops encircling each warp end (coil rod)

lower web

upper web

heddle rod with heddle loops

beater/shed opener

stretcher/temple

shed stick

shed

stick shuttle

back strap

front- or breast-beam of bamboo split lengthwise with the warp sandwiched in between

4

MIDDLE MOUNTAINS

LIMBU, RAI, NEWAR AND GURUNG

❖

Besinda, a village in one of the more northerly, stark regions of the Middle Mountains, the home of the *allo* cloth weaver on p. 126. Most villages in northern Sankhuwasabha are involved in *allo* harvesting and weaving. Here the *allo* grows in forests above the terraces which have been carved into the steep mountainsides to grow food crops.

Before the wide-scale settlement of the southern plains, *terai*, in recent times, most of the population of Nepal lived in the middle mountains: even today over 40 per cent still do. The region stretches from west to east of the country and includes the great valleys of Pokhara and Kathmandu. The astonishing contrasts and the beauty of this region of Nepal are illustrated by the comments made by Hooker (1854, I, 196) on seeing the Tamur valley:

> In one place the road ascended for 2,000 feet above the river, to the village of Chingtam, situated on a lofty spur of the west bank, whence I obtained a grand view of the upper course of the river, flowing in a tremendous chasm, flanked by well-cultivated hills, and emerging fifteen miles to the northward, from black mountains of savage grandeur, whose rugged precipitous faces were streaked with snow, and the tops of the lower ones crowned with the tabular-branched silver-fir, contrasting strongly with the tropical luxuriance around.

The mountains of the region rise to 2,400 m: the valleys are narrow and steep-sided, with valley bottoms at 300–800 m. There is thus great variation over a short distance. The climate, affected by altitude and aspect, varies from the subtropical to the cool temperate. The environmental range has nourished a richness of biological resources from which the different peoples have obtained a wide range of materials for their textiles. It is in these middle mountains that the greatest variety of textiles can be found. Here live, amongst others, the Mongoloid (Tibeto-Burman) Rai and Limbu in the east; the Newar from the Kathmandu Valley, who have also established urban areas in other parts of Nepal; the Gurung, Magar and Tamang

HM King Birendra is depicted on Nepalese stamps wearing the traditional topi.

Opposite A display of Nepalese textiles in the 1983–85 Himalayan Rainbow Exhibition in the Museum of Mankind. The window panels show a random selection of the infinite variety of dhaka cloth patterns on the 18 × 70 cm cotton strips from which the topis are made. The upper and lower centre includes blouse and shawl patterns.

in the west and also in some eastern areas; the Indo-Aryan people, including brahmin, Chhetri and the occupational castes, who came originally from India and over the centuries have diffused throughout the kingdom; and the people who migrated from Tibet. The dominant religion is Hinduism, but Buddhism is also strong, and in some areas traditional practices continue, for example, the worship of domestic and forest gods by Limbus (Caplan 1970, 66).

Limbu and Rai: Traditional dhaka-cloth weaving in east Nepal

Amongst the most remarkable and visible cotton textiles in the middle mountains are the intricately patterned, colourful panels which customarily are made up into caps, topi, for men and blouses and shawls for women. The topi is worn irrespective of rank or ethnicity and forms part of the national dress for men. This consists of a mid-thigh-length, plain white or light-coloured cross-over garment, *labeda*, with matching trousers, *suruwal*, which are tight-fitting from knee to ankle. On formal occasions and in winter a Western-style jacket is worn, sometimes with a waistcoat. The topi, the most distinctive part of the costume, is also worn on less formal occasions, sometimes with Western-type jeans and shirt, or, in the villages, with the *labeda* and a wraparound cloth and a waistband with the kukri tucked in at the front.

The traditional colours of dhaka cloth are black, white, red and orange, but no two topis or shawls are identical: each has its own individual pattern, reflecting the creativity and skill of the weaver. Strangely, this patterned cloth is known locally as 'dhaka cloth'. One story goes that the colourful topi, which has largely replaced the plain, often black, topi, was introduced by a minister who returned with the idea from Dhaka (Bangladesh); others believe that the name was given to the cloth simply because many items, such as cloth and thread, came to Nepal from or through Dhaka or because Dhaka muslin resembled the fine Nepalese weaving. However, the method of pattern weaving practised around Dhaka, called Jamdani, differs considerably from that practised by Nepalese weavers, as will be shown in later pages. It is also possible that Hindu weavers, fleeing from Dhaka at the time of the Muslim invasion, settled in or near Nepal and influenced Nepalese weavers. It is curious, though, that the main centre of dhaka weaving, Terhathum, is in an area of the middle mountains that was difficult to reach until quite recently and not in a border area. The few fragments of fine, handspun cotton inlay-pattern weaving in the collection of the National Museum, Kathmandu, are thought to date from as late as the early part of the twentieth century. Nevertheless, according to the elders of a Terhathum weaver, this type of weaving

has been known for generations, although formerly the patterns were applied mainly to the ends of sashes and waistbands rather than topis. Today some of the finest dhaka cloth is woven by Limbu women from eastern Nepal, though some Rai women are also involved. The majority of weavers are women: very few men weave dhaka cloth. The main area of dhaka weaving is in the town and around Terhathum, some eight hours' walk from a road-head.

The Limbu and Rai, together known as the Kiranti, form one of the largest single ethnic groups in Nepal. They are considered to be the original inhabitants of the middle mountain area and 'have been associated with the history of Nepal for thousands of years' (Bista 1980, 32). The Rais can be divided into a number of segments, *thars*, which were originally associated with a particular location and each had its distinct dialect; these are still identifiable, although nowadays the people increasingly intermingle (Bista 1980, 37–8). They live mainly to the west of the Arun river, the Limbus to the east. Urban settlements are few and small: most families live on isolated farmsteads, growing crops on terraced hillsides and raising small numbers of livestock. Most households have less than one hectare of arable land, and with limited areas of irrigated land crop production is largely rain-fed. Rice is grown where possible, the other main cereals being maize and finger millet. A range of pulses, fruit and vegetables is also grown: mixed and relay cropping are common. At higher altitudes potatoes can be an important part of the diet. Animals – cattle, buffalo, pigs, poultry and also goats and sheep – are a source of food, manure, draught power and income. Cotton used to be grown, and the women spun the thread and wove all the cloth needed for the family, but with the increasing population arable land has had to be used for food and some cash crops. Even so agriculture alone cannot give an adequate livelihood to many of the households, and alternative sources of income have had to be found. The most important of these are wage employment on other farms, portering (most areas are still accessible only on foot), and collection and sale of natural produce such as medicinal plants. Service with the Royal Nepal Army or with the Indian and British Gurkhas is a major source of income. So also, to a less extent, has been the income derived from the inventiveness and skill of the dhaka weavers.

Although throughout Nepal factory-made cloth has replaced much of the traditional handwoven material for clothing, the demand for the individually made dhaka cloth has continued. Most men invest in a new topi for special occasions such as harvest festival, the new year or Dasain. Often something unusual is sought, for example, a commission to design a topi with a new pattern to be worn at a wedding. Sometimes a bridegroom will wear full national dress made from dhaka cloth. At his own wedding HM

King Birendra of Nepal wore such a suit with silver braiding (Simha 1970).

The demand for traditional blouses and shawls is not as great as that for topis: although the style of the blouse remains unchanged, many women use factory-made, sometimes handprinted, cotton, instead of handwoven dhaka cloth. Among the Limbu weavers the most popular material is dark red velvet. However, at wedding ceremonies, particularly of the more affluent, the bride will often still wear a dhaka-cloth blouse and will be given a length of dhaka cloth as part of her dowry. The traditional blouse, the *chaubandi*, as the name indicates, is tied at four places (*char*: four; *bandi*: tie). The ties of this very practical garment allow for variation in size. The two parts of the front of the blouse overlap, so the right side crosses over the left, and each is tied near the armhole and at the waist. The cut of the blouse is in fact similar to that of the men's garment but it reaches only to the waist. In urban areas the blouse is worn with an Indian-style sari, but in most rural areas women wear a *lungi*, a tubular skirt (about 80 × 200 cm), or a wraparound length of cloth (80 × 400 cm or more) and a handwoven cotton waistband, *patuka* (40 cm wide and at least 300 cm long). This waistband is wrapped around the waist several times thus supporting the back and at the same time providing pockets for all kinds of valuables in its various folds. Recent research (Shah 1992) has confirmed that this *patuka*, by supporting the lumbosacral spine, could be one of the reasons for the low incidence of mechanical back pain in the *patuka*-wearing population of Nepal.

The dhaka shawl (90–100 × 200 cm) is usually worn round the shoulders with the ends crossed over one shoulder so that the whole upper part of the body is enveloped; sometimes it is draped over the head. Shawls of handprinted cotton lying between two layers of fine white muslin, acrylic shawls or, especially in Kathmandu in winter, pashmina shawls have become popular and have to a great extent replaced the traditional black, white and orange dhaka shawls. However, since the early 1980s an amazing upsurge of dhaka-cloth production has taken place since a wide range of yarns and colours became available to the weavers (see pp. 106–10).

The dhaka-cloth treadle loom

Most weaving takes place during the dry season, October to March, when little fieldwork is possible. Weaving forms part of the domestic scene: the children are with their mother – playing, watching, learning to weave or minding their younger brothers and sisters. Many girls know how to weave by the time they are ten years old. Often friends and relations work in groups, for companionship and mutual encouragement, and sometimes sharing some of the supporting posts for the loom.

A garlanded bridegroom wearing a Nepalese wedding suit made of dhaka cloth woven in east Nepal. In his waistband is the kukri, the traditional Nepalese knife. The guests are wearing national dress. (see p. 195)

93

Limbu dhaka-cloth weavers at Terhathum in the Koshi Hills, east Nepal.

Dhaka-cloth looms are of no standard size and there are regional variations of warping and weaving methods, but the basic principle is the same. The bamboo and woodwork are usually prepared by men who are members of the weaver's family or friends. The permanent features are the upright bamboo posts which support the loom and are anchored in the ground. Of the two posts nearest to the weaver one has a notch carved into the upper end and the other has a tongue (a protruding stick jammed into the hollow inner part of the bamboo post). The cloth beam rests in the former and slots over the latter. A little further in front of the weaver the next two posts support the crossbar to which the heddle horses are tied. Often a second crossbar is suspended from the top bar, and the heddle horses and reed beater are tied to this which allows for a free swinging movement. Several methods are used to hold the top crossbar securely: some weavers rest it in U-shaped notches on top of the posts; others split the (bamboo) posts for a short length. A bamboo stick across the split ends or string prevents the bamboo splitting further and acts as a rest for the crossbar, again making full use of the potential of bamboo: wood could not be split in this way.

The third pair of posts with a crossbar supports the length of the warp with the tension cord. Some weavers use just one post to support the warp, around which the length of the warp with the tension cord is folded. It seems incredible that the warp seldom gets entangled. The weaver sits in front of the cloth beam to which one

94

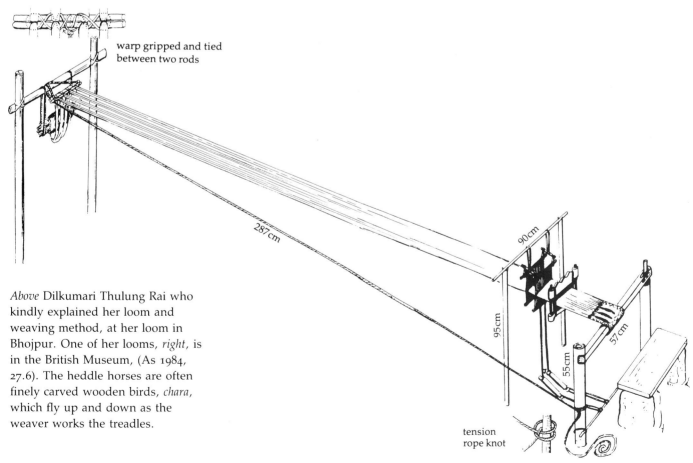

warp gripped and tied between two rods

287 cm

90 cm

95 cm

57 cm

55 cm

tension rope knot

Above Dilkumari Thulung Rai who kindly explained her loom and weaving method, at her loom in Bhojpur. One of her looms, *right*, is in the British Museum, (As 1984, 27.6). The heddle horses are often finely carved wooden birds, *chara*, which fly up and down as the weaver works the treadles.

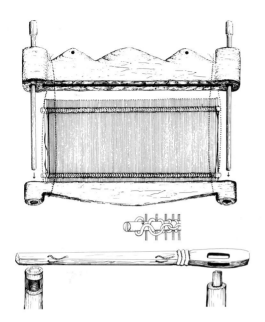

Above The two essential parts of the loom that most weavers own are one or two cloth-beams (bottom) and a reed beater (top). Their length depends on the width of the weaving.

For topi strips, the average beam length is 60 cm. Oblong holes are carved through all four sides of one end of the hardwood beam. The weaver can then wind on the woven cloth by quarter turns of the beam when it is slotted onto the tongue of the supporting post. The two holes carved through one edge of the beam are for the strings which hold the stick with the warp loops in place at the beginning of the weaving. The reed beater is used to space the warp threads and drive home the weft. Split bamboo strips 3 mm wide are lashed between two split bamboo rods: the spacing between the strips is determined by the thickness of the lashing yarn. The reed is fitted into a carved wooden frame, shaped for easy handling. The two holes at the upper part are for the string suspending the beater from the crossbar. The basic reed is usually made by an experienced reedmaker from the village, rather than at home. British Museum As 1984 27.6.

end of the warp is attached. The warp passes through the reed and the heddles to the warp beam, in this case two bamboo sticks tied together tightly, thus holding the warp in a cross. The rest of the warp, rolled up together with split bamboo sticks, is left hanging in loops tied to the crossbar. Two strings attached to either side of the bamboo stick (the warp beam) in a figure of eight are joined with the tension cord. This is tied to one of the bamboo posts supporting the cloth beam where the weaver can easily tighten or release it to adjust warp tension. As the cloth is woven and wound on to the cloth beam, the weaver loosens the tension cord and allows as much of the warp to move towards her as she requires before she tightens the rope again. This continues until the warp is almost up to the heddles so there is hardly any wastage.

At night-time the weaving is covered up. Sometimes it is taken inside the house for protection: to do this the tension cord is released, the warp loosely folded, the heddle-horse loops are slipped off the supporting bar, the cloth beam is unslotted from the front bamboo posts, and the treadles (part of the movable loom) are slipped off the bamboo crossbar at the bottom. It takes only a few minutes to set up the loom when it is used again.

Laying the warp

In warping, the threads which will run lengthways on the loom are arranged in uniform lengths and tension, and are separated into even and odd threads by the crosses formed between warping-posts. The crosses maintain the correct sequence of yarn and prevent the warp from becoming entangled.

There are various ways of preparing the yarn for warping: the handspun cotton yarn, which is the one traditionally used, is wound from the spindle on to a split bamboo cage spool to form a skein. This skein is put over a cone-shaped swift, which is yet another ingenious, home-made construction making full use of the flexibility and structure of split bamboo with its joints and hollow internodes. Mercerised sewing cotton thread, manufactured in southern Nepal, is now used by many dhaka weavers. As this is sold in rolls on cardboard cylinders, similar to bobbins, weavers can use them as they are, employing an even number at any given time in order to speed up the warping process. The cylinders are either all stacked on one bamboo rod or held in a fan on individual rods.

Traditionally the continuous warp is laid by winding it around a series of posts (about 1 m high) anchored in the ground. The distance between the posts at either end, which are particularly sturdy, determines the length of the weaving. This is usually 30 m or more, which would be sufficient to weave at least forty topi lengths of 70 cm. To prevent the fine yarn from getting entangled and to maintain the correct sequence of yarn over such a distance pairs of

Laying the warp over six warping posts along a path outside the weaver's house. A cross is formed at each pair of posts.

warping-posts are placed every few metres between the two end-posts, that is, the cloth- and warp-beam ends.

The weaver ties the ends of two rolls of thread together and slips the loops over the cloth-beam end-post. Then, walking back and forth between the two end-posts, the weaver forms with each individual thread a cross between every pair of posts. The rolls of thread spin easily on the rod or rods releasing the thread which the weaver is holding in one hand while the threads are separated and crosses laid with the other. Some weavers count the thread, but most know how many spools of thread or skeins they need for a given piece of weaving, for example, for topi strips from 300 to 400 warp ends.

When the warping is completed, the crosses are secured by inserting and tying sticks alongside them and often by tying a long cord around the cross. The warp is then slipped off the warping-posts starting at the distal, warp-beam, post. The warp is carefully folded and wound together with the cross-sticks and ties. It is now ready for threading through the reed beater. This is usually done by two women sitting face to face. One of them holds the warp-beam end with the bundle of warp in her lap. The reed is secured in an upright position on the ground in front of her or it is held by her helper, who sits on the other side of the reed. The weaver slips the warp yarn (cloth-beam end) over her hand or finger and, starting

97

at one side of the warp, selects from the cross-tie one loop after another and holds it against the reed where her helper picks it up with a hook through the appropriate dent of the reed and slides it over a bamboo stick. The sharpened end of this stick is used sometimes directly for picking up the loops. This means that two warp threads (= one loop) of the continuous uncut warp is threaded through each dent.

Dressing the loom

With the reed now resting in the warp the stick which carries the warping-loops is tied to the cloth beam. The warp is then held firmly at the second cross, stretched, shaken and spaced out. The warp at this point (second cross) is usually divided into four sections, tightly gripped between the cross-sticks and secured with string. These cross-sticks act as a warp-beam end to which the tension rope is attached going over a cross-bar to a point near the weaver's seat. The bundle of the remaining warp hangs in two loops from the horizontal bar. When only a single warp end-post is used, the warp bundle, securely tied, with the tension rope attached, is simply slung around this end-post, and again the other end of the rope is attached to the post near the weaver.

Heddle making. *Left* Putting the heddle thread through the shed. *Centre* Picking up the heddle loops between the warp threads. *Right* The interlocked heddle loops with the alternate warp threads in the eyes.

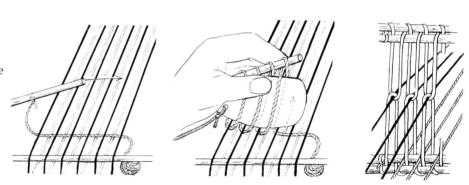

With the warp under tension the weaver now proceeds with making the pair of thread heddles which will help to form the shed and countershed through which the weft can be passed: the alternate warp ends, separated by the cross during warping, are picked up with thread loops which are gripped between bamboo rods (shafts). To form these loops a ball of strong thread is tied to one end of a bamboo rod which is slightly longer than the width of the weaving. This rod is passed through one shed which is obtained from the first cross, the ball of thread remaining on one side with the thread being slowly released as the rod moves. The rod is then brought back along the top of the warp, picking up in loops the heddle thread which shows as weft between the warp ends. The loops are formed over a measuring device, called *pati* in Limbu and *pirsa* and *pelau* in Rai, a carved piece of wood about 6 × 12 cm which

This weaver is forming the heddle loops for the second heddle with a measuring device, *pati*, and two heddle rods, encircling the previously formed loops and the warp thread before the warp is turned back to its original position. The reed without the frame is resting in the warp close to the weaver in front of the cloth beam.

ensures that all the loops are the same length. The weaver holds the rod with one hand whilst picking up the heddle thread with the other, leading the thread in front of the *pati*, then behind and back in front of the bamboo rod and down behind the *pati*. The same process is repeated for the next heddle loop. As more loops are formed, the others slide off the narrow part of the *pati*. The figure of eight between the rod and the *pati* is maintained by a cord which is tied to the narrow end of the *pati*. When all the loops are made, the cord is replaced by a bamboo rod, which is tied tightly to the top heddle rod. This keeps the heddle threads evenly spaced and prevents them from moving about. Many weavers put this second rod with the *pati* whilst forming the loops; in this case no cord is needed.

The heddles for the second or countershed are formed similarly.

99

The whole warp is then turned over so that the completed heddles hang down. Again the whole process of forming heddle loops is repeated, this time with the loops encircling the previously formed loops together with the warp thread, which is now caught in the heddle eye. When both heddles are made the warp is returned to its original position. (Some weavers use the same thread heddles for several lengths of weaving by simply tying in a new warp. The new continuous warp will have to be cut in this case loop after loop so that it can be tied to the old warp ends. For the narrow topi width most weavers save the heddle thread (unwinding the old heddle loops) and use it to make a new heddle for each warp.)

The two heddles are joined to each other at either end with thin cords, which are tied with lark's-head knots to the ends of bamboo rods or heddle horses about 12 cm long. These in turn are tied at the centre with a loop which is slipped over the cross-bar resting on the bamboo supporting posts. A cord, knotted round their centre, attaches the lower heddle rods to bamboo treadles. To serve as treadles weavers often use seeds which they can grasp with their toes, or they simply put the string loops, which were tied to the lower heddle rods, around their feet; the weaver can then achieve a change of shed by altering the crossing of her legs, either left over right or right over left.

Whichever method the weaver uses, if one treadle, seed or cord is pressed down, the heddle attached to it will be lowered and so also will be the warp thread caught in the heddle-loop eyes, while the unaffected warp ends in between slide up to form a shed. When the weaver depresses the other treadle, the second heddle rod, with the alternate warp ends caught in the heddle loop, will be brought down so that the countershed appears while the uncaught warp threads rise in between. Thus the treadles are worked alternately to obtain the shed and countershed needed for the plain-weave dhaka cloth.

Supplementary-weft inlay (brocade)

The best-known method of dhaka-cloth weaving is a plain ground weave with a supplementary weft of a different colour laid alongside the ground weft in the regular sheds in selected areas to create a pattern. For the white ground weft weavers use one or more strands of single cotton or one strand of two- or three-ply mercerised sewing cotton. For the supplementary weft they choose either several strands (six) single-cotton or mercerised cotton or stranded two-ply embroidery cotton, two or three strands at a time. The main traditional colours are red, orange and black with sometimes a little green and blue added. In the 1980s the locally manufactured acrylic yarn became popular: this brightly coloured yarn is preferred by many of the younger generation, especially for stiff taller topis.

The ground weft is put in either directly from a roll of thread or, more usually, the roll is first mounted in a boat-shaped shuttle: this helps to carry the weft through the shed swiftly. Mercerised sewing cotton rolls can be used as they are: the weaver threads the shuttle pin through the cardboard cylinder and just inserts it into the carved-out section of the shuttle. The inlay supplementary weft is woven in from either a loosely wound ball or a small bamboo stick shuttle or a type of 'butterfly' winding. The first half centimetre of dhaka cloth is usually a plain balanced (ground) weave – the most simple interlacing of warp and weft, where each weft yarn passes alternately over and under successive warp yarns with warp and weft of equal size in spacing and count. The thread count for dhaka cloth varies from about thirty to sixty warp ends per inch (2.5 cm). The weaver then proceeds with the weft inlay patterns, which involve four steps:

1 The weaver puts the shuttle with the ground weft half-way through the shed which she obtains by pressing down the first treadle.

2 Whilst the shuttle rests in the open shed (and helps to keep it open), she lays in the supplementary weft.

3 She then pushes the shuttle right through and beats the inlay and the ground weft into position with the reed beater.

4 She changes the shed by pressing down the second treadle, puts the shuttle with the ground weft half-way through the shed, and repeats processes 2–4. At every change of shed the weaver decides, without a chart or counting threads, where she is going to put the colour which forms the pattern.

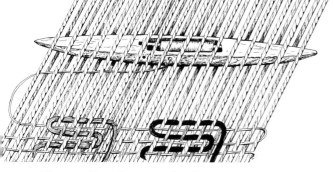

The 30–38 cm long wooden boat shuttle with the ground weft is put alongside the supplementary weft. The ground weft in the unpatterned area is pushed apart if thick inlay yarn is used. The fabric in these areas becomes semi-transparent. The removable pin on which the roll of ground weft is mounted in the shuttle is prevented from slipping out by inserting a feather quill into the hole at the side of the shuttle over the slot.

Tapestry

Although most dhaka cloth is woven with weft-inlay patterns, there are some weavers who employ various methods of tapestry. The coloured weft threads in this case are not supplementary but are woven back and forth in their own pattern area to form the actual structure of the textile. The warp is less visible in this type of dhaka, although not as hidden as in the textile generally referred to as tapestry, which is entirely weft-faced. One method of joining colour areas is that of dovetailing where two wefts go round a common warp end where the colours meet. But weavers also use inter-penetrated dovetailing where the wefts from adjacent areas alternately pass into the other area and turn on an adjacent warp-end, rather than a common one thus forming jagged outlines. Other weavers use double-interlocked tapestry methods where the differ-

A topi strip woven using the interlocked and interpenetrated tapestry method.

Above Tapesty pattern methods used for dhaka cloth. *Top to bottom* Dove-tailing, interpenetrated dove-tailing, double interlocking, and interlocking and interpenetrating.

Right Interpenetrated dove-tailing: traditional topi strips with the temple pattern.

Some of the many variations of the diamond motif. (This and the patterns on the following pages were all woven with supplementary weft.)

ent colour weft areas are joined by interlocking them in each shed: a ridge of interlocking loops will show at the colour joins on the working face – that is, the side facing the weaver – but is smooth on the other side.

Yet another method, where interlocking is combined with interpenetrating, is used for some intricate topi patterns.

Pattern motifs

The variety of dhaka patterns is almost infinite, from bold geometric shapes and temple outlines to complex floral patterns. Only some motifs are given specific names, such as the temple, *mandir*, and elephant trunk, *hatti sunr*. Others are interpreted by the individual weavers as diamond, zigzag, butterfly or flower, or are just referred to as *butta* (see p. 113). No two topi strips are identical, and within one length of warp the weaver usually changes the pattern every 70 cm (topi length). This not only makes it more interesting for the weaver but it means also that she can offer a passing customer or shopkeeper a choice of patterns. She will cut off the sections required, leaving at least 15 cm of woven cloth: this is dampened to ensure a good grip and then rolled around the cloth beam for the weaving to continue. Although some basic shapes are similar, colour and composition are decided upon by the individual weaver without any drawing or plan, thus making each piece of weaving a unique creation. Only some of the most common patterns can be touched upon here, but even these few demonstrate the complex interplay of shape and shade so prevalent in dhaka weaving.

One of the best-known topi-strip patterns is based on stepped diamond shapes, *inta*, along the centre. These are framed by broad, stepped lines and half-diamond shapes emerging from the selvage. According to Limbu weavers, this pattern is easy to weave and is often one of the first patterns for a beginner to practise on. An experienced weaver can weave one or two topi lengths per day with this type of pattern. A more complex pattern might take several days. The diamond appears in many other patterns and is arranged in such a variety of sizes, colours and outlines (smooth, jagged, stepped) and either joined up closely or kept separate that each woven strip has a different appearance, emphasised by the irregularities which occur in hand-picked patterns. Often patterns or colours are arranged diagonally, allowing the supplementary weft to continue upwards from pattern to pattern.

Diamonds or hexagonal shapes with a variety of centre patterns are woven into all-over designs or linked up to form new patterns, often in such a way that the background becomes the dominant pattern. Positive and negative forms are freely interchanged from one weaving to the other. There are many different types of zigzag patterns and an even wider range based on the outline of a Nepalese

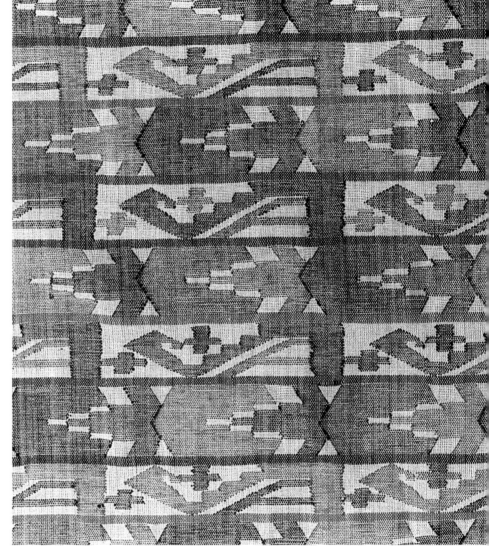

Above Motifs are often linked to form new arrangements in an interplay of positive and negative (background) shapes (see p. 110).

Above right Temple pattern alternating with the elephant trunk motif. In a recent innovation the motif has been reversed.

temple, *mandir*. Often this is arranged in stripes and alternated with the elephant trunk, *hatti sunr*, pattern interspersed with cross designs. Another truly Nepalese design is that based on the national flower, *Rhododendron arboreum*, or *lali guras*. Flowers have been the inspiration for many weavers and are incorporated in various shapes into a multitude of patterns.

It is interesting to compare this spontaneous invention and combination of patterns, which are unique features of Nepalese dhaka weaving, with the quite different approach adopted by the *jamdani* weavers from the Dhaka area (Bangladesh). Watson (1866, 79) described their method as follows: 'Two weavers sit at the loom, place a pattern drawn upon paper below the warp and range along the track of the woof a number of cut threads equal to the flowers or part of the design intended to be made and then, with two small pointed bamboo sticks, they draw each of these threads between as

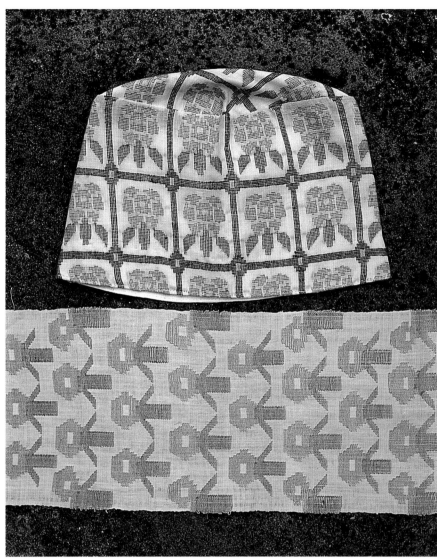

Above left Variations of the temple pattern.

Above right A topi strip and a topi showing the weaver's interpretation of the rhododendron with its distinctive red flower and downward pointing leaves. On formal occasions, women government servants wear white saris with a *lali guras* border.

Left Rhododendron arboreum – *lali guras* – the national flower of Nepal.

A Limbu weaver wearing the multi coloured shawl she wove. Woollen and acrylic winter shawls with similar patterns are the weavers latest edition to their range.

Opposite A shawl weaving sample. The weaver has tried out different warp and weft colours and a variety of patterns. This Limbu weaver was the first to start her own workshop, employing and training other weavers. (Further trials included woollen and acrylic yarns for winter shawls, which are now made and worn by many weavers.)

many threads of the warp as may be equal to the width of the figure which is to be formed. When all the threads have been brought between the warp they are drawn close by a stroke of the lay [reed beater]. The shuttle is then passed by one of the weavers through the shed and the weft having been driven home, it is returned by the other weaver.' This whole process is then repeated.

Today traditional dhaka weaving is flourishing: in addition a variation of this type of weaving is finding a market not only in Nepal but also abroad. This market was established through the combined efforts of a rural development programme, KHARDEP, the Koshi Hill Area Rural Development Programme of HM Government of Nepal and the UK Overseas Development Administration, and the weavers of the Koshi hills. In the early 1980s KHARDEP had been asked to assist in finding additional sources of off-farm income for the many families of the area who have not enough land to be self-sufficient in food. As weaving was one of the most widely practised crafts and was already the source of some income, it was decided both to assist the production of traditional items and to see if the techniques could be adapted for a wider market through using higher-quality yarns, which would do greater justice to the excellence of the weaving, and by making a wider range of colours available. But could this be done without harm to traditional designs and skills?

It was the weavers who provided the answer to this concern and made the decisions. A group of four carried out trials on the initial proposals in their own homes and adopting traditional methods and patterns but widening the range of inlay colours used they employed for the first time a black mercerised cotton warp. One of the great surprises and delights for the weavers was seeing how their traditional patterns appeared in a new light and seemed to glow on a dark background. Inspired by the challenge of using these yarns, the weavers arranged their patterns in many different ways and devised and discovered new shapes. Design development received a stimulus, enriching rather than harming tradition. The weavers' enthusiasm was infectious and passed to friends and relations, some of whom had not woven previously on a regular basis but only when a firm market was available.

At workshops the possibilities of new products were discussed with the weavers, for example, shawls of the traditional size but incorporating a wider variety of colours and designs, and scarves with borders and fringes based on the traditional 18-cm-wide topi strips. Small displays helped to test the market; as the demand for the new products became established and then grew, KHARDEP assisted the weavers by:

1 establishing a Cottage Industry Emporium shop in Terhathum to supply a wide range of yarn and equipment, act as a channel for orders and sales, and become the centre for discussions on

A traditional topi strip with white warp and weft on the left, and three trials by weavers using a wider range of colours and yarns in variations of the zigzag pattern, to be used for scarves and sari borders.

A Limbu weaver selecting the warp thread and laying in the colours which form the patterns. The 'wrong' side, with the small loop turns of the supplementary weft facing the weaver is as attractive as the other side.

Here the weaver has used a
different colour combination, but
the same pattern, and has added a
border to transform the topi strip
into a scarf.

109

The first experiments by a weaver using traditional patterns in a variety of colours on a black rather than a white warp.

Right A carpenter making wooden 4-shaft frame looms and spinning-wheels. The loom, with roll-on cloth and warp beams, has a fly shuttle attachment which consists of a track along which the shuttle runs from a throwing base to a catching base, propelled by means of a cord with a handle in the middle. By jerking the handle, the weaver can operate the shuttle much more quickly than she could by moving it through the shed by hand. It also allows cloth to be woven which is wider than the breadth of her reach. There are several variations of this type of frame loom but the basic principle remains the same.

product development, pricing, quality standards and marketing, initially this being supported by vso (Voluntary Service Overseas);

2 supplying labour-saving devices such as warping mills and roller shuttles;

3 arranging exhibitions and publicity material, establishing contacts between weavers and buyers;

4 assisting the Women's Training Centre, Dhankuta, with workshops which covered such subjects as weaving, health care and functional literacy as well as undertaking periodic visits.

A frame loom with fly-shuttle attachment was introduced at this stage, but most weavers prefer their lighter-weight and less bulky bamboo treadle looms. The frame loom works on the same principle as the bamboo treadle loom and has been used in Nepal for about seventy years. With their roll-on warp beam they can easily accommodate a 100-m warp, and the fly-shuttle attachment means that the weft on the spool can be carried swiftly through the shed, thus speeding up weaving. A disadvantage compared with the traditional bamboo treadle loom lies in the cost. This type of loom cannot be made at home but has to be built by a carpenter. Further, it cannot be kept outside and takes up much room in the usually small houses of the hill family. The loom is used mainly in urban areas, although some weavers in Terhathum use it for sari weaving.

By the time ODA financial support ended in 1986 some one hundred weavers were involved, and products, standards and linkages had been defined. The weavers had decided against a co-operative venture and continued working individually, within the family group or the training workshops which some of the weavers had established on their own initiative. In a number of cases, as weaving absorbed a greater part of their time, the weavers were able to afford to employ others to help with farm and household duties. Most weavers marketed their products through the Emporium, although some made direct contact with buyers from Dhankuta and, especially, Kathmandu, where dhaka cloth is used now by fashion designers as well as interior decorators and has found local as well as tourist and foreign markets. Following a small exhibition, 'Himalayan Rainbow' (1983–85), at the Museum of Mankind (British Museum), London, regular orders have been given for dhaka items for sale in the Museum shop. Such support from the various outlets and its encouragement of the production of original pieces of weaving have been highly beneficial in stimulating the inventiveness of the individual weaver.

It is a combination of factors – the weaver's creativity, the freedom to choose, in her own time, yarn and patterns, to use traditional colours or a wider variety, experiment or work according to market demand – that probably makes the dhaka cloth such a success.

110

Traditional Atpare Rai cotton shawl (100 × 180 cm). The main part of the shawl is embroidered with red and green stepped diamond *kothi* (house) patterns. Depending upon how many small diamonds are within the main unit, these are called 4-, 9- or 16-house patterns. The shawl above has 9-house patterns. The borders are embellished with two broad *chauko* (bench) patterns and one zigzag pattern and tassels. British Museum As 1984 27.

Atpare Rai girls from Santang, Dhankuta District, wearing their traditional home-woven shawls.

Variations

Two other types of dhaka-cloth weaving of different styles are of particular interest as they evoke comparisons and questions on the origins of the different types of dhaka cloth. The first involves a small but distinct group of Rais, the Atpare Rais of Santang, Dhankuta District, who wear specific colours and patterns as a means of self-identification. The second type is undertaken by people of several ethnic groups, including Chhetri, brahmin and Newar, in Palpa District, western Nepal.

The Atpare Rai women show their identity by wearing a white shawl with red and green diamond motifs. The natural off-white-coloured cotton shawls are woven on traditional bamboo treadle looms and are made up of two panels (each 200 × 40 cm) joined at the selvage. The interesting feature is that the motifs are either laid in with supplementary weft in the dhaka-cloth method or are embroidered on afterwards. Following along the lines of the weft thread of the plain balanced weave, groups of warp threads are picked up with a long needle and the stranded cotton embroidery

Right The traditional Atpare Rai patterns are now embroidered in a wide range of colours in a variety of materials. The reverse of the shawl is equally attractive.

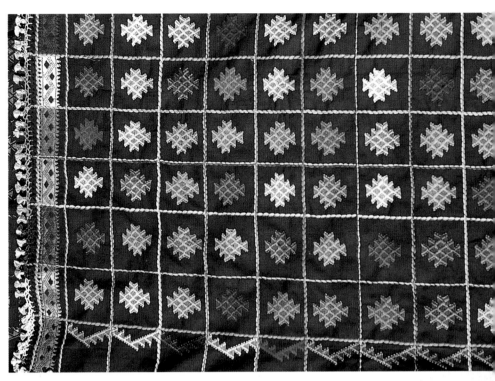

A Rai orange-seller at the weekly market. The check cotton shawl is embroidered with 4-house diamond patterns.

yarn is threaded through with a darning stitch. Some of the embroidery yarn floats on the front to form a solid relief, emphasising outlines. The delicate reverse side of the embroidery is as attractive as the front. The heavily embroidered ends of the shawl, with broad zigzag and line borders, are a dominant feature. The cut ends are folded in, stitched and secured with a type of knotted border with small tassels hanging in the end loops. Those tassels at the selvage border side serve the additional purpose of securing some of the border-line embroidery thread and add extra weight to the shawl so that it will drape well over the shoulder and show the richly decorated border to its best advantage. The woven and embroidered patterns are referred to in general as *butta*: this is translated loosely as 'embroidery' but there are also specific names. *Butta* is also used by Limbus to refer to their weaving patterns.

According to Santang weavers, pattern weaving and embroidery started within living memory but they claim that this was not introduced from outside. In this context it is interesting to compare the Atpare Rai patterns with those embroidered by another Rai group in Sankhuwasabha District (on p. 114). All inlay-patterned shawls used to be woven from home-grown, handspun cotton. The weavers say that a length of cloth equal to three and a half times the measure from elbow to fingertip can be woven in one day, that is, approximately 130 cm. Today little cotton is grown because of the pressure on land for food crops. Many Santang women buy full shawl-width, factory-made, white cotton material, available now in shops, and

113

Rai embroidered cotton head scarves from Sankhuwasabha. Some patterns with running stitches resemble those of the Atpare Rais from Santang, but here there is a wider variety of stitches and patterns, each woman inventing her own variation. Most of the patterns are along the borders. Knotted fringes and crochet panels are often added not only to decorate but also add weight so that the ends hang down. 132 × 38 cms and a 6 cm crochet border. British Museum As 1993 01.3.

embroider this with the traditional red and green motifs. Some women from nearby villages use the same motifs with their own colour schemes: the diamond motifs are sometimes incorporated into a check pattern.

Their embroidery skill has given many women an urgently needed source of off-farm income, which had previously been obtained by the exhausting and time-consuming occupation of cutting and selling firewood. This inevitably involved a daily absence from home for a number of hours which could have an adverse effect on the nutrition of young children. The practice was also harmful to the environment. The change was brought about through the formation of the Santang Women's Club, established as part of the extension programme of the Women's Training Centre, Dhankuta. The Club's programme included functional literacy, health care, vegetable production and other income-generating skills. The Santang women adapted their skills to develop a wide range of products by embroidering traditional patterns in a variety of colours on to handwoven and other high-quality cloth.

In Palpa District the Department of Cottage and Village Industries (DCVI) introduced dhaka-cloth weaving on wooden frame looms with fly-shuttle attachments. Following this training, many families, especially in the town area of Tansen, started their own small businesses, and local entrepreneurs invested in looms and warping equipment and engaged weavers, mainly women, on piece-work in their small factories. The supplementary-weft patterns are chosen often with the assistance of DCVI and in response to market demand. They are laid in by following either samples or charts, supplied by the employer, which the weavers come to memorise. Each line of inlay pattern is followed by two picks of ground weave, rather than a single pick as in eastern Nepal. Because of the width of the weaving (up to 1 m) often two weavers work together on a single piece. The cloth is sold in the local market, mainly in Kathmandu, by the metre as shawl and blouse pieces or the cloth is made up into topis. Most of the yarn, cotton as well as polyester in the traditional white, black, red, yellow and orange colours, comes from the nearby yarn factory in Bhutwal.

The richly patterned shawl being woven by Rita Thapa (below right) is now in the British Museum collection. There are about fifty

Below A Newar weaver from Tansen, West Nepal, teaches his daughter how to weave dhaka cloth on the big wooden frame loom. The treadles and fly shuttle are operated by the father.

Below right Dhaka shawl weaving at Pokhara. The wrong side of the shawl showing long floats is facing the weaver who carefully lines up all the bobbins with the supplementary weft and puts each back into place after having laid the colour into the section she selected. British Museum As 1992 10.36.

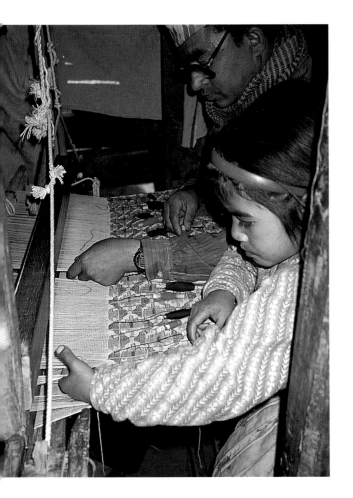

First trials by a dhaka weaver from Pokhara using a wider variety of colours. For the shawl pattern she usually weaves with white warp and weft, and yellow, red and black supplementary colours (p. 6). Weaving saris and lengths of colourful or all-white inlay-pattern material has been successfully taken up by some weavers.

warp ends and forty-two picks per inch (2.5 cm). The weaver used up to sixty-seven bobbins with the supplementary inlay weft in one single pick. Most weavers use the warping equipment from the DCVI training centre making warps of approximately 100 m at a time, sufficient for fifty shawls.

It takes about one month to weave three intricately patterned shawls. The weavers continue to follow the patterns, samples and charts they were taught on the DCVI training centre course but being self-employed they choose their own combinations. The potential for further development was demonstrated when the weavers were shown a colourful shawl woven in eastern Nepal, which incorporated similar designs to their own but with a wider range of colours. This inspired the weavers to make their own trials. Their enthusiasm for these was reflected in the results which gained them a ready market in Kathmandu.

In the same area a farmer involved in sericulture has made preliminary trials on the production of a silk dhaka topi cloth, using his own silk (see illustration on p. 58).

Float-weave-patterned cotton cloth
Less well known than dhaka cloth are the traditional 2/2 twill bird's-eye and diamond-patterned textiles which are woven by Limbu and Rai women on the same type of bamboo loom as that described on p. 95 but using four instead of two heddles and treadles (see p. 73). In spite of the impact of imported material this type of cotton cloth is still woven in the hill areas, although cotton is seldom produced locally any longer. Homespun and woven clothing is preferred, especially by the older generation, because of its qualities – softness, comfort and durability – as well as for economic reasons. Because there are fewer intersections of yarn the cloth feels more supple and flexible than plain weave and it drapes well, following the shape of the body: it is thus particularly suitable for waistbands and shawls. It is not known when this pattern weaving began but according to the weavers it has been passed on from generation to generation. Could it have originated in Nepal?

This unusual method of picking up patterns with loop heddles rather than threading each warp end through the appropriate heddle eye according to a predetermined diagram (the common method) merits a detailed description.

For the diamond pattern the warp is made using three instead of two warp sticks at the cloth-beam end, thus forming two crosses. Before lifting the warp off the sticks the crosses are secured by inserting the cross-sticks 1, 2 and 3. These are tied loosely to each other at the ends. The remaining cross-sticks are tied firmly to prevent the thread from entangling. The loops from the first stick are then passed through the reed – one loop = two threads in each

117

Traditional Rai cotton weaving patterns. *Top* 2/2 twill or *kes*. *Middle* Bird's eye or *kiring*. *Bottom* Diamond or *gimte*.

A weaver from east Nepal, wearing a diamond-patterned wrap-around cotton skirt, which she wove on her home-made treadle loom in the method described in the text. The skirt is made up of two 40 cm-wide panels which are joined at the selvage to form double width. The 4 m length of cloth is generously pleated at the front to allow for leg movement. The end of the cloth is wrapped over the pleated part, slightly hitched up to reveal the pleats and then tucked in at the waist. A length of cloth, some 4 m × 48 cm, is wrapped around the waist, either underneath, as here, or on top of the blouse.

Above Heddle-making for a diamond pattern. Picking up the heddle loops for the second heddle between pick-up stick A and cross stick 2.

Right The traditional way of laying the warp for the diamond pattern with two crosses (cross sticks 1, 2 and 3) at the front beam end and (*far right*) using the labour-saving warping mill introduced in 1984. The weaver is wearing her handwoven wraparound skirt and nettle jacket.

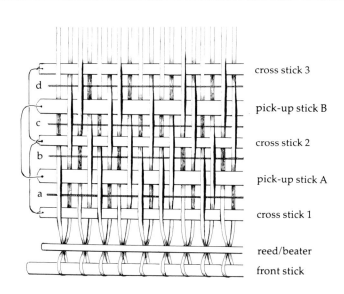

cross stick 3

pick-up stick B

cross stick 2

pick-up stick A

cross stick 1

reed/beater

front stick

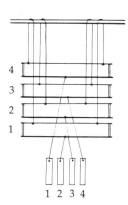

Above Using two bamboo pick-up stick, A and B, held open like shears, the weaver, starting from the left, picks up and puts down between the crosses, in succession, first a single and then four pairs of warp threads, as shown in the diagram. Sticks A and B are then tied loosely to each other at the ends, but are removed after heddle making. The weaver can now identify from the pattern formed between the pick-up and cross sticks (see heddle thread guides a–d) which warp threads are to be encircled with heddle loops, namely those which form a bridge passing over adjacent pick-up and cross sticks which, usually flat, can be put on their edges so that the bridge shows more clearly. The loops encircling these selected areas, the heddles, are made in the same manner as those described for the plain weave (see page 98). *Above right* After completing the heddles, the top heddle bars are joined in pairs, 1 with 4 and 2 with 3, and are suspended over a crossbar. The lower heddle bars are tied to the four treddles, heddle 1 to treadle 2, 2 to 3, 3 to 4 and 4 to 1. Two treadles are pressed simultaneously but the weaver only has to move one foot for each shed change. For the diamond pattern, treadles are passed in succession: 2 and 3, 1 and 3, 1 and 4, 2 and 4, 2 and 3, 1 and 3, 1 and 4, 2 and 4, 1 and 4, 1 and 3, 2 and 3, 2 and 4, 1 and 4, 1 and 3. With a change of treadling, the weaver can achieve a variety of patterns.

dent – and are placed over a strong stick which in turn is tied to the front or cloth beam. The rest of the warp is attached to the back beam and held under tension with the tension rope. The weaver now has the front beam, the reed and the three cross-sticks with two crosses in front of her. The subsequent process is very difficult to explain but should be clarified by diagrams and photographs.

A 2/2 twill or bird's-eye pattern requires different heddle threadings: these are made by slightly changing the pick-up method from the crosses, for example, for a 2/2 twill the pick-up sticks are inserted in between the crosses – in an under 2/over 2 pattern, showing the bridges which are going to be encircled with heddle loops.

A *rumal* or cover for offerings, also used at wedding ceremonies for gifts and the bridal dowry. This is a 2/2 twill weave cotton with supplementary weft patterns, made in east Nepal.

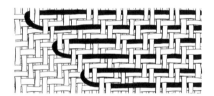

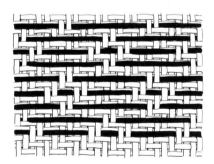

Above The method of using the supplementary weft for the corner of the star pattern. *Below* At the end borders the supplementary-weft pattern is often taken right across the warp from selvage to selvage.

Supplementary-weft-patterned twill

For shawls, headscarves and covering cloths 2/2 twill weaves are often combined with supplementary-weft patterns. A fine example of this type of weaving may be found in the British Museum collection. This exquisite shawl was woven about 1930 by a Limbu weaver from Telia, eastern Nepal. The shawl is made up of two panels (each 38 cm wide and 165 cm long), joined together by a type of herringbone stitch. Handspun, natural colour, single cotton has been used for both the warp and the weft of the 2/2 balanced twill, with fifty-five warp ends per inch (2.5 cm). The supplementary weft consists of eight very fine strands in faded yellow, grey-green and red. The inlay weaving differs from that used for topi cloth: although the hand-picked pattern is laid into the same shed as the ground weave in general, it floats on the surface in some parts and there is always an extra line of ground weft between each supplementary pattern weft.

Nettle (*allo*) textiles from Sankhuwasabha

The most unusual textiles in the middle mountains are those made from the Himalayan mountain nettle, *Girardinia diversifolia* (*allo*). The fibres of this plant have been extracted, spun and woven for centuries by Magar, Tamang, Gurung, the nomadic Rautye and, particularly, the Rais. The Rais live on small, scattered farms along the

120

Above A woman wearing a 2/2 twill supplementary-weft-patterned cotton shawl.

Above right Details – front and back – of a 2/2 twill supplementary-weft patterned shawl woven by the old lady on the right. British Museum (As 1991 28.1).

Right Three generations of Limbu in eastern Nepal (Telia). The women wear wraparound skirts, even if those of the younger generation are made of imported material. Shawls and waistbands are still woven locally. In town areas and for special occasions, the sari is becoming popular with younger women. For men, the topi remains an identification symbol for Nepal. The *labeda suruwal* is often replaced by Western-style clothes except at official functions.

Selling *allo* fishing nets at the annual *mela* at Dingla, Bhojpur District. The knotted circular casting net measures about 175 cm from top to bottom. It takes 7 to 10 days to make a net.

mountainsides above steep valleys, most of them several days' walk from the nearest road-head or airstrip. They carved the terraced plots of land for their crops out of steep, stony slopes. Some plots are so small they hold only a few plants of maize or finger millet, the staple diet, which is supplemented with potatoes, leaf vegetables, roots, fern tops and, at times, the young leaves and shoots of *allo*. For generations this plant has provided the raw material for making most of the textiles needed by the household, including clothing, mats, sacks, bags, fishing-nets, ropes and carrying-straps. The last three are made by men, while all the woven textiles are the work of women. In an account of the Kulunge Rai McDougall (1979, 68) states that 'rich households keep a large amount of decorated fibre cloth made locally' and that 'decorated fibre cloth is displayed on certain occasions with household ritual'. *Allo* textiles also used to be bartered, often for grain (to overcome the annual food shortage) at the local markets, *hat*, or annual fair, *mela*. *Allo* fishing-nets, porters' headbands, sacks, bags and mats are still in demand and in regular use. According to some fishermen, *allo* fishing-nets last longer than the synthetic nylon nets which have become available and they do not frighten the fish as the sparkling nylon nets tend to do.

Rai men used to wear the traditional *allo* jacket or *phenga*, and some, especially of the older generation, continue to do so. This type of jacket, sometimes without sleeves, is also worn by women and children. Often these jackets are beautifully embroidered for decoration as well as for strengthening joins and seams. McDougall (1978, 50) mentions distinctive sleeveless jackets with diagnostic designs on the back: 'Rais of different tribes can be distinguished by characteristic jacket designs.' A fine *allo* jacket in the British Museum collection was woven and embroidered by a weaver from Besinda, Sankhuwasabha. The jacket is made up of three pieces of fine warp-faced weave with about eighty warp ends (singles, z-twist) and seventeen picks per inch (2.5 cm). The main panel, forming the front and the back of the jacket, is 60 cm wide and 118 cm long with blue, green and orange narrow warp stripes at the selvage. The panel is cut open lengthways at the centre for the jacket front. The side panels are joined up to the armhole, and the cut edges and also the bottom of the jacket are folded over and hem-stitched with two-ply *allo* yarn. The sleeve panels (33 cm wide), which are woven separately, also with narrow green, orange and blue warp stripes near the selvage, are joined under the arm: towards the wrist the sleeve is narrowed by overlapping the two selvages. The left front panel of the jacket has a handwoven cotton double pocket (22 × 22 cm) stitched to the inside. The back opening is strengthened with three cotton panels, two small patches on the inside and an elaborately embroidered cotton panel on the outside – green, red, blue and orange diamonds with red pompoms all around joined below by a chain- and running-stitch flower pattern stitched directly on to the back of the jacket. All along the seams, except under the arm, the weaver embroidered the jacket with running- , chain- and herringbone stitches reinforcing the seams and decorating the jacket at the same time. Two chain-stitch 'bridges' with pompoms on each side seam add extra strength to a jacket which is both functional and beautiful, combining weaving and embroidery in perfect harmony.

Allo sacks and bags, with all their attractive different natural shades from beige to brown, are valued for their strength and durability. The bags, *jhola*, are made up of one length of warp-faced weaving (approximately 80–100 × 40 cm). The width of the weaving

A traditional *allo* jacket and handwoven cotton turban. Topis, crocheted and woven woollen mufflers and shawls reflect the diversity of Nepalese textiles at the Dingla *mela* or fair.

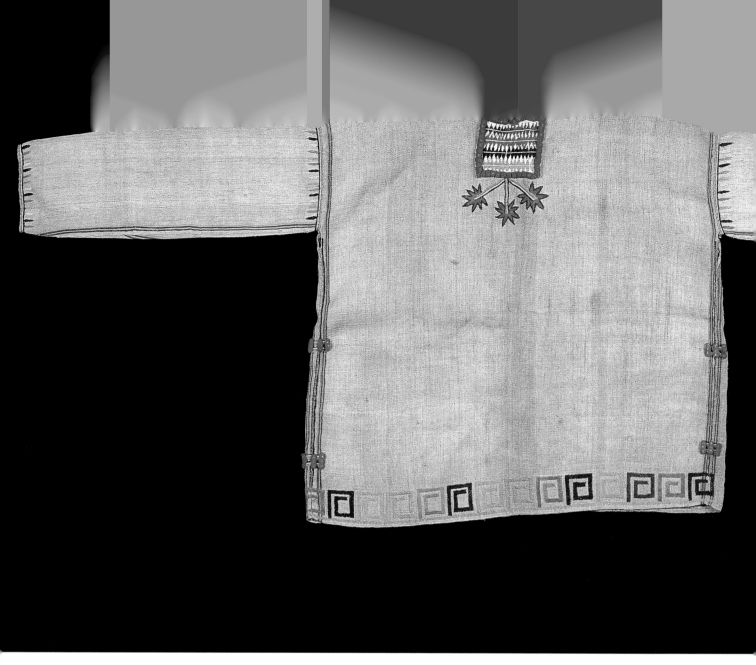

The back of a traditional *allo* jacket or *phenga* woven at Besinda, Sankhuwasabha (see p. 196). British Museum As 1992 01.2.

is the length of the bag: one selvage forms the opening; the other is firmly stitched at the bottom to form the base of the bag. A strap (185–200 × 5–6 cm) is stitched over the sides of the bag (over the seam and the folding line with the ends hanging down at the base as tassels). The carrying part of the strap is usually stitched up lengthways for extra strength. The bag is carried over the head with the strap resting above the forehead, thus leaving both hands free for the user, mainly a woman or child. Men often wear *jholas* as shoulder-bags. Colourful acrylic yarn crochet *jholas* have replaced the *allo jholas* in some areas. The strong sacks, much preferred to those of jute, are about 58 × 108 cm in size and made from one piece of weaving (216 cm long) with selvages stitched up to form the sides: the folding line is the base. Often the sack is woven in one piece with the circular warp uncut; 25 cm of the warp are left unwoven to form the mouth of the sack.

Traditionally all *allo* cloth is woven on backstrap or body-tension

124

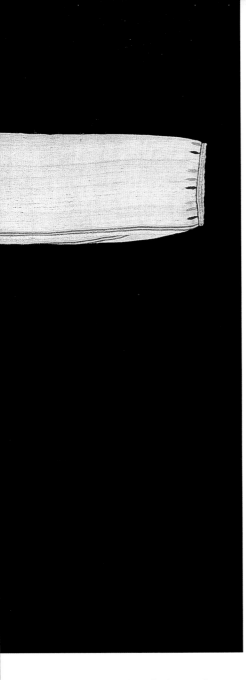

looms. Spindles and looms are standard equipment of every home. Weaving takes place mainly during winter when no fieldwork needs to be done. With the minimum of simple components this type of loom fulfils the basic function of keeping the warp threads under tension while the weft thread is interwoven with them at right angles. All parts of the loom, except the wooden beater, are carved from bamboo, often by the husband or a relative of the weaver. When a weaving is completed or at the end of the day, the loom parts can just be rolled together into a bundle which is easily stored in the roof rafters.

Most textiles are woven plain and are warp-faced – the most suitable method to use with *allo* on this type of loom without reed – and warp-faced material has a very firm texture which is needed for the jackets and waistcoats which are to give protection against the cold winds and for the bags and sacks which have to stand up to a lot of wear and tear. The warp for the loom is prepared in various ways. One of the methods used for the circular warp is similar to that described on p. 142 for Gurung wool weaving. The distance between the outer warping-posts is arranged according to the length of material to be woven: for a sleeveless jacket, for instance, they have to be four hand-spans, *bita*, apart, that is, from the tip of the middle finger to the thumb. Many Rai weavers, however, unlike the Gurung, incorporate the making of the loop heddle already into the warping process: two extra sticks are put into the ground at loop-heddle-length distance along the line of the warp and the loop-heddle yarn is tied to one stick. At every second round of the warp the loop-heddle yarn is laid around the warp yarn and then back around the stick thus encircling every alternate warp thread.

Right Forming heddle loops during warping over the pair of sticks on the left.

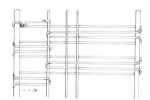

Warping with a warp lock stick. (If the beginning and end of the warp are tied to the warp lock stick rather than the front beam, the warp can be moved round without untying the knots.) See p. 142 for heddle-making.

Some weavers use yet another method, referred to by Emery (1979, 151) as the warp-lock method, which is also used by carpet and tablet-loom weavers (p. 160). Instead of circulating round the warping-pegs, the warp is looped around an additional axis rod or warp lock-stick in a u-turn, alternately from one side and then, returning in the opposite direction, from the other. If this stick is removed, the 'lock' will open and the weaving is spread out flat which is particularly suitable for mat weaving.

When the warp is wide enough, split bamboo pieces or the actual loom parts are put alongside the warping-sticks – sometimes secured with ties – and the warp is slid off the pegs, rolled up and taken to the place of weaving. The Rai weaver, who made her warp with a warp lock-stick (as can be seen in the illustration above at the lower web, the start of the weaving), attached her back beam

to a bamboo bar on a frame. The warp in the front is sandwiched between a split bamboo section (74 cm long and 3 cm in diameter), the front or breast beam. This is tied with a cord to the backstrap – a ply-split band, the making of which is described on p. 128. In front of the weaver are the heddle loops with the rod, the bamboo shedstick (82 × 4 cm) and one cross-stick. She leans slightly forward, releasing warp tension, and pulls up the heddle rod with the loops whilst passing a stick down behind them to counteract the shedstick opening. With the shed opener she is just about to open the shed, the passage for the weft to be passed through. She uses a bamboo stick shuttle to lay in the weft. The shed opener is also used as a beater to drive the weft home. To open the second shed she leans back to put the warp under tension; the shed will now show in front of the bamboo shedstick, as the warp ends slide up between

Above Weaving *allo* mats (*jilima*) in Besinda, Sankhuwasabha. This, one of the Rai weaver's looms, is now in the British Museum collection. The loom measures 113 cm from breast to warp beam. Both warp and weft are Z-spun single strands with 18 warp ends and 7 picks per inch (2.5 cm). British Museum As 1993. 01.

Above right Weaving a bag-carrying strap (5 × 200 cm) on a backstrap loom. For this narrow warp, the weaver uses the heddle loops for one shed; for the other, a long loop.

the loop heddles. To prevent the *allo* yarn from getting fluffy the weaver brushes the warp occasionally with water using a shelled maize cob as a brush. (Some weavers use a type of starch, rice or millet water, to smooth the *allo* yarn.)

After a few centimetres of weaving she moves the temple forward, poking both pointed ends of the split bamboo into the selvage again to keep an even weaving width. As the weaving progresses, she opens the gripping front beam and moves the warp around so that the woven part becomes the lower web. (The beginning and end knot of the warp had been untied from the breast beam earlier after weaving about 15 cm in order to be able to move the warp around. Sometimes these beginning and end threads are threaded along the selvages of the lower and upper web respectively to secure them.)

Another *allo* item, also made by men, which is still produced and

Pushing the bamboo needle through the 3-ply warp strands. Only one of the three strands is picked up by the needle.

The *namlo* (carrying strap) worn here over the topi, is attached to the basket or *dhoko.*

sold, is the porter's headband or tump-line, *namlo*, used to support the traditional carrying-basket, *dhoko*. Portering, like trading and army service, remains one way of earning the supplementary income that is so essential in these areas of scarcely subsistence level farming. The headbands are also made from other fibres – jute, 'sisal' or bark – but those made from *allo* are particularly strong. The method used for making *namlos* is that of ply-splitting (Collingwood 1987, 86). Parallel plied warp strands are joined by crossing elements which do not interlace as in weaving but split each warp strand in turn. This method is particularly suitable for making the band strong yet flexible so that it will mould itself comfortably over the porter's forehead. This flexibility is also appreciated by *allo* weavers who often use a *namlo* as a backstrap. An important part of *namlo* making, therefore, lies in the yarn preparation. An even number of s- and z-plied warp strands, double the length of the intended *namlo*, which will be about 70 cm long, are required, together with one long two-ply strand for darning through the warp strands, a kind of weft. On average the *namlo* is made of twelve warp strands, namely six strands folded in half. Of these three are s-plied, made up of three z-plied singles, and three are z-plied, made up of three s-plied singles. To begin, the strands are folded over at their mid-point and plied or braided together to form a loop, the neck of which is secured by winding the yarn into a type of Turk's-head knot. The *namlo* maker holds this loop with twelve parallel warp strands in front of him, together with the darning (weft) yarn, which is attached to a small, round bamboo rod, sharpened at one end ('bamboo needle'). For the narrow initial part of the *namlo* all s-plied strands are split in one direction, with the bamboo needle and darning yarn, and the z-plied in the opposite direction, thus forming a two-layer fabric for 2–3 cm. The twelve strands are then arranged in s-ply and z-ply alternately: the bamboo needle now passes under one ply of each of the s- and z-twist strands, darning the weft yarn through to the other side. At the selvage the strand is stitched through the double selvage at the fourth row down and up again between the double selvage at the third row down. The *namlo* is then turned over to the other side and the return passage is made with the darning yarn passing again under one ply of each of the twelve warp strands. At each passage of the darning yarn the *namlo* is turned over, and each time the darning yarn passes under only one ply, resulting in a connected double layer with a v-shape pattern. Although this is the most common method, there are variations. When the *namlo* length is completed – the ply-split section is about 50 cm long – the same two-layer method is used as at the start in order to narrow the fabric. The strands are then bound with one of the cords or are divided to form another loop. The final tying up is usually done with one of the warp strands which is fastened

Purba Kumari Rai's house at Lamuwa, Bala, Sankhuwasabha. Most houses have woven bamboo walls and thatched roofs. Purba's daughter accompanied by her sister and neighbour is weaving on the traditional cotton loom.

by becoming a darning (weft) cord and ply-splitting through the remaining warp cords for one or two rounds.

This method of ply-splitting is used in a simplified way for many other purposes – for instance, by the silkworm raiser at Rupse who makes his silk cocoon frames by splitting a two-ply cord with bits of straw, and by the farmers who make hexagonal-patterned bamboo muzzles for their buffaloes and goats by ply-splitting the holding cord at the point where the basket fits comfortably over the animal's mouth, using a knot to prevent the cord from slipping out of the ply-split.

A new type of *allo* cloth began to be developed in the 1980s, when some weavers of Sankhuwasabha asked if KHARDEP, a rural development programme operating in the area, could assist them with improved processing and marketing of the traditional *allo* products, for which the returns were very low. (It was calculated that it required a total of twenty working days from *allo* harvesting to finished product to make three sacks, which would sell for 54–60 Nepalese rupees, a gross return of 3 rupees per day (US$ 0.20 in 1983).) Product development began in one of the weaver's homes in Bala, Sankhuwasabha. Purba Kumari Rai, an experienced cotton and *allo* weaver, made the first trial of putting an *allo* warp on her four-shaft treadle loom, which she had previously used only for

The Bala workshop in Sankhuwasabha explores the possibilities of processing, weaving and knitting *allo*. The weaver on the right is using the backstrap loom, weaving an *allo* and wool twill. The other weavers are experimenting with *allo* yarns on their traditional cotton weaving looms.

cotton weaving. For *allo* she had always worked with her backstrap loom. The traditional *gimte* pattern she wove with *allo* warp and wool weft aroused much interest among *allo* producers on surrounding farms, who subsequently requested that a workshop be held. This took place in 1984 and gave an opportunity both to explore new possibilities for *allo* processing, dyeing, weaving and knitting, using traditional and adapted looms and equipment, and to assess, together with the weavers, the most successful way of using *allo* fibres and yarns for traditional as well as new products.

A warping-mill was the most appreciated piece of equipment to be introduced and has since been in continuous use. Two sturdy frame looms which were tried were adopted by some weavers, especially for heavyweight cloth and for greater width. The most remarkable feature of the workshop, though, was the way the weavers adapted their four-shaft looms and traditional 2/2 twill and diamond patterns to *allo*. Previously these had been used only for cotton, with *allo* being woven in a plain warp-faced weave on a backstrap loom. Twill *allo* cloth and especially *allo* and wool tweed found an immediate local market. The traditional winter outfit for men in urban areas includes a type of tweed jacket, which had always been made up previously of imported cloth: the *allo*/wool cloth was an admirable alternative. The same cloth was also used in combination with leather for bags and purses by a Nepalese charity, Himalayan Leather (Leprosy Trust). *Allo* mats, based on traditional weaving and also cloth with cotton warp and *allo* weft, found a ready market among visitors and tourists. The workshop also enabled a variety of shuttles, metal reeds and bobbin winders to be tried, and work on bleaching and also dyeing yarns, as well as milling, rolling and softening cloth to be undertaken.

Further training courses, which included such subjects as health and functional literacy, were held by the Women's Training Centre, Dhankuta. As the demand for *allo* products grew, the weavers asked for help in building a weaving centre for finishing cloth and for organising marketing. The building was constructed at the riverside at Sisuwa Tar on a self-help basis, with financial support from the British Ambassador's Special Fund. The weavers in the area formed a Weavers Society which was supported in the first three years by a weaver from Voluntary Service Overseas, Liz van Rensburg. She described (1992) the method of cloth finishing at the Centre as follows:

> Until recently there was no tradition of cloth finishing among the *allo* weavers of Sankhuwasabha. However, several new technical processes have been adopted by the weavers following training courses at Sisuwa Tar. The *allo* tweed cloth is first burled so that all knots and loose warp threads are carefully mended. Then the cloth is washed and wet finished by trampling with the feet in a thick soap solution until it felts and shrinks to a prescribed measurement. It is then thoroughly rinsed and rolled onto a slatted drying roller. The cloth hangs in the shade and is rewound every day until completely dry. Then it is passed through a mangle with steel rollers. This beetling process makes the cloth soft and smooth. It is then ready for sale.

The mangle was designed and built in Kathmandu by Akkal Nakarmi, with funds donated by the German Embassy.

Other small village groups have established themselves as the DCVI have conducted training courses, which have included the weaving of cotton and *allo* on the larger wooden frame four-shaft looms with fly-shuttle attachments. In these areas *allo* textiles have become a valuable source of supplementary income. In Solukhumbu and Sankhuwasabha Districts the development also links in with the proposals of the Department of National Parks for an extension to the Sagarmatha National Park (Makalu-Barun) which places much emphasis on the involvement of resident and neighbouring communities. 'In order to protect this ecosystem of the Nepalese Himalaya and to develop a participatory model of sustainable economic development for the surrounding communities' (Shrestha and Campbell 1990, Foreword), the Makalu-Barun Conservation Project is partly supporting the Sisuwa Tar Weaving Centre as a place of

A coat made up by a Dhankuta tailor from one of the first *allo* and wool tweed weaving trials. In the background is an *allo* plant.

Allo products: lengths of *allo* and wool tweed and a lacey-knit *allo* shawl, an *allo* and leather bag and *allo* mats, cushion covers and open work curtain weaving trials.

training and information for the Park area communities. Thus the encouragement of and building on traditional skills will both assist with the improvement of the livelihood of the people and help with the conservation of forests within which *allo* thrives.

Newar

The Kathmandu Valley is the historic home of the Newars, where they have long-established traditions as farmers, businessmen, artisans and government servants. From there also numerous merchant families have migrated to other parts of Nepal and are now found in many of the major towns and villages. The Newars' fame as artists in wood, stone and metalwork spread centuries ago as far as China, where they were engaged by Kublai Khan (see p. 28). Newars have their own language and script; their religions, Buddhism and Hinduism, are practised with much mutual integration.

Textiles are involved in many of the numerous rites and festivals performed by Newars every year. (Much information on these can be found in Anderson 1971 and Slussor 1972 and 1982.) There is, for instance, the sacred bejewelled waistcoat, thought to have belonged to the serpent king, which is displayed in the presence of the Royal Family from a high chariot at the 'Rato Machendranath'

The Kathmandu Valley. The traveller Dr Kurt Boeck described his first view of the valley from Chandragiri Pass as 'a picture of fairy tale beauty, such as is not to be found anywhere else in the world . . . the most magnificent mountains on earth in front of which, Great Nepal, the fertile valley of Bagmati river with the capital Kathmandu, lay at my feet.'

festival, a festival designed to ensure a successful monsoon rain. At Holi, the important spring festival, a ceremonial pole is erected in the Durbar Square, Kathmandu, and hung with tiers of coloured strips representing the saris which Lord Krishna took and hid in a tree to tease the cowherding maidens as they bathed. There are also prayer-flags and precious cloth draped around idols at festivals and the elaborate costumes of the dancers. At one time these might have been woven by a particular set of weavers. Although not mentioned as a specific caste, Chattopadhyay (1923, 551) believed that Hindu weavers may have existed as a special group, at least as temple menials, although he leaves open the question of whether these weavers were men or women. He cites Oldfield's reference to Tatti, who made dresses for idols, and the Tatee, who wove the cloth to wrap the dead (see p. 38), but he accepts Hodgson's view that 'there are no other weavers in Nepal', then remarking 'all the spinning and weaving necessary for household needs having been performed up till now at least by Newar women'. However skilful this work may have been, apparently it was not ranked as professional weaving. It was merely an integral part of a Newar woman's life and religion.

Oldfield (1880, 66) describes how Newar women visit the shrine on 'Mount Pulchoak [Pulchowki] taking their girls as soon as they have learned to use the *kirkha* or thread machine, the handle of

133

which is presented with fruit, flowers etc as an offering to the deity'. Wright (1877, 20) mentions the same shrine and adds that nearby the pilgrims deposit weavers' shuttles.

The earliest detailed account of the type of textiles produced is given by Campbell (1836, 219 *et seq.*) who records a variety of cotton cloth manufactured by the Newars, including plain-weave, check and bird's-eye patterns, *punika*. Although he sounds rather dismissive about some of the weaving techniques, he had to admit (p. 223) 'that the Nepal loom, and the arrangements of the weaver, are superior in some respects to those of the unrivalled manufacture of the Dacca muslins'. He describes (p. 222) how

. . . the weaver sitting on a bench, with the loom in front of her, plies the shuttle alternately with either hand, pulling forward the swinging apparatus for laying the woof [weft] thread close to its predecessor, and plies the treddles [*sic*] with her feet. . . : instead of footboards moving on a fixed point, to be depressed alternately, so as to make one layer of the warp threads cross the other, and thus incorporate the woof with it, we find two small buttons suspended from the lower margin of the netting, which the weaver seizes between her great and first toe, alternately depressing each foot as the woof thread is delivered by the shuttle. The weaving is carried on under a shed, with a small verandah, or in the house; and as the roofs are generally low, the treddles are made to play in a hollow dug in the earthen floor under the loom.

He adds in a footnote (p. 223) 'the different parts of the loom are not connected so as to form one complete machine. For instance, the swinging beam and netting are generally suspended from the roof of the house', the swinging beam presumably being the reed beater and the netting the heddle shafts. From the description the loom appears to be similar to the dhaka loom except for the warp-beam arrangement. The warp for the loom was prepared similarly to the methods described on p. 96 for dhaka cloth. Campbell (p. 221) records the length of the warp as 'from 6 to 12 and 14 yards' (5.5 to 11 and 12.8 m) and the width of cotton cloths as about half a yard (0.45 m). A photograph taken in 1957 by Dr C. Rosser in Sankhu, a Newar village in the Kathmandu Valley, shows a woman walking along a path in a similar way holding up a bobbin rotating swift. As the warp yarn is released, she appears to lead it over the reeds with a stick in her right hand, without having to bend down. Today most of the warping is done on warping mills and the weaving on wooden frame shaft looms with fly-shuttle attachments. Weaving is still a major activity in some parts of the Kathmandu Valley – for instance, in Bhaktapur and Kirtipur – but the cloth is woven often for income rather than home use. Some weavers sell this cloth individually; others work under contract and are paid by the metre

Laying the warp in Sankhu village, near Kathmandu. Weaving is still a major activity in some parts of the Kathmandu Valley.

Jyapu women planting rice near Bhaktapur, Kathmandu Valley. They are wearing the traditional black sari with a red border. The folded mat in the foreground is a type of umbrella. It is attached with a string over the forehead and gives complete protection from the rain, leaving both hands free. To make the rainshields waterproof the leaves of the camel foot climber *bhorla* (*Bauhinia vahlia*) are sandwiched between two layers of open-weave bamboo sheets. See p. 138.

by cloth merchants who supply them with yarn and market the products. The Department of Cottage and Village Industries encourages local small-scale handloom production, but the competition from factory-made cloth is very strong.

Nevertheless, the women of one group of Newars, the farmers, Jyapu, still use their traditional homespun and woven cotton cloth, their distinctive dress showing their occupation and social status. The most characteristic part of the outfit is the black, wraparound cloth, *parsi*, or (the older term) *patasi*, about 700 × 75 cm, with a strikingly colourful border, *kinara*, 3 to 10 cm wide. The predominant colour is red with orange, yellow and sometimes green and golden strips or patterns incorporated in various ways. 'Through these variations, the women seek to distinguish one village from another' (Toffin 1977, 180).

The *parsi* is draped around the body in a special way which differs from the way a sari or other wrapped skirt is worn. It is pleated both at the front and behind and hitched up sufficiently to allow for easy leg movements while working in the field: this also reveals the decorative tattoo designs above the ankle. One way of tying the *parsi* is to hold one end of the cloth at the left hip and carry the rest of it round the back to the front. Here a bundle of pleats is formed and tied with a cord. The remaining cloth is then again taken round

135

the body before more pleats are formed which are placed at the back. The end piece of the *parsi* is wound in an upward spiral to form an elegant curve, below which the pleats protrude, before the end is tucked in at the front. The upper garment is usually the traditional cross-over, tied, waist-long blouse, which has been described earlier. A white waistband, *patuka* or *jani*, about 550 × 65 cm, is wrapped round the waist several times to keep the *parsi* in place and provide pockets, or a seat for a baby – it completely hides the waistline. The waist is further disguised by the way the shawl, *ga*, is worn. This cloth, 350 × 90 cm, which is often printed and lined, is also wrapped around the waist with just the end put over the shoulder to hang down the back. Silver necklaces and gold ear-rings are used as ornaments. Karunakar Vaidya (1990, 112) in one of his folk tales, *The Story of the Bamboo Cutter*, recounts how some Newar farmers believe that the very presence of the black *parsi* helps to drive away evil spirits. Jyapu men wear the Nepali suit, often with a black waistcoat, and a white cotton waistband but, unlike other men in the hills, they never wear the kukri tucked in at the front of the waistband. Their way of transporting goods is quite different too: Jyapu men do not use *dhoko*, the popular cone-shaped basket, but carry loads in two baskets suspended at either end of a yoke which is borne across the shoulders. Other Newar men wear either the Nepali suit or Western-style clothing, the women wear mostly Indian-type saris and blouses, and the young girls long tunics and matching trousers similar to the Punjabi outfit. Shawls are worn, especially during the cooler season; amongst them are the luxurious pashmina shawl, dhaka shawls and the three-layer cotton shawls, handprinted cloth between two layers of fine muslin.

Hand-block printing by a specific Newar caste, the Ranjitkar, has a long tradition in the Kathmandu Valley. Hand-blocked saris, once greatly in demand, are rarely worn now; however, handprinted shawls, blouses and waistbands are still much in evidence. Unfortunately, the white cotton cloth with the distinctive black and red block-print patterns has now to compete with cheaper, imported copies.

Printing patterns are numerous and are generally referred to as *butta*, a floral motif and, by extension, all motifs of elaborate decorative designs. These include fish motifs, stars, flowers, lines and dots and a rich combination of small geometric patterns, often arranged diagonally. The wooden block (average size 18 × 13 cm), into which the designs are carved, is fitted with a handle. The white cotton cloth to be printed is washed and beaten to remove any starch. It is then put on to three or four layers of jute cloth and a smooth sheet as padding. The printer presses the block on to a sheet soaked with the dye inside a box and from there on to the cloth. An experienced printer can print fifteen to twenty 2-m-long sari lengths in

A Jyapu farmer carrying his children in the traditional Newari baskets, *khamu*.

Block printing patterns on a shawl
(between two layers of fine muslin),
a blouse and a traditional purse,
thaili. British Museum As 1992
10.33, As 1993 01.9, As 1992 10.34.

Newar straw and jute shoes from
the Kathmandu valley. British
Museum As 1992 10.29.

one day (Gajurel and Vaidya 1984, 150). This traditional printing by Ranjitkars continues on a small scale. Several organisations – for example, the Women's Skill Development Project and the Association of Craft Producers in Kathmandu – have trained various groups in block printing as a means of income generation using traditional and new designs for making dress material and home furnishings for the local, tourist and export markets. Through these developments block printing has become a craft which is no longer caste-related.

One Newar textile, rarely seen now, is the *chunari*, zigzag-patterned tie-dye cloth, used during marriage ceremonies for wrapping up dowry articles. Dyeing among the Newar was always undertaken by a special caste, the Chippah. Gajurel and Vaidya (1984, 144) reported that nettle thread was used to tie the cloth into bundles before dyeing. Batik painting and printing are more recent introductions to the Kathmandu Valley and have become popular mainly as tourist items.

A textile-related structure, the weft-twined straw and jute shoes made by Newars (Jyapu) and worn by women in winter, should be mentioned to illustrate the wide variety of textile techniques practised in the Kathmandu Valley. The straw shoes are made of two pieces – a three-plait braid stitched together sideways to form a sole (3 cm thick), and an upper part. To weave the upper part two-ply warp strands are stitched in and looped round at the outer edge of the sole at a spacing of about 1 cm. These warp strands are kept in place by weft-twining straw strands all around for several rounds. The front and heel sections are built up separately. The shape is controlled by varying the thickness of the straw weft: finer straw is

137

A young Newar girl sheltering under a rainshield (*ghum*). The shawl, *ga*, (*c*.90 × 350 cm) is usually worn wrapped around the waistband with the other end draped over the shoulder and hanging down at the back.

used towards the top of the shoe where the warp strands move closer together. The shoe is finished with a row of sisal-strand weft twining. The bent-over warp ends are secured by the twists of the two weft strands.

The jute shoes are worked in a similar way but the sole is made up of three to four thick, jute-wrapped straw bundles which are wrapped, coiled and interlaced rather than plaited. The bundles are tapered to form a fine point at the toe. The jute warp is stitched and looped into the sole and held in place with one line of jute weft twining. Starting at the toe, the shoe is again built up in two sections. The added element is the small green weft twine inset at both sides, the green weft-twine border catching the warp yarn, and the small embroidery pattern.

Gurung

In west central Nepal along the slopes of the Annapurna mountain range and scattered in some other parts of the kingdom live the Gurungs. Some legends tell how they came in ancient times with their flocks from the high pastures of Tibet; others recount the long migration from the mountains of western China to Burma and then from the east of Nepal to the west. Indian descent is claimed by some Gurungs. Both views may be correct as the Gurungs appear to incorporate elements of both Tibeto-Burman and Indo-Aryan origin (Macfarlane 1976, 12). Ethnically they are related to other Tibeto-Burman groups – Magars, Thakali, even to the Kiranti of east Nepal (Bista 1980, 75), and to the Tamang (Macfarlane 1976, 12). Gurung textiles have a unique character which bears little resemblance to those of any of the surrounding countries, thus pointing to an independent development of textiles over centuries. Historically until the 1930s the Gurungs were pastoralists, and those living at the higher altitudes (1,800–3,000 m) continue the tradition of transhumant stockraising, particularly with sheep as a source of wool, milk and meat. Their diet would also include millet, buckwheat and potatoes. In addition to agriculture they engage in barter trade. As the population grew, many Gurungs moved farther south, hewing out spectacular terraces into the steep hill slopes, planting them with maize, millet and vegetables, and irrigating the lower terraces to grow rice in summer and wheat in winter.

The Gurungs' high reputation as soldiers dates back at least to the eighteenth century when the Shah kings of the western state of Gorkha unified Nepal. Their continued employment in the Nepalese, Indian and British armies is a valuable source of income for the community. A smaller, but even longer-established source of income is based on the extraordinary skill of the Gurung weavers

Trading woollen blankets, rari, at Terhathum *hat* bazaar in east Nepal.

The highly practical sling-bag is worn over a western-style shirt by a young Gurung who makes rainshields (see p. 194).

who very probably brought about the first recorded trade transactions from Nepal – namely, the export of woollen blankets to India in the third century AD (see p. 24). The traditional Gurung blankets, rari, are still valuable trade items today at village markets as well as in the streets of Kathmandu. However, the once-flourishing trade with woollen, handwoven garments has almost ceased, except amongst the communities in the far north. The availability of cheap, ready-made clothing at local bazaars, the shortage of wool, the switch to arable crop production, contact with urban areas, and, through the army, with other parts of the world has led to a gradual change in the style of clothing.

Nevertheless, traditional dress is still worn by most Gurung women in rural areas, although it is often made up from bought rather than homespun material. It consists of a cross-over blouse, a full wraparound skirt pleated in the front and held by a black, cotton-lined, velvet square, which is folded into a triangle to cover the back, and a waistband. A cloak is worn over the left shoulder and a headcloth completes the outfit. Gold and semi-precious stone necklaces, bracelets and gold ear- and nose-rings are an essential part of the outfit, especially on festive occasions. Red glass or plastic bangles are worn by married women (Macfarlane and Gurung 1990, 8).

Men's dress comprises a kind of cotton kilt held by a waistband, a short shirt tied across the front, a sling-bag and a cap. In winter,

A Gurung tie-dye design waistband, *c.* 16 × 265 cm. The warp is of single wool, the weft of single wool for the patterned section and cotton and mixed fibres (acrylic) for the light coloured stripes. One tied section shows how the weaver ties the design with cotton thread before dyeing. The design has to be carefully folded to produce the cross effect. Most weavers now use Indian direct dye. To improve the fastness of the colour, the Manang Gurung weaver of the above design added *chuk*, which she obtained by boiling lime juice in a copper pot until it turned into a paste. Dye and *chuk* were boiled for three minutes before the tie-dye cloth was added, simmered for a further three minutes, left to cool, rinsed and left to drip off before the tied parts were opened. British Museum As 1992 10.4.

especially in the northern areas, woollen jackets or coats are also worn. Today the younger generation favour either Western dress or a mixture of the two, which often includes the traditional sling-bag. This is a most remarkable combination of a garment and a bag: it provides the wearer with a safe pocket which can expand to almost sack size, yet be carried comfortably without strain. It provides protection against wind and cold from the back and warmth for the hands. When not being worn, it can be used as a cover or be neatly folded up, as it is simply an almost square (some 120 cm) piece of cloth. It is made up usually from four handwoven cotton, nettle fibre or hemp, plain-weave panels, joined at the selvage – often with a fine, decorative stitch. The square is folded in half along the selvage of the centre panels, and the two corners at each side of the rectangle are knotted together. The arms are put through the openings thus formed, and there is thus a knot on each shoulder, with the main bulk of the cloth lying down the back. Each knot is then in turn taken over the head to the other shoulder, thereby forming a cross and pocket openings below the arms and at the back. The sling-bags are also worn by women of the Tibeto-Burman Magar group in central and west Nepal and by some Tamang women. It is interesting to note that the Gurungs from eastern Nepal never wear sling-bags but they are the predominant wearers of the jackets and coats described below.

The colourful, striped, woollen waistbands (Nepali: *pogi*; Manang Gurung: *mindu dari*), often tie-dye-patterned, are some 16 to 23 cm wide and up to 360 cm long. They are wound around the waist several times, providing support to the back, warmth and a storage place for small belongings as well as a kukri, which men wear tucked in at the front. For waistbands with multicoloured patterns the weaver ties fractions of dry powdered colour into the design before dyeing the cloth; the drop of moisture that soaks in dissolves the dye and causes it to spread until it meets with resistance from the tie-string. The problem of retaining a lighter colour during the dyeing process is solved by weaving these stripes with a different type of yarn – tight twist cotton and acrylic which do not take dye as the wool weft which is used for the rest of the weaving.

The woollen, sleeveless jackets, *lukuni*, worn mainly in the east by men, women and children, are made up from two panels (each approximately 27 × 128 cm) folded into half at the shoulder-line. The panels are joined at the selvage, often with a decorative figure-of-eight type of cross-stitch at the back, and from the waist to the armhole openings at the side. Some jackets are made from just white or black wool, but often the different shades of the Baruwal sheep wool are arranged to form stripes and attractive border patterns. Most jackets and coats have a cotton pocket stitched on the inside of the front left panel.

Festival at Gosainkund. Magar women wearing sling-bags made of red cotton panels. The woman on the right is wearing a tie-dyed woollen waistband and a back apron with colourful cotton piping and borders. The little woollen cloth caps are decorated with patchwork and embroidery.

Onlookers wearing *lukuni* watching the Gurung weaver inserting the backstrap loom parts beside the warping sticks.

The coat, *bakhu*, is of a similar cut but is made up of panels about 35 cm wide, and the triangle which was left open at the back for the neck in the *lukuni* is filled with a gusset. For each sleeve a panel (about 26 cm wide) is folded into half and stitched up at the selvage to form a sleeve.

An all-enveloping, hooded blanket (Nepali: *ghum rari*; Gurung: *boku*) is worn for protection against wind and rain. It is, in fact, a blanket folded into half and stitched up along one half at the selvage. The hood so formed hangs down at the back over the seam, while the unstitched sides hang down in the front giving the appearance of a cloak: in cold weather the hood is worn over the head.

The blanket/rug, rari, is the best known of all woollen woven items. The size of a rari varies upwards from the 70 × 150 cm of the small, fringed sleeping-mat, *burkasan*. Larger raris are made up from two or more panels joined at the selvage. The manufacture of raris has been associated with Gurungs for centuries (see pp. 24 and 37). Used by almost all Gurungs in one way or another – to sit or sleep on or as a travel rug – they also form an important part of the dowry. The most treasured raris are used as a seat for honoured guests. At the final memorial rites for the dead, *pai*, which are considered to be an expression of good relationships between the deceased's lineage and that of his affines, an occasion of gift giving, the host will give the affines the best rari to sit on. To retrieve the rari at the end of the ceremonies the host has to give a token payment in coins (Messerschmidt 1974, 101). According to Gajurel and Vaidya (1984, 126), when a member of a family passes away thirteen days of mourning are observed during which the mourners sleep on the rari in an isolated corner of the house. Unfortunately, no further details are given. A mother who has given birth usually sleeps on a rari for ten days.

Humphrey (1980, 83) lists some of the many barter exchanges for raris made by Gurungs from northern Sankhuwasabha, east Nepal. They bartered raris for metal vessels made by Newars, for example, *chang* (local beer)-making equipment, water-carrying vessels, for cotton in Dharan (in the *terai*), for raw wool, tobacco, watches, and even cattle and goats. 'Some enterprising people take raris to Assam and come back with shawls.'

The local Baruwal sheep is the main source of raw material for Gurung weaving. The fleece is short and rather hard but is easy to felt, which makes it particularly suitable for hard-wearing, rain and windproof outer garments and for raris. Garments are woven mainly from the soft wool of the first and second shearings of the Baruwal sheep and raris from the later shearings, as well as from goat and yak hair. The different shades of the Baruwal fleece, from white, beige and brown to black, are made full use of by the weavers for a wide variety of stripes and checks. The woollen yarns for the tapestry-type patterned blankets are sometimes dyed with ochre, obtained from walnut shell, and light red from madder.

Most weaving is done by women, when their agricultural and household duties allow. Gurung men used to weave blankets (Hamilton 1819, 27) but today only a few do so or help with the warping or the heavy wool embroidery which is applied after weaving. The finishing/felting process, however, is entirely men's work. The main components of the loom are similar to those used by Rai weavers, but some Gurung weavers in east Nepal use cross-sticks rather than the coil-rod warp separator, and the warp is laid without the warp lock-stick.

Several warping methods are used to prepare the continuous circular warp for the loom. For a plain weave in one method the warp is simply wound around the warp and breast beams which are held in position by pegs and string. The even and uneven threads are put alternately over and under two cross-sticks during the winding process. A more common method is to lay the warp around warping-pegs (wooden sticks in the ground). For a plain weave six warping-pegs are used dividing the warp into even and uneven threads. A continuous loop heddle is made for one set of threads; for the other a shedstick is used to obtain shed and countershed as described on p. 86.

The warping method for the 2/2 twill is unusual and very sophisticated. The warp yarn is wound round seven warping-pegs in four

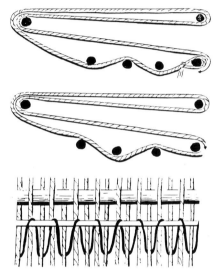

Laying the warp for a plain weave, *chitre*, around six warping pegs in two successive rounds. Below, the heddle rod with heddle loops and shedstick. The heddle loops are formed in a similar method to that described on p. 98, except that the weaver uses no measuring device for the loops, which are formed simply over a single rod.

successive movements. How did the weavers find this ingenious solution to the problem of incorporating a twill pattern sequence, whilst laying a circular warp? One could argue that a similar method is also used in Dolpo and parts of Tibet and the method might have originated there, but the twill-weave tapestry blanket patterns described below seem to be unique to Gurung weavers.

When the warp is wide enough, the breast and warp beams of the loom are slipped in beside the appropriate pegs and bamboo sticks are put alongside the pegs with the crosses; these are usually secured with ties. The warp is then slid off the warping-pegs and, often rolled up, taken to the place of weaving. The warp beam is attached either to a lintel or other structure of the weaver's house or to a wooden or bamboo frame. To bring the warp under tension the weaver attaches a backstrap to the breast beam in front of her and then passes the strap round her waist. The pairs of warp threads

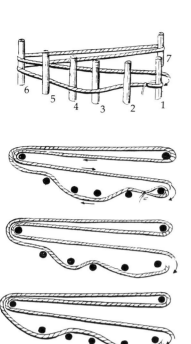

Laying the warp for a 2/2 twill *mandre*. The crosses formed during warping enable the weaver to obtain the four sheds required for this type of weave. At the bottom is one of the three loop heddles with pairs of warp threads in each loop.

Above right A Gurung rari weaver outside her home. The back beam is attached to the roof structure. The angle of the warp is usually 20 to 30 degrees.

showing up clearly on the bamboo sticks are picked up by the weaver with three loop heddles: the fourth stick is replaced by a shedstick. Inserting the weft with a stick shuttle for the first time from the left, the weaver picks up heddles numbered 2, 3 and 1 in succession (heddle 1 is the nearest to the weaver). To obtain the fourth shed she puts the shedstick on edge and leans back: the fourth shed will then show in front of the three heddle loops. Using these four steps, the weaver achieves a perfect selvage, overcoming the problem of an unconnected weft thread which is often encountered in a twill selvage. To help with spacing the warp some weavers start their weaving with a plain basket weave, alternately weaving over 2 and under 2, lifting heddles 2 and 1 in succession.

A distinctive feature of the blankets is the striking geometric pat-

A Gurung weaver who settled in Kathmandu weaving a 2/2 twill muffler in the rari weaving method. Leaning slightly forward, she is releasing the tension on the warp so that she can lift up the second heddle to obtain a shed. With the shed opener in her right hand she opens up the passage for the stick shuttle with the weft yarn (in her lap) to travel through.

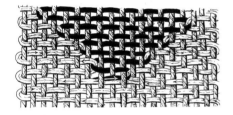

Interlocked tapestry in a plain weave (above) and a 2/2 twill weave (below).

terns based on triangles, squares, crosses, meander and key motifs amongst others. These are created by independent weaving of different-coloured wefts not from selvage to selvage but back and forth, each in its pattern area and interlocking it with weft of the adjacent area on the return passage, thus forming the structure of the cloth – a tapestry method not in the usual weft-faced but in a balanced plain weave or a 2/2 twill weave. All patterns are built up to the same level in each shed.

When the weaving is complete, it is slid off the loom and the unwoven warp threads (12–20 cm long) at the end or between the panels are looped around each other to form a secure border with warp fringes when the circular warp is cut. The cloth panels are then ready for finishing, joining or tailoring, but there is still some work to be done on the raris before they undergo their more unusual finishing/felting process. The raris used for sleeping, *burkasan*, are usually woven full width and need no joining. Where they have fringes all the way round, these are added at this stage. Woollen, two-ply yarn strands (15–20 cm long) are knotted into both the selvage sides with lark's-head knots. Larger raris are joined at the selvage to form a complete pattern. Before the stitching a lot of pulling and stretching often has to be done so that the pattern will actually meet, although some eccentricity can add character.

For the highly valued double blanket/rug two single raris of the same size but with different patterns are placed one on top of the other and joined by knotting the fringes through both layers of selvages. The two blankets will adhere completely during the felting process, giving the impression of a single piece of weaving and concealing how this rug with two completely different sides was woven.

Right Securing the uncut warp threads by crochet-type looping. In the centre are the warp-end fringes after crochet looping, and on the far right, the knotted-in selvage fringes.

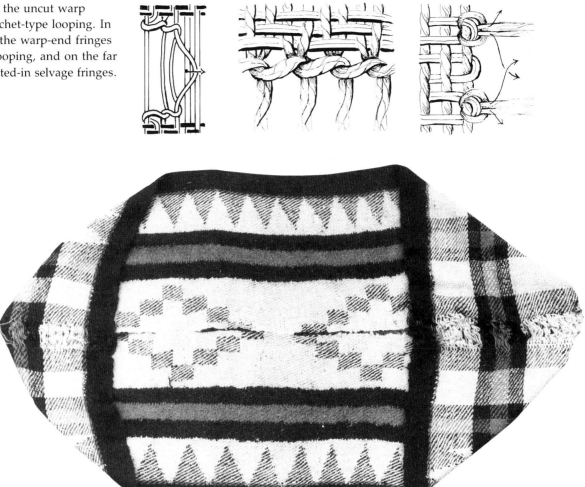

A balanced 2/2 twill-weave rari with interlocked tapestry patterns which has just been taken off the loom. The warp is made up of black, beige and white 2-ply S-twist Baruwal wool. The weft is made up of two single strands. There are 11 warp-ends and 7 picks per inch (2.5 cm). After securing the warp-ends the unwoven parts will be cut at the centre and the selvages of the two panels and joined to form two diamonds at the centre of the rari.

The quality of the rari, including its wind and waterproof characteristic, depends, to some extent, on the finishing – the felting process – which might take a whole day. According to Bhadra Maya, a Gurung weaver of Bhojpur District, the less tired the man who felts (usually the husband or relative of the weaver), the better will be the rari. A large, preferably flat stone, brought from the hills or selected from an area nearby, is used by most Gurungs in east Nepal. Where such stones are not available, felting takes place on bamboo mats. Either hot water is poured over the folded rari on the stone or the rari is put into a big vessel with water, heated up and then placed on the stone, where it is trodden on until most of the water has come out. This process is repeated three times. The felter, supported by two long bamboo sticks, shifts his weight from one foot to the other in a rhythmical dance movement – graceful to look at but exhausting if done for hours. Where piped water is available, the process may be undertaken at a tap. Raris shrink considerably during felting and, through the matting of the yarn

A 2/2 twill rari with tapestry centre patterns and borders (meander and crosses) with chain stitch embroidery. The embroidery is not detectable as it was applied before felting and at first glance appears to be a weaving pattern. British Museum As 1992 10.71.

fibres, the texture becomes so close that sometimes one cannot recognise it as weaving. Campbell (1836, 226) mentioned that 'to add to the warmth and thickness of the Rhari it is frequently improved by beating wool into it, which gives it the appearance of felt', but he gave no further details about the procedure.

In some parts of Nepal Gurung weavers have adapted their rari weaving skills to new ventures. A Gurung weaver who settled in Kathmandu now weaves warm mufflers (about 34 cm × 2 m) for

Tamang hemp (*Cannabis sativa*) jacket, *phenga* and cotton skirt. The striped, warp-faced skirt is traditionally woven and worn by women of the Tibeto-Burman speaking Tamang community living and farming in the mountains surrounding the Kathmandu Valley. The man's hemp jacket, rarely woven now because of the restrictions on hemp growing, is made up of 23.5 cm-wide, warp-faced, plain-weave panels. These are joined with green and red acrylic yarn decorative figure-of-eight stitches. All panels are woven on backstrap looms which are also employed to weave woollen blankets and garments similar to those made by Gurungs. British Museum As 1992 09.1 and 1982 22.17.

the local market. They are woven in a 2/2 twill with a two-ply cotton warp: the wefts are two single pashmina strands (approximately sixty warp ends and twenty-two picks per inch, 2.5 cm). The attractive greyish colour of the cotton yarns is obtained by dyeing with *harro* (*Terminalia chebula*), *barro* (*T. bellerica*) and *amala* (*Phyllanthus emblica*). The fine warp yarn is kept in place and prevented from becoming entangled by a carved warp spacer which also ensures an even width. The other loom parts are the same as those for woollen rari weaving. On cold winter days such mufflers are often worn wrapped over the topi and around the neck.

Another Gurung weaver, in Bhojpur District, who still weaves raris, used the same loom to weave colourful acrylic wool shawls (76 cm × 2 m) for her own use. The acrylic yarn (called *uni* whilst wool is called *un* in Nepali), manufactured in Kathmandu, is available now in many villages throughout Nepal. To maintain even width and a perfect selvage on such a wide piece of backstrap weaving assisted only by a bamboo temple is a demanding task. Devi Gurung, the weaver, seemed to surmount it without too much difficulty.

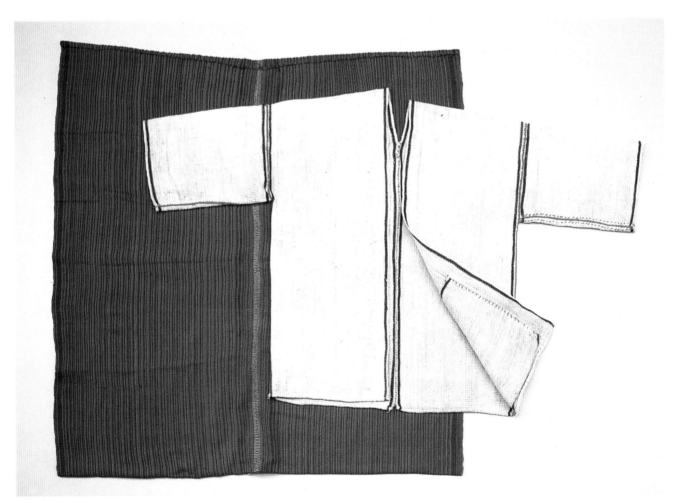

5

HIMALAYAN NORTH

SHERPA AND DOLPO-PA

Wool-weaving on the frame-treadle loom or *thag*.

In northernmost Nepal, among the majestic mountains of the Himalayas, along slopes, in valleys and bare plains above the tree-line, live the people who over the centuries migrated from different parts of Tibet into Nepal or became Nepalese citizens when the border between Tibet and Nepal was changed in the course of history. They are often referred to collectively as Bhote, *bhot* being the Nepalese term for Tibet. The term may be misleading, for within this alpine region there are many different groups and clans with widely varying customs, linguistic dialects and distinct textiles. Among them are the Lhomi, the Lopa of Mustang, the Baragaunle, the Manangba, the people of Dolpo in the west who live in some of the highest human settlements in the world, and the Sherpa of the Sagarmatha region in the east. All, though, share to some extent their Buddhist faith and cultural background from Tibet, as well as the hard life of an inhospitable environment. Temperatures can drop down to −20° Celsius and the land can be awe-inspiringly bleak, except for a short time in summer when the plains burst into colour, displaying a spectacular carpet of bright alpine flowers.

Livelihood depends on a combination of a barely subsistence level of crop production, livestock husbandry and trade. All three are needed, for crops and livestock alone can scarcely sustain a family. Until recently the centuries-old barter trade with Tibet provided the major means of obtaining additional food (see p. 28). Trade transactions were long and involved and required much courage and mercantile skills. The main item of trade was grain, but madder, dried potatoes, handmade paper, incense and other items were also bartered. Using yak caravans, the goods were transported over most

149

difficult passes to be exchanged in Tibet, principally for salt and wool. Weight for weight grain is of much higher value in Tibet than the local salt, which is gathered from deposits on the shores of lakes in western Tibet. By contrast, in the grain-growing middle hills of Nepal the Tibetan salt could be exchanged for a greater weight of grain, on occasion eight times the weight.

Sherpa

The Sherpa had such links not only with Tibet and the middle hills but even with the *terai* and India. Salt and wool from Tibet were exchanged at a favourable rate in the south, and the profit was increased by weaving cloth from Tibetan wool and trading that rather than just the raw material. Nepalese madder, the dyestuff, was also taken to Tibet and bartered for wool at variable rates, sometimes even pound for pound. For some trading was undertaken only on a small scale and the goods were carried in large baskets by the farmers and their family, often without the help of pack animals. Fürer-Haimendorf (1975, 65) describes the combination of trade, barter and cash employed by a Khumjung Sherpa farmer in 1957: in April the farmer and his son and daughter went into the lower Dudh Kosi valley, Rai country, with a woollen blanket, a yak-hair mat, Tibetan salt and also some cash which he had obtained earlier from the sale of salt. The wool and hair for the blanket and mat had been spun by the family, but a Khamba woman (a recent immigrant from Kham in Tibet) had been hired for the weaving. The family sold all their goods and bought maize and millet. In June the farmer's son went to Tibet again to barter grain for salt. He then made another trip to a Sherpa village to collect wheat in exchange for woollen apron material which his father had left on an earlier occasion.

Wool and textiles formed an important part in most trade transactions. To obtain wool from Tibet Sherpas would venture as far as India for unrefined sugar, which would be exchanged in Tibet for an equal weight of wool. Sheep's wool from Tibet is the main yarn which is fashioned into the warm and protective clothing needed in this climate. Other raw materials for textiles are supplied by the local sheep, the goat and especially the highly valued yak. Its long, hard outer hair is made into ropes and harnesses, waterproof tents, durable mats and sacks. In former times it was even used for protection against snow-blindness, long before snow goggles appeared. 'The commonest eye preservers consist of a gauze netting of closely plaited black yak hair' (Waddell 1899, 179). The soft, down-like inner hair of the yak is woven mainly into soft blankets. Some clothing is made from the hair of the young, two-and-a-half to three-year-old yak. Yak-hair items are highly regarded by the Sherpas as items of trade as well as for use at home and as part of the dowry.

A yak caravan returning from Tibet. Goats and sheep take over as pack animals farther south, where the temperature and altitude are unsuitable for yak.

The sacks and bags carried on the trading expeditions from country to country on the backs of pack animals have to stand up to extreme conditions: the yak-hair bags and sacks are the most valued because of their durability. They are still woven and in demand today. One such grain bag, which may have travelled through blizzards along mountain trails and passes on the back of a yak, is now in the British Museum. Colour, design and function form a perfect combination. The natural yak-hair colours, brown, fawn and grey, are arranged in stripes in a plain, warp-faced close weave which renders the bag hard-wearing and, especially as the unwashed hair still contains all its natural fat, also waterproof. The bag has two particularly interesting features – the colourful corners, patches of woollen cloth which are stitched on with *allo* (nettle) thread, to strengthen the bag, and the line of white yak-hair twining on one of the panels near the bag opening which helps the owner to identify his bag. The twining line encircles two warp yarns at a time, and immediately after this line the weaver changed her weaving method for about 9 cm, using paired warps rather than singles as before. For the last 3 cm only the double warp thread (not the weft) is paired again to make four strands, thus giving the appearance of a weft-faced weave. To finish, the warp ends are woven back and forth to form a strong edge with eight loops which help to secure the load on the animal's back.

The long-established practice of trading transactions between Nepal and Tibet was seriously disrupted following the imposition of Chinese military rule in Tibet in 1959. During that period also traditional trade diminished further as cheap Indian salt became available in Nepal. Tibetan salt, once the most important trade item, no longer held its monopoly. This was because Indian traders, who had been reluctant to enter malaria-infested southern areas and the almost inaccessible hill areas of Nepal, were now able to bring in their goods, especially cheap salt, following the almost complete eradication of malaria and the construction of motorable access roads into the middle hills. With much imagination and initiative some Sherpas switched from the diminishing barter trade to mountaineering and tourism at a most favourable time. Nepal was opening her borders to foreigners, and the first successful ascent of Mount Everest (Sagarmatha) had stimulated the interest of aspiring mountaineers from all over the world.

Prior to the 1950s all the textiles needed by the family in the Sherpa community were made at home. Both men and women spun and, according to Fürer-Haimendorf (1964, 15), it was not unusual even for rich men in Khumbu to walk about the village holding a piece of sheep's fleece in the left hand and a spindle in the right while gossiping with friends. However, weaving has always been done by women, mostly in the winter when no fieldwork can be undertaken. In Khumbu this season may last for five months, as the snow may not melt until March.

The dwindling cross-border trade (one result of which was a shortage of wool), increasing commitments to tourism and the availability of imported clothing, led to a decline in weaving from the 1950s. Today only a few Sherpa women weave. Some families employ Khamba women, Tibetan immigrants who have no land and earn their living by weaving those items which are still in demand: amongst these are yak-hair blankets and bags and multicoloured aprons. But sadly the woollen cloth for the traditional garments is rarely woven now the style of dress is changing.

The Sherpa men, especially those who engage in mountaineering, often adopt the kind of foreign clothing used on climbing expeditions; others wear the Nepalese national dress. Nevertheless, at ceremonies such as marriages and at festivals some Sherpa men still dress in the traditional fashion – a cross-over shirt/jacket, *thedung*, woollen trousers and, the main item, the long, generously cut, long-sleeved coat, *chuba*, also called *bakhu*. This is crossed at the front and hitched up to calf- or knee-length with a sash at the

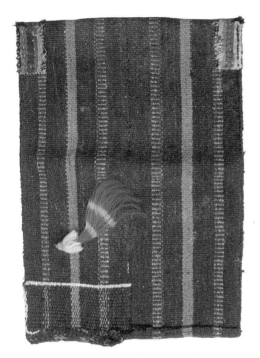

A natural coloured yak hair bag used on trading expeditions, which takes three days to make. The white stripe acts as a kind of luggage label. The bright coloured tuft of the tie-dyed yak hair, which is put into the pierced ear of the *bri* (female yak) both decorates the animal and helps the owner to identify it. Hooker (1854, 213) observed of the yak, 'their ears are generally pierced and ornamented with a tuft of scarlet worsted'. 48 × 68 cm. British Museum As 1992 10.75.

waist, with the surplus length gathered at the back to form a large pocket above the sash. On journeys this is handy for keeping boot-repair materials such as yak leather and wool, as well as dried yak cheese as an emergency ration. It is unusual to wear both sleeves of the coat except to honour a person. On other occasions only one sleeve is worn, whilst the other hangs down the back or, depending on the type of work being done, both sleeves are knotted together at the waist. In severe weather sheepskin coats are worn but these are usually bought in from Tibet and rarely made at home (see p. 165).

Many Sherpa women still retain their traditional way of dress, even though handspun and woven woollen material of the ankle-length wrap-over type coat-dress, *angi*, is often replaced by imported material. A silk or cotton blouse, *shemjer*, is usually worn under the coat-dress. The traditional blouse is only of waist length and has a broad shawl collar attached around the neckline. The loose, set-in sleeves are so long that they cover the outstretched hand and are folded over several times to below elbow-length. The blouse has no buttons: it is crossed over at the front, the left side crossing over the right. This is usually done at the same time as the left side of the 280 cm-wide coat-dress is folded over and fastened under the right armhole with two narrow ribbons or a round metal button. The shawl collar of the blouse is folded inwards over the neckline of the coat-dress. The full width of the dress is then held in each hand and folded into two pleats at the back which are secured with a handwoven waistband: highly ornamented bands are often used over the already securely tied coat. Two borders, usually of all the colours of the spectrum, frame the black, white, red and green centre section with a wide variety of patterns. These include simple geometric designs and zigzag and stripe patterns for those parts of the belt which will not be visible when it is tied around the waist twice. The end parts of the belt, which do show and reflect the skill of the weaver, are adorned with meander bands, and patterns representing the swastika, the Chinese long-life symbol and religious symbols, including the butter lamp, bell and the thunderbolt (*vajra*) amongst others.

The most characteristic and beautiful parts of the costume are the multicoloured aprons, *dongtil* (*dong*: front) worn at the front and the *gyabtil* (*gyab*: back) behind (see p. 74). The front apron is made up from three colourful panels which are joined at the selvage. Although the colour combination of the three panels is the same, the placing of the colours and the width of the stripes varies, resulting in a completely new design of perfect harmony, staggered stripes and hues of colour blending when the panels are handstitched together. The arrangements of stripes and colours are not woven according to a plan, as one would presume seeing some of these perfect

A Sherpa woman in c.1890, wearing the traditional *sikok* with a long sleeved coat, *chuba*, and a blouse underneath. A large amulet necklace and others made of coins, silver and glass beads, a silver belt and bracelets complete the outfit. The *sikok* is now always worn open without a belt. Photo: P. A. Johnston and T. Hoffman. Royal Anthropological Institute.

Opposite A Sherpa ceremonial coat or *sikok* (see p. 195). British Museum As 1992, 16.1.

designs, but made up intuitively by each individual weaver. It is not surprising that no two aprons are alike, especially when all the colours are obtained from vegetable dyes, prepared by the weaver herself. The fine woollen, home-dyed yarn is now often replaced by ready-dyed and often harsh-coloured acrylic or cotton yarn. In the early 1990s there appeared to be a change in fashion even in traditional garments. The trend was towards narrow stripes, wide stripes being worn only by older women (A. D. Sherpa, personal communication). The apron is fastened over the coat-dress with two ribbons which are attached to the apron and crossed at the back and then knotted at the front. Special front aprons, with embroidered or brocaded corners, are worn on festive occasions.

The larger back apron is usually less colourful, in darker tone stripes, and is made up from five panels. Cotton piping is sometimes put all around the apron to decorate and strengthen it. Unlike the front apron, the back apron is worn with the selvages parallel to the waistline, thus giving the appearance of vertical stripes. It has no ribbons but is fastened at the front with a clasp and/or a sash. As the apron is rather long, about one and a half panels are folded inwards – some women, especially the young, fold it in half: the panel ends are brought to the front, overlapping the front apron, and are fastened with a metal clasp or a sash.

In severe cold weather two aprons are worn for extra protection, the more beautiful one on the outside. When doing heavy farm work, the front apron is seldom worn, while the back apron is often folded into a triangle and worn with the point hanging down at the back. The other two folded ends are tucked in or are fastened with a belt or a clasp in front. Some aprons have a smooth upper side, which is singed, and a fluffy/hairy underside, which is brushed, giving extra warmth and adherence to the garment beneath. This is usually done by two women, facing each other, who pull the panels over a round bar which rests at a certain height over an open fire: in the process the underside is singed whilst the upper side is brushed with carders.

Sikok

One particularly beautiful garment, a sleeveless, ankle-length coat, is worn by Sherpa women on special occasions only – festivals, marriage ceremonies, and when honoured guests are received and offered drinks. The coat is always worn open and is usually just draped over the shoulders, except during the marriage ceremony, when the bride, bedecked with jewellery, wears it like a coat. The Sherpa names for the garment, *sikok* or *angi tangtza* (*angi*: woman's dress; *tangtza*: ornament or tassel), indicate that this garment, though of Tibetan origin, has been worn by Sherpa women for generations. It is rarely made by Sherpas, however, but is either

Above A woollen panel with woven-in supplementary weft patterns, intended to be made into a ceremonial dress.

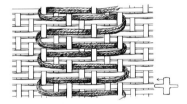

Laying in the supplementary weft for the cross pattern.

handed down from one generation to another or obtained from Tibet. Women from Manang in north-west Nepal have traditionally worn a similar type of ceremonial dress at the Horse Festival but only a few continue to weave and dye it themselves.

The garment is made up of 2/2 twill, handwoven, woollen, plain dark red or black panels alternating with striped and cross-patterned, multicoloured panels: there is a brocade covering over the shoulders. All panels are weft-faced, the plain coloured ones felted. The multicoloured, weft striped panels have blue and red cross patterns, *thig ma*, which are tie-dye patterns of a most unusual kind and achieved by folding the four arms of each cross and tying them up. The tips are then pulled through holes in the bottom of a big pot so that they protrude through the base. The base of the pot with tips is then dipped into a bath of dye. The other parts of the cloth are protected from the dye by the pot (Müller and Raunig 1982, 157). According to Jest (1992, personal communication), this particular method originated from the province of U Tsang, central Tibet. As there are only a few specialists who know this type of dyeing, cross patterns often are simply printed with small wooden blocks. Sometimes they are woven in the cloth with supplementary weft, giving the appearance of an embroidery pattern. The raised surface texture of the pattern is achieved by the three span floats of the supplementary weft being anchored to the 2/2 twill ground weft under each fourth warp end only. This 3/1 interlacing of the double-strand supplementary weft completely hides the ground weave in the front of the cloth and is hardly visible at the back. (This is quite a different method from the float weave patterns described in Chapter 4, where the supplementary weft follows the 2/2 twill ground-weave pattern.) The number of ground weft picks between the supplementary 3/1 picks varies; the latter are anchored under the same warp end at the points where it floats over two weft yarns. According to Sermaya Buddh Thoki from Jumla, who wove the panel, such woven-in cross patterns in woollen panels as fine as this (175 picks and 12 warp ends per inch (2.5 cm) are made for their own use only. The tie-dye cross patterns and stripes were developed later for trade purposes.

Boots

Colourful boots worn by men, women and children complete the traditional outfit. They comprise an all-in-one, fascinating mixture of weaving, embroidery, appliqué and, in many cases, leatherwork. Only some Sherpas know how to make these boots but all know how to repair them. Most boots are made in Khumbu or by boot-makers from Kham, Tibet, who settled in Nepal. Some boots have corded soles. Six layers of plain-weave sack material (although in most cases scraps of woollen material would be used) are stitched

The sole of an unfinished boot and a complete boot with a garter. British Museum As 1992 15a, b and 16a.

closely and firmly together with high-twist yak hair or nettle yarn. The stitching is so tight that the sole becomes waterproof. The most common boots, *khadzan*, have an outer sole of yak hide for which the inner sole stitching need not be so tight.

The sackcloth sides around the sole are shaped upwards by using several rows of very tight stem stitching. The black woollen leg of the boot, with the red and blue strengthening and shaping strips, is attached to the sole and instep with rows of decorative stitching. The embroidery and appliqué patches of rectangles and triangles have been applied to those parts of the boot which have to bear the most strain, thus strengthening and decorating at the same time. A length behind the upper calf is left open to make it easier to put the boot on. A colourful woven strip is stitched on to reinforce the back, while the top upper part is lined with red cotton cloth. The boots are fastened by winding a 4-cm-wide garter, *hamdog* (Tibetan: *lham drog*), round them just below the knee. The length of the garter varies from 60 cm to 1 m. These colourful, warp-faced, striped bands are usually woven on backstrap looms. The weaver uses an ingenious way of weaving such lengths with a circular warp: front and back beams are kept under tension solely by the weaver's body and her feet. The uses of these bands have been greatly increased recently as they have been turned into tourist items ranging from belts to jacket facings.

The frame-treadle loom
(Sherpa: *tijang*; Tibetan: *thag* or *khri thag*)*
All traditional woollen garments are made up from panels, *nambu*, 2/2 twill, weft-faced cloth woven from Tibetan wool. Without any wastage these are joined together to form garments appropriate to various purposes as well as the size of the wearer. The weft-faced 2/2 twill panels used to be woven on backstrap looms until earlier this century when the Tibetan horizontal frame loom was introduced into Nepal, probably by Tibetan immigrants. The panels woven are narrow, about 23 cm, which is a width easy to weave on this type of loom. The backstrap loom is still used for some weaving, especially yak-hair blankets, but most other cloth is woven on this sturdy wooden Tibetan treadle loom. It is widely used also by other groups of Tibetan origin. The loom is extremely versatile: with two or four treadles either plain or patterned cloth can be woven. The loom can be assembled or dismantled easily and transported even along difficult trails. This makes it possible for weavers to share a loom or to travel with it to undertake commissions or obtain employment.

The frame loom consists of four sloping legs, which are tenoned

---

* The name *thag* suggests the sound of a weaver beating.

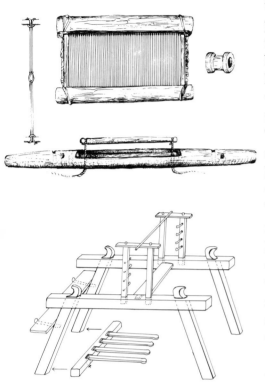

through two side beams. These are connected with a slot-in cross-plank, thus stabilising the frame. The leg ends sticking up above the side beams are carved so as to hold the front and the warp beams. The two front legs, usually slightly shorter than the back legs, are fitted with two large wooden pegs which support the weaver's seat (a wooden plank) and give further support to the frame. Two upright structures are slotted into the side beams. The crossbar resting on these structures, and connecting them, serves as an axle for the pulleys, which are made from a section of bamboo. The string around the pulleys connects two heddle shafts which, in turn, are connected with string to the treadles below. When the weaver presses down one treadle, the heddle shaft connected to it is lowered also, which simultaneously raises the other heddle shaft. Thus, alternately pressing each treadle, shed and countershed are opened in the warp for the weaver to put in the weft thread for a plain weave. For the 2/2 twill weave, which is used for most of the cloth weaving, two extra heddle shafts and treadles are added. These are strung over an additional crossbar resting on the upright structure.

The working of the loom is in principle the same as the bamboo treadle loom described earlier but has the following differences. The heddles of the frame loom are of a more permanent nature: they consist of knotted strings forming slots and eyes through which the cut warp ends are threaded according to the pattern required. In addition the surplus warp is rolled up over a warp beam rather than stretched out a long way and kept under tension with a rope. The warp tension on the frame loom is obtained with two hooked metal rods or sticks, which are inserted into the holes provided in the front and warp beams and then rested on the appropriate pegs, which are slotted into the upright structures.

The most common weaves are either plain or a 2/2 twill. For a plain weave the warp ends are threaded alternately through the eyes of heddles 1 and 2. For a 2/2 twill weave heddles 1, 3, 2 and 4 are threaded in succession. Heddle 1 is that nearest the weaver. Heddles 1 and 2 are joined over the pulleys on the front bar on the uprights, and heddles 3 and 4 over the back bar. Heddle 1 is connected with treadle number 1 (first left from the weaver), 2 with 2, 3 with 3 and 4 with 4. Two treadles are put down at a time in four successive movements: 1 + 4; 2 + 4; 2 + 3; 1 + 3. Each foot rests on the same treadle for two picks.

A new warp is made by tying it to the last 30 cm of the old warp. This is done by two women (the weaver and a helper) as follows. The warp beam is taken to a distance equivalent to the required warp length: there it is weighed down with one or two heavy stones. The inner warp beam, secured with two knotted strings to the outer casing, is rested upon two stones, which are high enough for a ball

Above The wooden frame-treadle loom. Although there are regional variations, the basic principle remains the same. All parts slot into each other; no nails are used. To prevent entanglement, the treadles are put into carved-out slots in the beam and secured with string threaded through the holes in the treadles and the bar. The reed (top) is made of wood and 4mm-wide bamboo strips. The ends are put into the carved-out channel of the top and bottom reed bar, and are spaced and held in place with string and split bamboo and secured with scraps of cotton cloth which act as caulking (5 dents to 1 inch (2.5 cm)). In the centre is a warp beam with casing for the inner warp beam, and at the top, a 6-ply cotton thread heddle (left) and a pulley, a section cut from the hollow bamboo stem.

Left A frame-treadle loom (in the basket) on the way to Sankhuwasabha to be used for *allo* weaving (see p. 130).

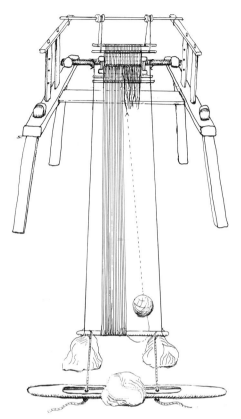

Tying in a new warp.

of yarn to pass underneath. Both ends of the inner warp beam are connected to the front beam with a length of string in order to keep tension and an even distance. The weaver then ties the beginning of the new warp yarn ball to one outer warp end. Her helper then takes the ball around the inner warp beam and back to the weaver who cuts the loop, ties one end to the second old warp thread and holds the other end from the ball of the warp yarn, aided by teeth or feet. The helper then takes the ball round the warp beam and back again in a loop to the weaver, who ties the previously held thread and cuts the loop holding one end again. When all the old warp threads have been tied to the new warp, the inner warp beam is put back into its casing and the warp is rolled up and transferred to the loom. Before the new weaving is started, the old warp with the knotted joints is pulled gently through the heddle eyes and reed and is then rolled on to the front beam.

When a new warp has to be set up, some weavers simply prepare a short warp (each warp thread about 70 cm long), doubling and knotting each thread to the front inner casing beam: each warp is threaded through the reed and the heddle, and to this new short warp the new long warp is tied in the same way as described above.

Tablet weaving

Tablet weaving, the ancient method of weaving ornamental belt and apron bands (p. 153), is assumed to have come to Nepal from Tibet. It is practised only in some northern areas and in Kathmandu, where numbers of Tibetan refugees have settled. Here tablet weaving has become more tourist-oriented: rather than adorning a traditional dress or apron a tablet-woven band might appear around a tourist's neck as a camera strap or as a tie-belt around jeans. Although the method is employed by only a few people, a brief description is justified. A definitive account of the technique can be found in Collingwood 1982.

In tablet weaving the warp yarn is threaded through holes in flat tablets instead of through the eyes of heddles. By manipulating the tablets – giving them a slight turn – shed and countershed can be opened for the weft yarn to be inserted. Depending on how the colours are threaded and which tablets are turned, a wide variety of patterns can be achieved. In Nepal, usually four-hole leather tablets are used.

The warping for a belt, as witnessed in Kathmandu, was done on a wooden board with five nails. Starting at nail number 1, the weaver threaded the tablets and led the warp yarn around the nails using the starter nail as the turning-point where colour changes took place and new warp threads were tied in. This starting- and turning-point or axis is referred to as *srog thur* (life post) as, if it were withdrawn, the circular warp would open up (Ronge 1978).

A wood and metal beater and two of the 36 leather tablets (5.7 cm²) which were used for weaving the cotton 'tourist' belt (above). British Museum As 1992 10.4–11.

In the centre, the fine traditional belt (6.3 × 183 cm), with 260 warp-ends, has a range of motifs including waves, bird's beaks, swastikas, meanders, thunderbolts and bells.

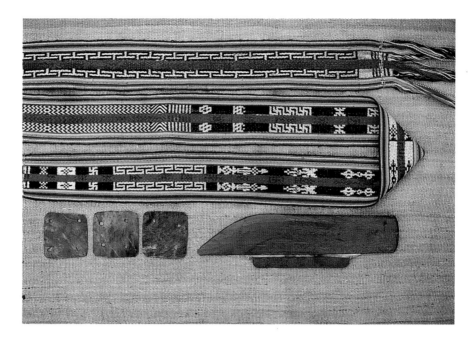

The weaving takes place on a backstrap loom. The loops from the starter nail are transferred onto a stick and the warp is placed over the breast beam and two wooden bars, one some 80 cm above the other. These are fixed with strong loops to a wall. The weaver sits in front of the wall with the breast beam held by the backstrap and the warp forming a triangle in front of her. This method is particularly suitable for tablet weaving as the weaver can control the tension of the warp – leaning slightly forward when turning the tablets and leaning back when beating in the weft. The beating is done with a small wooden beater with a metal edge set in on one side. When some weaving has been completed, the warp is simply slipped around the three poles to the position the weaver requires.

Dolpo
(FOR ALL THE INFORMATION ON THIS REGION I AM GREATLY INDEBTED TO DR CORNEILLE JEST, CNRS, PARIS.)

In north-western Dolpo – far from motorable roads, five days' walk from the nearest airstrip (which was opened as late as 1990) and unaffected as yet by tourism – spinning and weaving are still major activities. Homespun and woven, as well as hide, garments are worn by everybody. Within majestic scenery, at an average altitude of 3,800–4,200 m, lie the scattered villages of people whose religion and way of dressing and living portray their Tibetan origin. Life is harsh: the land consists of dry, unstable slopes and the rainfall is limited. The people of Tarap, one of the four Dolpo valleys, can grow only one crop of barley a year. Wild plants, like nettles and the roots of *Chenopodia* and *Potentilla*, milk, cheese, but rarely meat, supplement the diet. The people rear yaks and their cross-breeds,

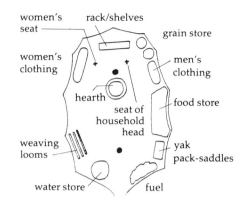

women's seat   rack/shelves
                                grain store
women's
clothing   men's
                                clothing
        hearth
            seat of   food store
        household
            head
weaving
looms   yak
                                pack-saddles
    water store   fuel

Above Summer camp at Tarap, a drawing by Kungya. In early summer, yak, cattle, sheep, goats and horses are taken up to graze at higher altitudes. During this time the herdsmen and their families make their home in woven, water-proof yak hair tents (*right* and *top*). A tent, made up from 40 cm-wide panels and covering some 15–20 m² of ground, is supported by two centre posts in between which is the fireplace. Drawings courtesy of C. Jest.

Weaving in winter in the shelter of some rocks. The weaver in the foreground has just opened one of the four sheds for the 2/2 twill weave. The three heddles and the shedstick show behind the shed opener. The man on the left is wearing a traditional Dolpo blanket. Behind the weavers, amongst the rocks, are two chörten or places of worship.

cattle, sheep, goats and horses: livestock represents both livelihood and status. Barter trade has always been an essential factor for survival. Dr C. Jest (1975, 160–4) describes some of these trade transactions, which took place within one year, starting in the spring.

First stage: local barley is taken by yak caravan to Tibet and bartered for rock salt, wool, yak hair, yak tails, butter and cheese.

Second stage: rice, wheat, maize, buckwheat, millet and spices from inhabitants south of Dolpo are obtained in Dolpo by exchange for Tibetan rock salt and wool.

Third stage: the people of Dolpo go to the middle hill areas in winter and barter Tibetan salt for local cereals at a favourable rate. They also sell horses.

Extra income is gained from wool, yak hair and goat-hair products. These are made not only for their own use but also for sale or barter. Blankets are especially valued in the more southern region of Nepal and as trade items.

Interruption of the long-established cross-border trade in the late 1950s, together with the loss of some Tibetan winter pastures as a result of political disputes, and the arrival of refugees from the north, made life even harder for the people of Dolpo. Nevertheless, the close ties with Tibet could not be broken: trade soon resumed and was adapted also to some new types of consumer goods. However, wool and yak hair remain major trading items, providing the raw material for most of the textiles.

Sheep's wool is used to weave clothing and blankets. The wool of the six-month-old lamb is especially valued for its softness. From the yak the hard, outer hair is made into ropes, slings, guy-lines for tents, tent panels, bags, sacks and even a kind of protection against sunlight (see also p. 150). The down-like inner hair is woven

163

A Dolpo man cutting the panels for a woollen coat or *chuba* (see p. 193). For a sheepskin coat or *slog-pa* all the pieces of skin are joined like a jigsaw puzzle. This skilful tailoring is always performed by men. Coats are also made of goatskin, (*raslog*) with the wool or hair worn on the inside.

into carpets and blankets. It is also felted into soft, saddle-cloths for horses, or pack-pads for the yak. The goat's hard outer hair is used only for ropes and sacks, whilst the fine cashmere-type inner hair is woven into garments.

During the long, cold winter months, between the middle of October and February, when the frozen ground makes fieldwork impossible, men and women work together in sheltered enclosures protected by stone walls, whilst the children play, watch, learn and help. Men make ropes, bridles, halters, slings and baskets. They also spin, prepare hides, do all the tailoring and sewing, and felt saddle-blankets. The women spin and weave all the textiles needed for the home and family.

The woollen, handwoven clothing is mainly of natural colour but some is dyed red or maroon. Red is used by lamas. Dark blue, the colour reserved for gods, is never dyed in the valley. If this colour is required, women dye it far from their village, so that their homes are not harmed if the anger of the gods is aroused. Chemical dyes, traded in from India, have replaced most natural dyes.

The clothing for men consists of a vest, trousers and the greatcoat, *chuba*, together with the traditional home-made boots. For festive occasions a cotton or wild silk cross-over, waist-long shirt is worn. The vest is made up from one panel, 40 × 102 cm. This, folded lengthwise into half, forms the shoulder-line. A cut is made along one shoulder-line and around the neckline. The side of the vest with the folded shoulder is stitched from the waist for about 35 cm up to the base of the armhole opening. The other open side and shoulder are fastened with six and two cross-ties respectively. The trousers consist of two panels (60 × 80 cm) for the legs and two panels (80 × 16 cm) which are folded lengthwise to form the crutch and back and front inset: these overlap. The trousers, which are fastened with a draw-string at the side, are worn with the legs tucked inside the boots and are prevented from slipping out by garters. An interesting feature is that certain areas of Dolpo can be identified by the patterns of the garter. The rest of the costume is identical throughout the district.

The style of the coat, *chuba*, is the same as that worn by Sherpas but it is made mostly of wider panels (40+ cm); that is, the usual width woven on backstrap looms rather than the narrow panels woven on the treadle looms employed by Sherpas. According to Dr Jest, a *chuba* is made up of about 16 *khru* (a cubit or forearm length, approximately 40 cm), that is, a panel some 640 × 40 cm. This would take about four days to weave. As with all garments, the panels are cut and sewn in such a way that there is no wastage of cloth.

The shirt is made up from one panel (54 × 96 cm), folded length-ways to form the back and the front, one inner front panel (27 × 48 cm) and two sleeve panels (each 30 × 52 cm). The main panel is

The panelled back cloths or blankets seen here at the Dolpo Tarap Festival form part of the traditional clothing for Dolpo women. The metal headdress, silver rings and earrings often enhanced by turquoise, and protective charms inside leather sachets and pendants, complete the festive dress. The men are wearing greatcoats dyed red with madder.

cut at one shoulder and along the neckline so that it can be crossed over and tied under the right armhole. The inner front panel, top right-hand corner, is cut to follow the neckline.

The women's costume is similar to that of the men but the maroon/brown-coloured trousers are longer and of a different cut. The two leg panels (each 80 × 90 cm) are joined with a gusset 38 cm square. The *chuba* is not hitched up as high as a man's but worn near ankle-length. A striped, coloured apron is worn at the back. An apron is worn at the front only on special occasions. The most striking feature of the Dolpo women's costume during festivals is the wide-striped, colourful blue, reddish-grey and yellow shawl/ blanket (Nepali: *kamlo*). This is draped over the back and shoulders and fastened in front with a decorative *vajra*-shaped clasp. These attractive and warm shawls have gained recognition far beyond Dolpo and have become a valuable item of barter trade.

In winter everyone wears ankle-length coats of sheepskin, *logpa*, or goatskin, *ra-slog* (pronounced 'ralog'), instead of the woollen coats. These are prepared in an unusual way which has been recorded by Dr Jest (1975, 189). The work is usually done by men. The skin is first air-dried for several days with the wool side upper-most, care being taken to avoid overheating. The skin is then folded with the wool again on the outside and left for about ten days before tanning, *mnes-pa* (pronounced 'nye-pa'). For this the skin is

165

stretched out and lightly moistened. A mixture of soil and horse dung, *rta-sbans* (pronounced 'tabang'), is spread on to the skin, which is then thoroughly trampled, the tanner steadying himself with a stick. This stretches the skin and makes it more supple, a process which is continued by stretching it with lengths of wood, which are either notched or have the horns of an antelope attached on which to hook the edges. Any remaining pieces of flesh are removed with a stone or knife. The skin is then coated with the brains of the sheep and left for four to five days before being trampled once more. It can then be used for clothing, with the wool being worn on the inside. The skin is cut and joined in a kind of patchwork so that not a single scrap is wasted.

All weaving was done on backstrap looms until recently when the Tibetan frame-treadle loom was introduced to Dolpo. On religious grounds this loom was met with considerable opposition and was introduced only gradually. The women from Tarap considered that weaving on this *khri thag* (pronounced 'tritag'; literally 'seat loom', the seat being part of the frame) would be a grave religious error because only a lama has the right to use the raised seat or *khri*. To the present day Dolpo women who use the *khri-thag* abstain from weaving on this loom from the third to the eighth months – the time of field cultivation – in order to avoid a bad harvest.

The backstrap loom, *pan-thag* (pronounced 'pangtag'; literally, 'breast loom'), is still widely used. It is similar to that employed by Gurungs for rari weaving (p. 143) but the warp beam in this case lies near the ground. It rests on, and is weighed down by, heavy

Spinning and weaving in a sheltered enclosure. After weaving, to give the cloth a compact fibrous surface, it is soaked in a wooden container for half a day, trampled, wrung and dried. It is then brushed with a split-bamboo brush to soften it, rolled up round a stick and pressed in order to straighten it out.

Laying the warp for a 2/2 twill weave. The weaver is wearing the traditional woollen *chuba* and the Dolpo metal headdress with a shawl draped over it.

stones. To prevent the long circular warp from trailing on the ground a wide piece of wood is placed upright just beyond the heddle bar. This gives the warp a slight slant downwards towards the breast beam. It also creates an easier angle for the weaver to work and supplies a foot brace for the weaver.

The warping method for the backstrap loom differs from that of the Gurung weaver, as most Dolpo women include a warp lock-stick and spacer/coil rod: every warp end is wound once round this rod, thus keeping the warp correctly spaced and preventing entanglement. The arrangement of the warp-stick differs also in so far as Dolpo weavers use the same sticks both for forming the cross and for lengthening the warp. The warp crosses formed during warping are for either a plain or twill weave. The transfer of the warp to the loom, the making of the heddles and the weaving method are similar to those practised by Gurungs.

Manang and other northern areas

The blankets, *phe*, worn in Manang are similar to those of Dolpo, but usually a two-ply cotton rather than wool is used for the warp, whilst the double-strand weft is single, hand-spindle spun wool. These blankets, which are wrapped round the body and sometimes the head, also serve as baby-carriers. Some blanket weavers have recently adapted their products for a wider market. The panels, often decorated with embroidery or supplementary-weft patterns, are tailored into multicoloured jackets, with garter facings, mainly for the tourist trade.

A woman weaving a belt. The colourful warp-faced, plain-weave garters and belts are woven on portable back-strap looms. The warp is held under tension by the back beam resting against the weaver's outstretched feet. The weaver is wearing a *shuba* a woollen blanket strip round her waist and traditional boots and garters. Her partner is dressed in a sheepskin coat.

A plain weave Manang Gurung blanket from north west Nepal is made with cotton warp and wool weft, used as a wrap to keep warm and to carry babies. British Museum As 1992 10.73.

One type of blanket, the soft, warm loop-pile blanket, is woven solely for home use, principally for bedding. When made of natural-coloured wool it may look, at first glance, like an actual sheepskin. The soft, flexible blankets are woven on backstrap or treadle looms, in either a plain or twill ground weave and are made up of panels (35 × 170 cm) joined lengthwise for various widths. The method of forming the loop pile is very similar to that of making loop heddles (see p. 142), but instead of a heddle rod a gauge rod is used. The size of the gauge determines the length of the pile. The weaver holds the gauge in one hand whilst with the other she picks up the pile yarn, one after another, in between each pair of upper warp threads and slips each as a loop over the gauge, pulling it tight. In this way she moves the head of the gauge rod along the entire warp until she reaches the side where the ball of pile yarn has been continuously releasing the yarn required for the loops. The gauge rod, now covered with a spiral of loops, is then beaten in with a beater and two, sometimes three, picks are woven. These ensure that the loops stay in place when the weaver cuts them along the open U of the gauge and then removes the rod. The process is then repeated.

This is not the only method used by weavers. Some form the loop pile in a 2/2 twill weave; others use a round rod to form the loops which are not cut. Yet other weavers incorporate a simple pattern

168

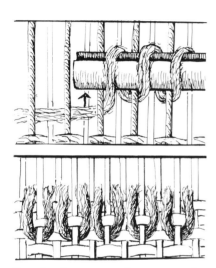

Forming loops over the gauge rod.

Patterned woollen plain-weave cut
loop carpet from North West Nepal.
British Museum As 1981 26.82.

by changing the colour during looping. An example of this is illustrated on the previous page.

Sling

A simple woollen sling from Manang may serve as an example of

'Bhotiya rug loom' bought at the Coronation Exhibition of 1910 by H. Ling Roth for the Bankfield Museum, Halifax. The pile rod with loops and two picks of 2/2 twill ground weave show in the front of the completed woven panel (45 cm wide). The dense woollen pile is 1 cm deep.

the range of textile structures employed in the northern areas. Such slings are also made by Sherpas and other Tibeto-Burman groups, particularly in the north, where they are used to direct sheep and to scare away birds, monkeys and other animals. In the past they were used as weapons of war. Jest (1974, 78) records that a Tarap boy will be given his first sling, *urtu* (or *urdo*), at the age of seven:

Petite fronde en laine	Small sling of wool
jouet d'enfant	joy of the child
fronde bariolée	sling of many colours
fronde de berger	sling of the shepherd
fronde à huit tresses	sling of the eight strands
fronde à guerrier	sling of the warrior
fronde à neuf yeux	sling of nine eyes
fronde de magicien	sling of the magician

A Tarap boy wielding a woollen sling, drawn by Kungya from Tarap.

The nine-eyed sling refers to the one used by lamas during festivals. Such slings have a cradle of nine stripes woven from black hair. The evil spirits which have been trapped within a *torma* by some magic words of the lama are removed from the village when the lama places the *torma* in his sling and casts it away.

The standard sling consists of a cradle in the centre and two long

170

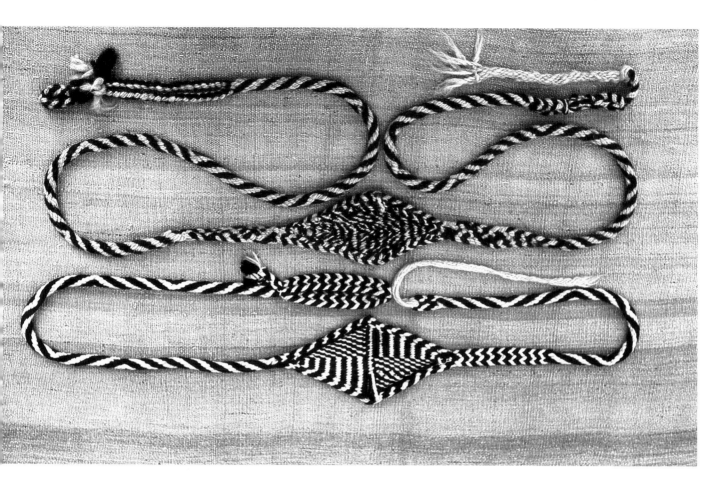

Above Two woollen slings from north-west Nepal, made in various ways of ply-splitting and braiding. The unusual pattern of the sling cradle, below, was achieved by darning through the 2-ply (1 black, 1 white) warp-strands in such a way that either the black or the white strand would show at the top as required. British Museum As 1993 10.1.

From left to right S-twist and Z-twist yarn; ply split darning through a Z-and a S-ply yarn; tubular ply split darning for the end piece of the sling at the top; 4-strand round braiding employed for both slings.

ends, one of which has one or two loops. Both ends of the sling are held in one hand with the loop over either the index finger or the hand. The missile, usually a stone, is placed into the cradle which is then whirled violently around before the loopless end is released allowing the missile to fly with tremendous speed at its target – if one is a skilful user.

On closer examination of the sling one discovers that knotting, flat and round braiding and two different types of ply splitting as well as two colours are incorporated into this one length of an apparently simple sling, illustrating just one of the countless different types of braiding and knotting known to the people of Nepal.

Carpets

Textiles of a different nature, knotted, woollen pile carpets, have probably been produced in the most northern areas of Nepal for centuries. Snellgrove and Richardson (1968, 158) believe the weaving of carpets in Tibet must have been a quite ancient craft, though coming under Chinese influence possibly even earlier than the Ming period (that is, prior to 1368). Under King Song-tsen Gompa (AD 620–49) 'Tibetans were ranging from the plains of India and the mountains of Nepal to the frontiers of China' (Snellgrove and

171

A cross-patterned carpet woven by Tibetan weavers on a large frame loom leaning against the roof. British Library MSS EUR 80/S1 196 R88.

Richardson 1968, 25). If the Tibetans were producing such carpets at that time, it is conceivable that the practice was taken up in areas which are now part of Nepal although this remains speculative. A saddle-carpet appearing in a Nepalese mandala painting of 1564 demonstrates that they were known in Nepal certainly over 400 years ago. The people of northern Nepal today use the carpets mainly as seat-pads, beds and saddle-blankets. They may occasionally be used also as door curtains and pillar wraps.

Much more substantial production of carpets has occurred since the 1960s. Following the Lhasa uprising of 1959, many Tibetan refugees came to Nepal, a number of whom brought their ancient carpet-making skills with them. Through refugee centres, workshops and training courses carpet knotting was introduced into many areas, with major centres and factories developing in Kathmandu, Pokhara

A medaillon carpet with border pattern, woven in Kathmandu. 74.5 × 61 cm. British Museum As 1992 10.24.

A tiger-pattern carpet made in Kathmandu with cloud-band and mountain motifs on the borders.

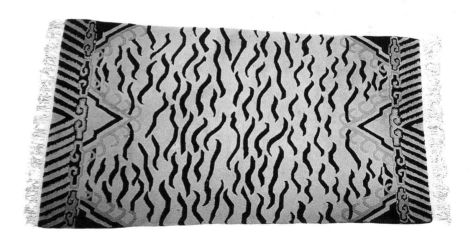

and Solukhumbu. The equipment needed to establish such an enterprise was relatively cheap to make and operate, and this also enabled many individual home weavers, Tibetan immigrants and Nepalis of various ethnic groups, to start working for a contractor or a small family business.

The carpets are woven on sturdy, frame looms in a vertical or slightly sloping position. Irrespective of size, the main components of a loom are the same – two movable beams, held in position by wooden blocks or pegs which are fixed to the rigid wooden frame,

A Manang carpet weaver, who settled north of Pokhara, knotting wool round the iron gauge rod. She follows the paper pattern hanging in front of her.

made from wood 8–10 cm thick. The average size of a home loom is 150 cm square. Factory looms are much larger, varying with the size of carpet to be produced.

The tools required for carpet knotting are:

1 One or more metal gauge rods, depending on how many weavers are working on the carpet. The pile length (average 1.25 cm) is determined by the diameter of the rod.
2 Cutting tool or knife to cut the loops on the gauge rod.
3 Comb beater to beat down the weft.
4 Mallet to beat down the rod with the loops.
5 Shuttle for the warp yarn.
6 Scissors for trimming.
7 Wooden wedges, which can be pushed between the pegs and the warp beam if the tension needs adjusting. The wedges can be removed temporarily when the weaver wants to release the tension in order to move the woven section down and thus slide the whole warp around the two beams to present a section of unwoven warp to the weaver.

To lay the warp the loom is placed horizontally on the ground. The weaver squats inside the frame and leads the ball of warp yarn, usually six-ply cotton, around the beams, over and under the cross-sticks and in u-turns round the warp lock-stick (axis rod). When the warping is completed, the loom is put upright against a wall. The warp lock-stick is pushed down to the bottom of the frame with the two cross-sticks above showing the alternate warp threads. For one set of warp threads a loop heddle is made; the other cross-stick is replaced with a flat shedstick. Some carpet weavers make a loop heddle for each shed, and in this case the two heddle rods are tied to a heddle horse (a flat bar about 20 cm long) which rests on a raised bar fixed above the frame: the heddle horse, like a seesaw, is pushed backwards and forwards over the bar, thus tipping up and down and lifting each heddle alternately.

The weaver – or weavers for a wider carpet – sits on a low bench or a pad in front of the loom. The design of the carpet is usually drawn on graph paper and hangs down from the top of the loom or is unrolled, row by row, as a guide to the weaver. Sometimes an actual carpet is used as a sample to follow or the weaving is done from memory: some house weavers make up their own pattern variations. On average there are forty-five knots to a square inch (= 675 per square decimetre). The weaver (most often female) begins to weave, usually with a row of end binding followed by four lines of plain weave using double or treble thickness of the warp cotton thread for the weft. (Before 1914 warp, weft and pile in Tibet would have been from Tibetan wool. However, by the 1950s Indian cotton was being used largely for the warp and subsequently increasingly for the weft also (Denwood 1978, 16).)

175

Dolpo pilgrims in their festive garments. Their horses are covered with tie-dye patterned blankets. The decorative pile carpets over and under the saddles provide padding and comfort, and feature medaillon, cloud, mountain, phoenix and floral motifs. Some under-saddle carpets have stepped or rounded corners, similar to the saddle carpet shown in the mandala on p. 31.

The successive steps, as recorded at the Department of Cottage and Village Industries Training Centre, Dhankuta, east Nepal, in the 1980s are:

1 A line of knotting with woollen yarns, using the colours required for the pattern.
2 Beating down the rod with the mallet.
3 One line of cotton weft.
4 Beating in the weft with the comb beater.
5 Cutting the loops by leading the sharp knife or cutter along the metal rod.
6 Trimming with scissors where necessary, for example, the loose ends where colour changes have taken place.
7 Edge binding: the outer two pairs of warp threads are bound

176

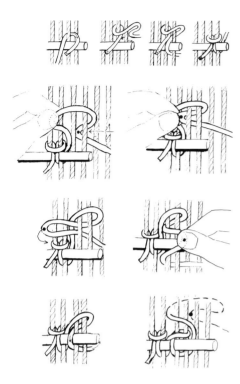

From top to bottom Successive steps in weaving a carpet. For the first and last knots of each row, and when colour changes take place, a type of Ghiordes knot is used. The wool is held with the left thumb and index finger or the loop is slipped over the little finger. A second loop is pushed with the right hand under two adjoining warp threads from right to left. Letting the first loop go, the second loop is held, pulled to enlarge it, and is slipped over the rod with the right hand; the end is pulled down over the rod and then up behind it. The rod is moved to the right as required and the steps are repeated.

with carpet wool between the wefts (alternately around two pairs and three pairs).

Stages 1–7 are repeated until the carpet has reached the required size. Then, after four lines of plain weave and a line of edge binding, the carpet is taken off the loom and shorn with scissors to level out any irregularities. Often the patterns are then outlined by cutting a v-shaped groove with small scissors all around: this contouring is usually done by specialists (men).

Traditional Tibetan designs include geometric shapes, crosses, medallions, meander – cloud and mountain borders – peony and lotus, phoenix, dragon and tiger motifs and Buddhist symbols, for example, the *vajra* shape on the seat carpets used for meditation. It is quite conceivable that along the ancient trade routes linking China, India and Persia there was much cross-fertilisation of ideas and practices on motifs and designs. J. and B. Ford (in Lipton (ed.), 1988, 151) state that the kinds of designs and colours most often found in Tibet clearly group them within the Chinese cultural empire but 'it is beyond dispute that the Tibetan rug is no mere appendage of Chinese art. Not only is the weaving technique entirely different, the treatment of the motifs and the style of coloration are unique and readily recognizable'.

Today designs in Nepal are a blend of this Tibetan tradition and Chinese and Western influences, with a Nepalese adaptation. The markets influence design and, indeed, carpet exporters stress the flexibility of their designs which can be adapted to meet the buyers' requirements. Some buyers specify design, colour and size for implementation in the exporter's workshop. In some cases new designs may be required each year. The orientation is often towards Western home-furnishing taste. Nevertheless, traditional designs, based on Tibetan carpet traditions and Nepalese adaptations (for example, inspired by old carvings), continue to be made for the home, tourist and export markets. (Nepalese carpets have been exported to more than thirty-five countries and in 1984–5, for example, totalled 227,000 sq. m). The most popular sizes are the square (40 × 40 cm) seat-pad and the rectangular (180 × 90 cm) carpet.

Colours were obtained originally from plants, chiefly madder, rhubarb and indigo, together with the natural colours of the wool. Many different shades of red were possible using madder plants of different ages and a range of mordants. Synthetic dyes have to a large extent replaced these natural dyes, although an increasing demand for natural-dye carpets has revived interest in age-old dye recipes and has led to some manufacturers using plant dyes for all their carpets.

6

SUBTROPICAL SOUTH
THARU, RAJBANSI
AND GEOTEXTILES

A traditional warp-faced Jute panel.

For generations Nepal was defended naturally from hostile invaders by the Himalayas to the north and along its southern border by the *terai*. This is a relatively flat area, only 70–300 m above sea-level, which runs almost continuously from west to east. *Terai* means 'the land of fever', and it was for centuries notorious for the existence of a particularly virulent form of malaria. For a long time it was sparsely inhabited, and much of it was swampy and under forest. There was some seasonal exploitation by outsiders for timber and food cropping. Its wildlife included the Royal Bengal Tiger and the Greater One-horned Rhinoceros, and so in the nineteenth and early twentieth centuries it was the setting also for big game hunting by the ruling classes and their guests.

Nepal's greatest place in history rests with the fact that within it was the birthplace, Lumbini (to the south-west of Kathmandu), in 543 BC of Prince Siddhartha Gautama who was to become the Buddha. Lumbini today is a place of pilgrimage for Buddhists from all over the world. Janakpur, to the south-east of Kathmandu, is, according to legend, the birthplace of Sita who was to marry Ram, the hero of the Hindu epic *Ramayana*, and is a place of Hindu pilgrimage.

Since the start of mosquito control in the 1950s, most of the forests of the *terai* have been cleared. Although the *terai* covers only 14 per cent of Nepal, it has much of its cultivable land, a subtropical climate and is well-watered: it has become the major agricultural and industrial region of the country. Over half the population now lives there. In addition to food crops it also has substantial areas of industrial crops including jute, sugar-cane and cotton. The cities of Nepal,

179

other than Kathmandu and Pokhara, are found in the *terai*. The government also appreciated the need for forest and wildlife conservation and established nature reserves.

Inevitably, since the Indian border is so close and Nepalese factory-made cloth so readily available throughout the *terai*, very little traditional weaving is still practised. Nevertheless, the indigenous Nepali people, who are considered to have developed immunity from malaria, though now outnumbered by immigrants from the mountains and the south, have retained their distinctive identity in some areas of the *terai*. They include the Tharu, a generic term relating to one of the largest groups found throughout the region (Bista 1980, 118), and the Danuwar, Dhagar and Rajbansi, who are found largely in the two easternmost districts of Morang and Jhapa. The Tharu of western Nepal continue with their fine patchwork and embroidery and, although they have ceased to weave in the east, they have become well known for their basketwork.

Tharu

The Tharu are found throughout the length of the *terai* and are probably amongst the longest-established people in the area. They have been divided into thirty-two groups, each of which historically has been more or less confined to a specific area. Before the large-scale clearing of the forest they farmed under the most difficult conditions, living in forest clearings and at risk of disease and such wild animals as tigers and snakes (Bista 1980, 118 *et seq.*). Today these dangers are greatly reduced, but the massive influx of settlers has left little opportunity for shifting cultivation, and as few Tharus own land, many now work as tenant cultivators, usually on a share-cropping basis. Most of the textiles that they require are factory-made, often imported from India. Nevertheless, some Tharu groups, particularly in western Nepal, have retained their distinctive style of dress, even though the cotton from which it is made is no longer handwoven. Tharus in Bardiya District wear finely embroidered, appliqué handstitched blouses/jackets with wraparound-type skirts made up of colourful cotton panels. These are sometimes gathered before being stitched together to give full flare to the skirt. Silver anklets, necklaces and coins are the ornaments. The short blouse illustrated opposite, gathered in the front, is tied at the back of the neck. The delicate lines (0.2 cm wide) are white cotton strips which are stitched on to the black cotton twill-patterned background and appear like relief work with their rolled-in hems. The red, green, yellow and blue cotton strips are attached to the black background with running stitches. Small v-shaped and herring-bone stitches and minute white appliqué triangles add another decorative element.

Coiled and stitched baskets made by Tharu women. British Museum 1992 10.55 and 1993 01.5.

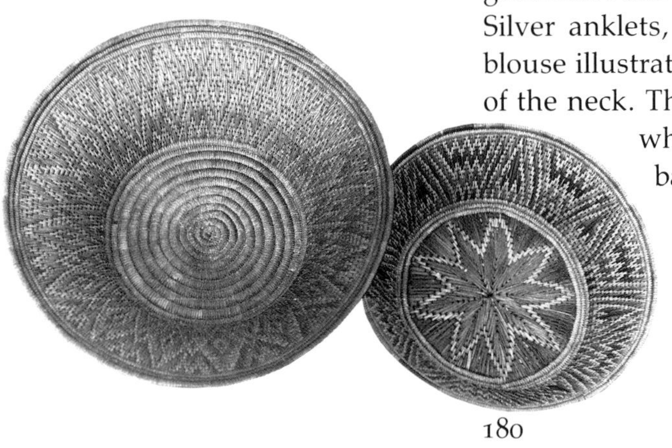

180

A Tharu hand-stitched embroidered appliqué cotton blouse or jacket from the Bardiya District, west Nepal.

The intricately patterned, coiled grass Tharu baskets are made in a wide variety of shapes to carry sweets and fruit to festival gatherings, to bring gifts to a bride and to provide storage. A whole set of baskets usually accompanies the bride to her new home. Most baskets are carried on the head. Some are decorated at the rim with a net-like border incorporating jingling shells and seeds. The baskets are made in the coiling method – stitching/wrapping the stem of *siki* grass around a coil of *khar* (*Saccharum spontaneum*) grass. The designs which are stitched over the basic shape with dyed grass include diamonds, triangles, flowers, fish, bird and elephant motifs.

Rajbansi jute products

The Rajbansi in the east are often referred to as Koch or Koche, which is said to be their original name and refers to a people who are mentioned in the ancient Hindu epic *Mahabharata*. Bista (1980, 134 *et seq*.) states that the Rajbansi/Koch are said to have been a very powerful nation during the seventeenth and eighteenth centuries and, quoting Hodgson (1880, 107), says that their territory

181

included the western half of Assam and the eastern half of Morang and the land between. Subsequently the area was taken over by the British from the south and King Prithvi Narayan Shah, who annexed Jhapa and Morang in 1774. The people then divided into three groups: one retained their traditional beliefs, one adopted Hinduism, and the third embraced Islam. In Nepal the people remained predominantly farmers, some of whom grew cotton and wove their own materials. Hodgson (1880, 110) states that 'the clothing is made by the women and is in general blue-dyed by themselves with their own indigo, the borders red-dyed with Morinda. The material is cotton of their own growth'.

Although very little cotton cloth is woven now, Rajbansi women still spin jute fibres into lustrous yarn and weave the traditional

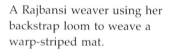

A Rajbansi weaver using her backstrap loom to weave a warp-striped mat.

warp-faced colourful floor mats, *dhokra*, carrying-bags, *jhola*, and also double bags which are used for animal loads. The jute items are sold at local markets, but women also receive payment for their weaving skills within the community: 'unmarried, widowed and landless women were given jute fibre by the head of the village who took a percentage of the profits from the resulting work' (Hurle 1984, 3). Spinning and weaving skills are considered great assets and are learned by girls when they are very young, often by just watching their mothers. Traditionally all the weaving was done on backstrap looms. The warp is wound directly around the front and back beams which are secured by pegs or tied to supporting bars. The weaver, squatting beside the beams, leads the two-ply warp yarn around the two beams and alternately over and under two cross-sticks and around the warp lock-stick in u-turns. With a separ-

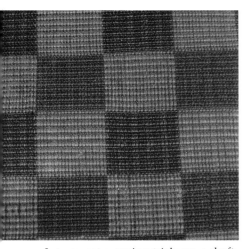

Jute carpet weaving trials on 4-shaft frame looms at Jhapa Training Centre.

Weaving jute mats for soil conservation. While two women press down the heddle frame and push the shuttle through the shed, the other two push the previous pick into place. To obtain the countershed the women will lift the frame in order to raise the warp threads which rest in the twisted-wire heddle eyes.

ate ball of yarn she encircles each second warp thread with a loop over a rod, thus forming the heddle loops whilst warping. The average size of a mat panel weaving is 35 × 180 cm, with about eighteen warp ends and eight picks per inch (2.5 cm). Three strips are joined together to form a mat.

In the 1980s the Jute Development Corporation, the Jhapa Training Centre and the Women's Development Section tried to develop the market for local jute products, as the majority, mainly floor coverings, are imported from neighbouring countries, having often been made from jute grown in Nepal. Two- and four-shaft frame looms were introduced to some jute weavers with the aim of encouraging a parallel development to the traditional backstrap weaving. The attractive mats/carpets, woven on the shaft looms, are marketed through co-operatives and might eventually replace imported carpets.

Geotextiles

A jute textile of an entirely different nature is produced by a group of self-employed and self-organised women in east Nepal for the Dharan-Dhankuta Road Maintenance Project (HMGN/UK Bilateral Aid Programme). Low-grade jute is purchased from the farmers and spun into a yarn (5–7 mm in diameter) which is woven into open-weave mats (10 × 1 m). The loom consists of two bamboo bars fixed horizontally, 10 m apart, and a rigid twisted wire heddle. (The jute

warp strands are threaded through the heddle and looped over and tied to the bars). In 1992 2,000 to 4,000 m per month were made. The mats are laid on steep, bare roadside slopes to stabilise the soil and help to establish a permanent vegetative cover. Seeds or small clumps of grass are planted under the netting. In the early stages the netting provides effective protection against the heavy monsoon storms which could otherwise cause serious surface erosion. By checking the run-off of rain-water the netting also ensures that more penetrates the soil and it also reduces the high temperatures at the soil surface, thereby helping the establishment of the young plants. The jute biodegrades in twelve to eighteen months – rather sadly, as it is an attractive textile – but by then a good vegetative cover should be established (Clark 1992).

Laying jute mats on a roadside slope
in east Nepal to stabilise the soil,
particularly during the heavy
monsoon season.

7

CONCLUSION

❖

A small selection of the wide variety of baskets made in Nepal. The brown, smoked bamboo storage basket is interlaced diagonally with no side or wall strands added. The shallow, footed baskets with the traditional cross-type base pattern are adaptations of the taller storage basket or *dalo* in the centre. By using two colours, natural and smoked, the base pattern can appear in many different ways, depending upon the arrangement of the strands.

Describing the textiles in this book made me increasingly aware both of those of other ethnic groups which deserve appreciation and of the fields of study which await attention, for example, textiles in the context of rituals and ceremonies, and the diverse textile-related structures which are made in every mountain village from bamboo and other locally available materials. They form an important part of Nepal's material culture and are entirely suited to sustaining the environment, but can only be touched upon in this book.

Each technique is employed with ingenuity to serve a particular purpose, resulting in a perfect marriage of material, structure and function. Most of the bamboo structures are made by men, lightweight mats and leaf plates by women. The items are made in each rural household as they are required. There are also some professional basketmakers who sell or trade their goods at local markets and, recently, further afield. Certain types of baskets are unique to specific regions or ethnic groups, with methods and technology being passed on from generation to generation. Evidence of the use of the well-known carrying basket, the *dhoko*, was recorded 200 years ago by Kirkpatrick. A woman carrying this type of basket appears on a nineteenth-century relief carving at a house at Changu Narayan in the Kathmandu Valley. This hexagonal, strong, yet lightweight bamboo structure is also used for the round, flat-bottomed pairs of carrying baskets, *kharpan*. Variations of the technique are shaped to make, among other items, a house or cover for small chickens or to carry oranges or a live cock, a bag-type container, *perungu*, for smoked fish or spices and, among the Limbu, for meat as part marriage payment (Caplan 1970, 217) as well as for animal muzzles, *mohla*. Gurung rainshields are of a similar structure. It could be a revealing study to compare this semi-circular Gurung rainshield with the rectangular plain-weave shield, *ghum*, of the Newars or the big, circular hat/shield made by Tharus, and discover the reason for employing such different methods for the same purpose.

Amongst the wide variety of techniques employed for making sieves, filters, cradles, mats, leaf plates and storage baskets, two of the most commonly used basket methods are of particular interest; each shows an entirely different method of achieving a twill-patterned basket, both starting at the base centre. One method is used for lightweight and solid double-layer storage baskets and lidded rectangular containers: with these, the base strands are interlaced diagonally to form sides. The other method is employed for various-sized baskets, especially the commonly known *dalo* storage basket, which is wider at the top than at the bottom and stands on four feet. The base strands of those baskets are bent vertically upwards to be interlaced horizontally with additional strands to form the sides. Both methods are known amongst Sherpas, Rais and most other Tibeto-Burman ethnic groups. By using natural coloured, off-white bamboo, together with the rich brown, smoked bamboo, these two basic patterns are not only enhanced in their appearance but also protected from insect attack. The bamboo strands are smoked simply by being placed above the fireplace for a period.

Changing times, bringing easier access to town by road and air, together with the arrival of factory-made goods or plastic, do not inevitably bring decline of traditional skills. For the local market, the durable and versatile bamboo products, which can be made for a specific purpose without any cash outlay, cannot easily be replaced with a mass-produced item. Amongst the basketmakers who are now earning an income from their skills, in which they have also involved other smallholder farmers, are Rais from Ankhisalla in Dhankuta District. They continue to sell their bamboo products locally, while extending their market to Kathmandu, which is now within reach by bus. There the traditional mats and baskets, especially the adapted shorter version of the *dalo*, are sold to urban households and hotels as fruit and bread baskets. By combining craftwork and farming, the basketmakers have obtained sufficient income to remain on their land, which, as a sole source of income, could not support their families. They have also planted bamboo on non-arable land to ensure an adequate supply of raw materials and, at the same time, protect the soil.

A much greater change, bringing a decline in some traditional skills, has taken place in textiles used for clothing in some areas close to the Indian border or exposed to Western influence. Here saris, Punjabi-style dress, shirts and trousers have become popular.

Spinning-wheels and handlooms, once part of every household in Kathmandu, have become less evident. But textiles expressing identity with the nation or an ethnic group are still made and worn: the topi, or cap, as part of the national dress for men, the black and red cloth of the Jyapu women, the white and green embroidered shawls by Atpare Rai or the colourful blankets of the women from Dolpo. Textiles for the home, among them the woollen rari made by Gurungs and the Rajbansi jute mats, are still used and identified with the groups who make them.

In most rural areas of Nepal some textiles or textile structures are made or some particular raw material is available which could become a source of income. Both government and non-governmental organisations (NGO), aware of this, are supporting small-scale village projects, where help has been requested by the communities. Two such programmes have been mentioned in previous chapters – dhaka weaving and *allo* cloth production. Dhaka weaving has become the best known of Nepalese textiles: both the traditional black, white, red and orange topis and blouses and, to complement, not replace, this long-established cloth, modern dhaka textiles using a wide range of colours and yarns. Each of these pieces of weaving is a creation integrating new ideas with the old. The artist-weavers of these textiles need not fear competition. No power loom, geared towards mass production, could produce such a wealth of colours or patterns and diversity of design within a short length of weaving. However, there is also a demand for lower-priced dhaka-type cloth. This is met by Jacquard loom weavers and power-driven loom factories and workshops in urban areas where electricity is available. Thus there is a parallel development of the fairly expensive handwoven dhaka textiles (it takes about a week to weave a fine inlay-patterned shawl) and the low-priced repetitive patterned cloth, each meeting the demand of its own market.

The other true Nepalese textile, *allo*, has undergone similar development. Traditional items continue to be woven, especially sacks and bags, while a new type of nettle cloth is woven alongside. At the request of the *allo* weavers of Sankhuwasabha a training and cloth-finishing centre was established. *Allo* in combination with wool has become for some the treasured winter tweed. With easier and speedier processing of fibres and yarns, *allo* could become an alternative to the more luxurious linen. The use of water power for a spinning mill by the centre has been suggested. With this revival of *allo* cloth, the sowing and planting of the *allo* both as a source of raw material and for soil conservation has been given much attention. In some small ways the continuation of traditional skills can thus help to safeguard the fragile ecosystems of the Himalayas, managed and sustained over the centuries by the people of Nepal. Protecting the environment is becoming increasingly difficult. With

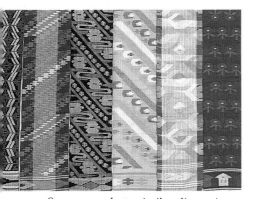

Scarves made to similar dimensions as the traditional topi strips, using a wider variety of colours and adding a border pattern and fringes.

the rising population, most land suitable for food crops is already being used in the mountain areas, and converting forest would further endanger the environment. Some families face the alternatives of migration to the lowlands or towns, which are hardly able to accommodate them, or finding some additional source of income. This may be from a traditional skill, especially where integrated government or NGO assistance was given, covering research into raw materials, technology and marketing of products together with help with education, health care, trail improvement and water supplies.

Supporting tourism development in such areas, with craft activity as a potential focus of interest and source of income, is more controversial. Nevertheless, the Annapurna Conservation Area Project (ACAP) has demonstrated that, with careful planning, tourism can be beneficial to both the host country and the tourist. Special textile study tours could bring deeper understanding and appreciation of Nepalese textiles. This could be helped further by a living craft centre and textile museum, which might be established in the future and could serve also as an inspiration and give pleasure to those who have no opportunity to admire the ingenuity of Nepalese weavers, embroiderers and basketmakers in their remote homes. Their wealth of skills and knowledge will ensure that the heritage of Nepalese textiles will be not only preserved but enhanced and enriched with every generation.

Details of a
supplementary-weft-patterned
shawl.

TRADITIONAL GARMENT PATTERNS

An arrow inside the pattern indicates warp direction
in handwoven cloth.
Folding lines are represented by a dotted line, ...
stitching lines by a line of dashes. _ _ _ _ _ _ _

collar

4   2

Traditional crossover
tied blouse, *chaubandi
cholo*, worn by
women, with a
waistband and long
wrap-around cloth,
skirt or sari.
BM 1993 As 01.9.

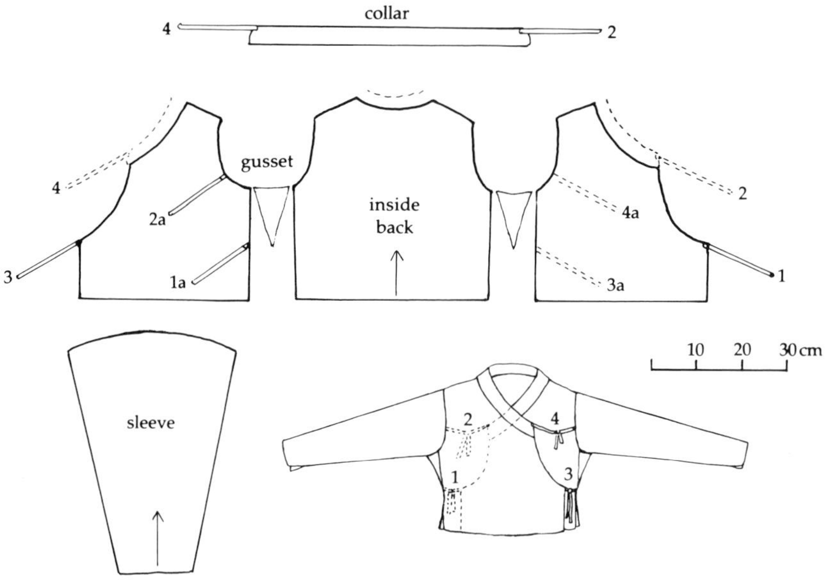

gusset

4

2a

3

1a

inside
back

4a

2

3a

1

10 20 30 cm

sleeve

2   4

1   3

A1   B1

back

C1

sleeve

C

Blouse or *shemjer* worn under the
coatdress shown opposite.
BM 1992 As 10.18.

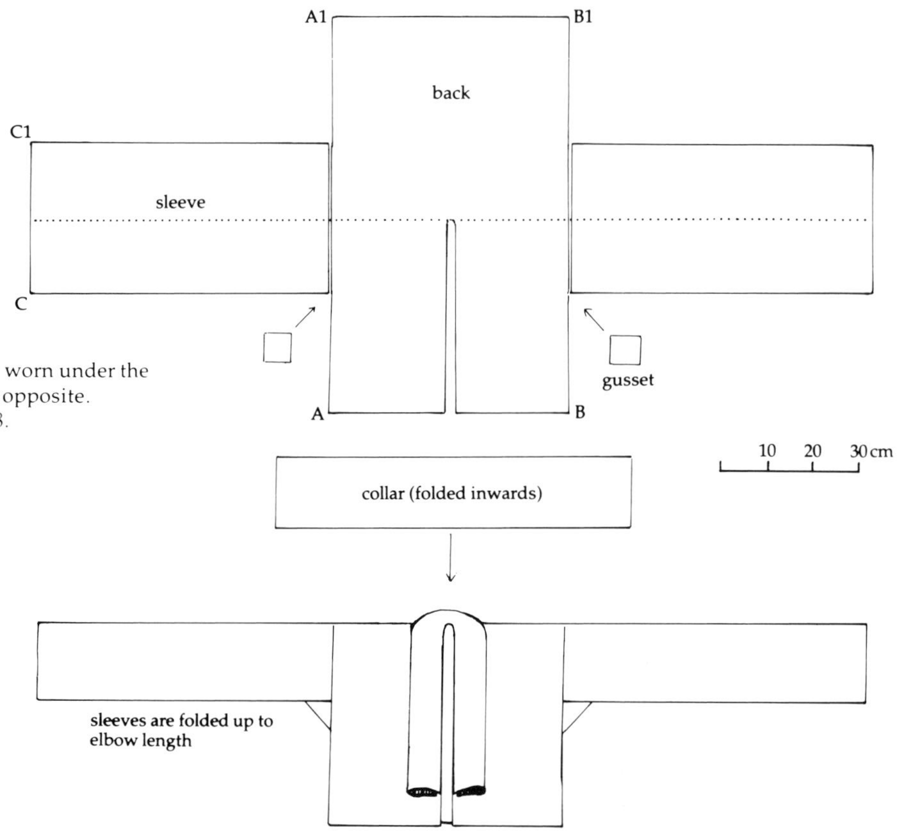

gusset

A   B

10 20 30 cm

collar (folded inwards)

sleeves are folded up to
elbow length

192

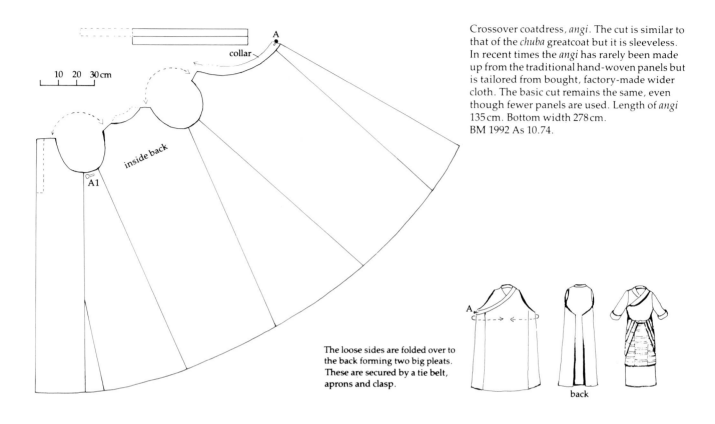

10 20 30 cm

collar

A

inside back

A1

Crossover coatdress, *angi*. The cut is similar to that of the *chuba* greatcoat but it is sleeveless. In recent times the *angi* has rarely been made up from the traditional hand-woven panels but is tailored from bought, factory-made wider cloth. The basic cut remains the same, even though fewer panels are used. Length of *angi* 135 cm. Bottom width 278 cm.
BM 1992 As 10.74.

The loose sides are folded over to the back forming two big pleats. These are secured by a tie belt, aprons and clasp.

A

back

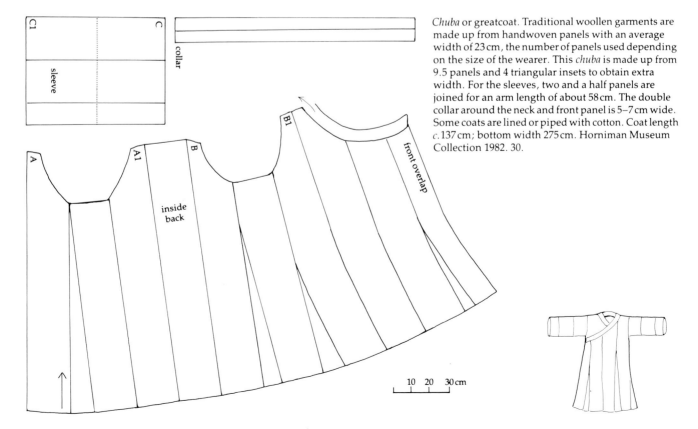

C1   C

sleeve

collar

A   A1   B   B1

front overlap

inside back

Chuba or greatcoat. Traditional woollen garments are made up from handwoven panels with an average width of 23 cm, the number of panels used depending on the size of the wearer. This *chuba* is made up from 9.5 panels and 4 triangular insets to obtain extra width. For the sleeves, two and a half panels are joined for an arm length of about 58 cm. The double collar around the neck and front panel is 5–7 cm wide. Some coats are lined or piped with cotton. Coat length *c*.137 cm; bottom width 275 cm. Horniman Museum Collection 1982. 30.

10 20 30 cm

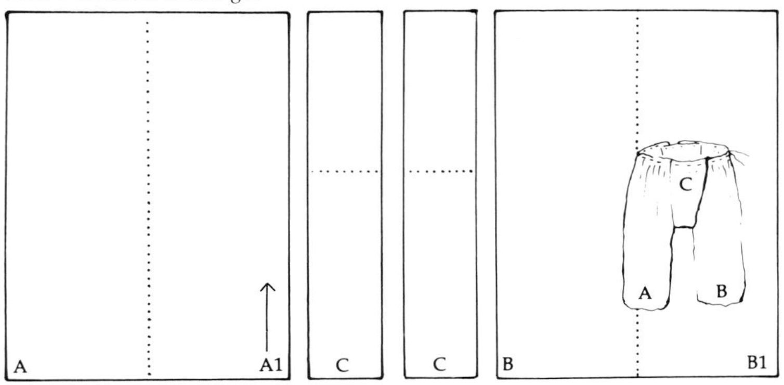

Sling bag or *renga*. The one in the British Museum (1992 As 10.77), is made up of four natural coloured cotton panels, 30.5 × *c.*120cm. of warp-faced plain weave, each with a narrow black and red stripe in the centre (1 black, 1 red warp thread alternately four times in succession). The panels are joined with a treble strand of black cotton by a figure-of-eight type looping round the selvage edges. The ends of the panels are folded over twice and hemstitched.

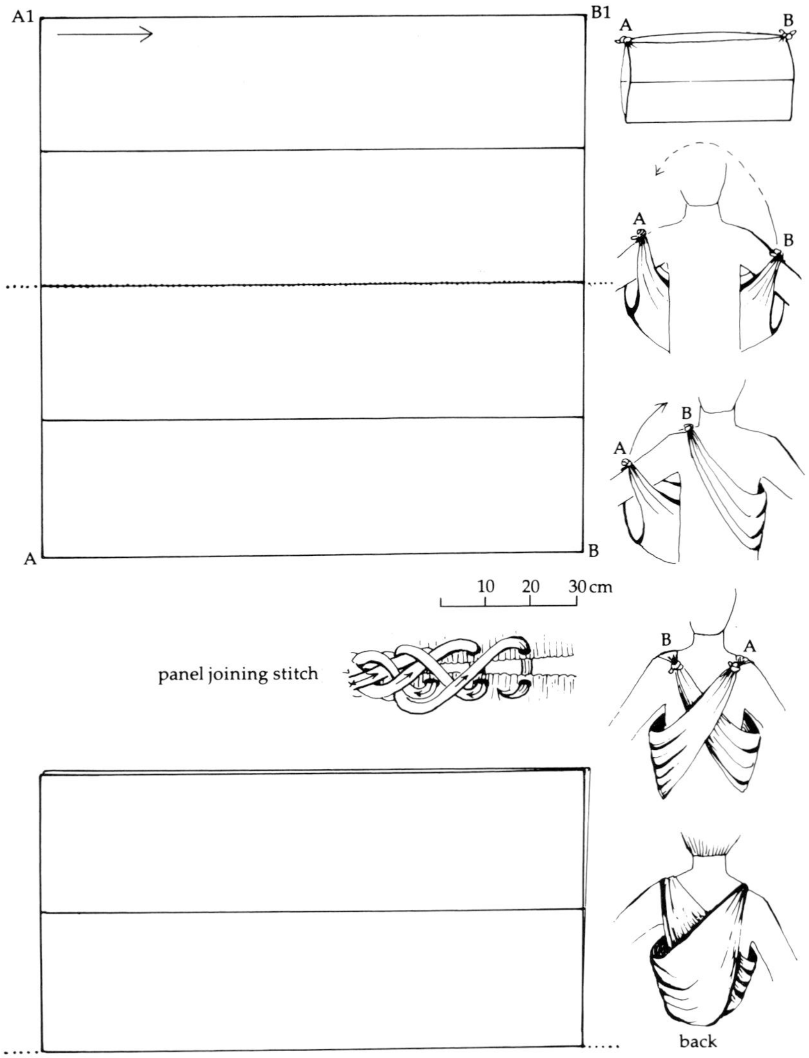

panel joining stitch

back

Women's trousers or *mo-gos*

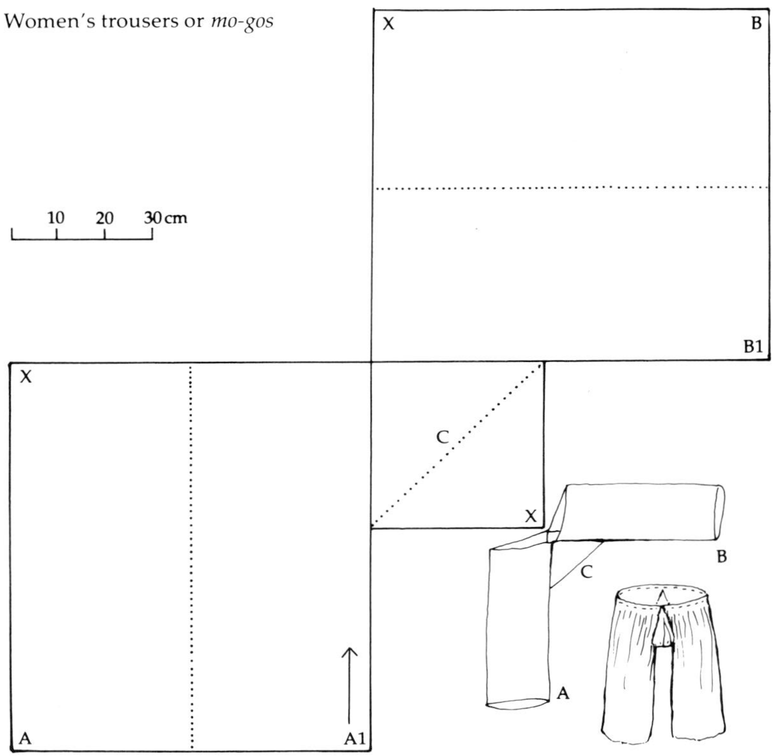

Men's trousers or *nan-gos*

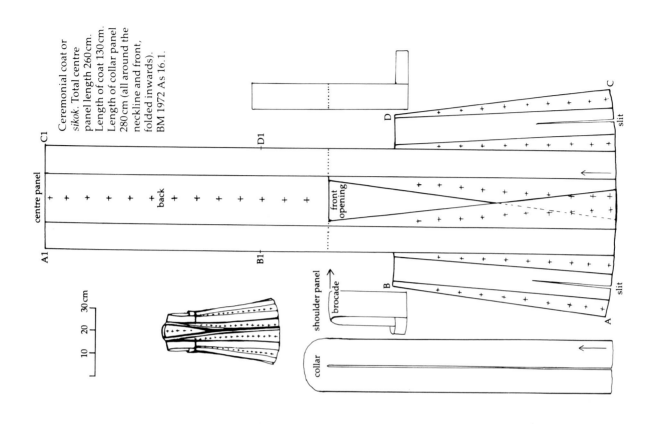

Ceremonial coat or *sikok*. Total centre panel length 260cm. Length of coat 130cm. Length of collar panel 280cm (all around the neckline and front, folded inwards). BM 1972 As 16.1.

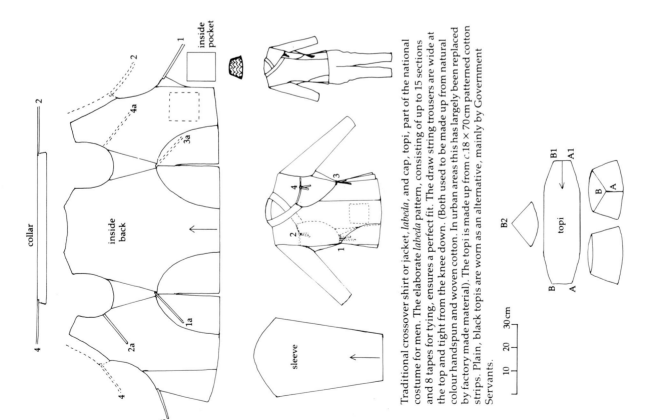

Traditional crossover shirt or jacket, *labeda*, and cap, topi, part of the national costume for men. The elaborate *labeda* pattern, consisting of up to 15 sections and 8 tapes for tying, ensures a perfect fit. The draw string trousers are wide at the top and tight from the knee down. (Both used to be made up from natural colour handspun and woven cotton. In urban areas this has largely been replaced by factory made cotton. The topi is made up from *c*.18 × 70cm patterned cotton strips. Plain, black topis are worn as an alternative, mainly by Government Servants.

A1 Vest or *stod-thun*

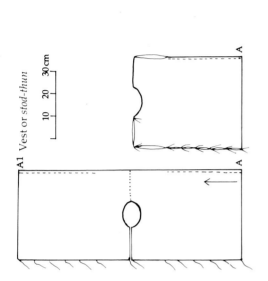

Sleeveless jacket or *lukuni*. The striped 2/2 twill *lukuni* in the British Museum (1992 As 18.5) has ten 2-ply warpends (2 brown, 2 white alternating and 8 brown at the selvage) and eight picks of white double strand (singles) per inch (2.5 cm). For the check border pattern the weaver changed from using white weft to alternating 5 brown, 5 white followed by 4 brown, 4 white.

inside pocket

back

Nettle jacket, *phenga*
BM 1992 As 01.2.

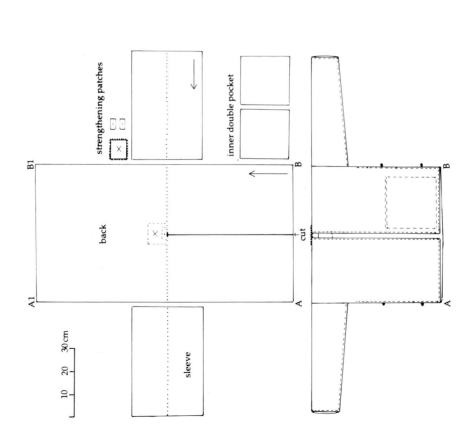

strengthening patches

back

inner double pocket

sleeve

B1

B

A1

A

cut

BIBLIOGRAPHY

ACHARYA, B. (1977) 'A brief account of ancient and medieval Nepal', in Malla, K. P. (ed.) q.v., 8–13

AMATYA, SAPHALYA (1991) Art and culture of Nepal. An attempt towards preservation, Nirala series 12, New Delhi, Nirala Publications

ANDERSON, MARY M. (1971) The festivals of Nepal, London, George Allen & Unwin

ARAN, LYDIA (1978) The art of Nepal, Kathmandu, Sahayogi Prakashan

ATTENBOROUGH, DAVID (1984) The living planet. A portrait of the earth, London, Collins & BBC

BAINES, P. (1977) Spinning wheels: spinners and spinning, London, Batsford

BALLY, W. (1955a) 'The role of jute and its substitutes in world markets', CIBA Review 108, 3886–90

BALLY, W. (1955b) 'Jute growing and fibre extraction', CIBA Review 108, 3892–900

BANERJEE, N. R. (1968) 'Parvati's penance as revealed by the eloquent stones of Nepal', Ancient Nepal 2, 27–34, Kathmandu, HM Government of Nepal

BANERJEE, N. R. (1980) Nepalese architecture, Delhi, Agam Kala Prakashan

BANERJEE, N. R. and RIJAL, B. K. (1968) 'Three early sculptures in stone from the National Museum, Kathmandu', Ancient Nepal 4, 37–43, Kathmandu, HM Government of Nepal

BANGDEL, LAIN S. (1989) Stolen images of Nepal, Kathmandu, Royal Nepal Academy

BARTHOLOMEW, MARK (1985) Thunder dragon textiles from Bhutan: Bartholomew Collection, Kyoto, Japan, Shikokosha

BEAL, S. (Trans.) (1906) Si-Yu-Ki Buddhist records of the western world. Translated from the Chinese of Hiuen Tsiang (629 AD), two vols, London, Kegan Paul, Trench, Trubner

BENDALL, CECIL (1883) Catalogue of the Buddhist Sanskrit manuscripts in the University Library, Cambridge, Cambridge University Press

BENDALL, L. C. (1903) 'A history of Nepal and surrounding kingdoms', Journal of the Royal Asiatic Society of Bengal, Calcutta, LXIII, 1–32

BERRY, M. J., LAURENCE, J. F., MAKIN, M. J. and WADDAMS, A. E. (1974) Development potential of the Nawalparasi area of Nepal, Land Resource Study 17, Surbiton (UK): Land Resources Division, Overseas Development Administration

BHATT, DIBYA DEO (1977) Natural history and economic botany of Nepal, second ed., New Delhi, Orient Longman

BHATTARAYA, C. (1962) 'Cultural Heritage' in Nepal. Monograph on Nepalese Culture, 37–46, Kathmandu, HM Government of Nepal, Ministry of Education

BISHOP, LILA M. and BARRY C. (1971) 'Karnali. Roadless world of western Nepal', National Geographic 140, 5, 656–89.

BISTA, D. B. (1980) People of Nepal, fourth ed., Kathmandu, Ratna Pustak Bhandar

BOECK, K. (1891) 'Himalayische Wanderungen. Zeitschrift des Deutschen und Östreichischen Alpenverein', Band XXII, Vienna

BOECK, K. (1903) Durch Indien ins verschlossene Land Nepal, Leipzig, Ferdinand Hirt & Sohn, 253

BRAUEN, MARTIN (ed.) (1984) 'Nepal. Leben und überleben', Ethnologische Schriften Zürich ESZ 2, Zürich, Völkerkundemuseum der Universität Zürich

BROUDY, ERIC (1979) The book of looms. A history of the handloom from ancient times to the present, London, Studio Vista

BROWN, PERCY (1912) Picturesque Nepal, London, Adam & Charles Black; reprinted 1971 New Delhi, Today and Tomorrow Printers

BURBAGE, M. B. (1982) Report on a visit to Nepal: the medicinal plant trade in the KHARDEP area – a study of the development potential, London, Tropical Products Institute, Overseas Development Administration, report R103(A)

BURNHAM, DOROTHY K. (1981) A textile terminology. Warp & weft, London, Routledge & Kegan Paul

BURT, B. (1977) Weaving, London, British Museum Publications

BYROM, P. C. (1980) KHARDEP Cottage Industries Programme (Textiles). Consultant's report to the Overseas Development Administration, London

CAHLANDER, A., ZORNE E., and ROWE, A. (1980) 'Sling braiding of the Andes', Weaver's Journal Monograph IV, Boulder, Colorado, Colorado Fiber Center

CAMPBELL, A. (1836) 'Notes on the state of the arts of cotton spinning, weaving, printing and dyeing in Nepal', Journal of the Asiatic Society of Bengal, vol. 5, 219–27

CAMPBELL, A. (1840a) 'Note on the Lepchas of Sikkim, with a vocabulary of their language', Journal of the Asiatic Society of Bengal, vol. 9, no. 100, 379–93

CAMPBELL, A. (1840b) 'A note on the Limboos and other Hill Tribes hitherto undescribed, Journal of the Asiatic Society of Bengal, vol. 9, part 1, no. 102, 595–615

CAPLAN, LIONEL (1970) Land and social change in East Nepal. A study of Hindu-tribal relations, London, Routledge & Kegan Paul

CAPLAN, L. (1974) 'A Himalayan people: Limbus of Nepal', in Maloney, Clarence (ed.), q.v., 173–201

CARSON, B. R. (1990) Proposed agro-ecological classification for Nepal and its significance to the horticultural master plan formulation, Kathmandu, Master Plan for Horticulture Development Working Paper 1

CBS (1988) Statistical Pocket Book Nepal 1988, Kathmandu, Central Bureau of Statistics

CHANDRA, MOTI (1950) 'A painted scroll from Nepal', MARG IV, I, 42–49, Bombay

CHANG, G. C. C. (trans.) (1962) The hundred thousand songs of Mila Repa, New York, University Books, 1977 Boulder edition

CHATERJI, SUNITI KUMAR (1951) 'Kirata-jana-Kriti' Journal of the Asiatic Society of Bengal, XVI, 2, 143–233

CHATTOPADHYAY, K. P. (1923) 'An essay on the history of Newar culture', Journal & Proceedings of the Asiatic Society of Bengal, New Series XIX, 10, 465–500, republished in 1980 by Educational Enterprise Pvt Ltd, Kathmandu

CHEMJONG, IMAN SINGH (1967) History and culture of the Kirat people, (two parts), Phidim, Nepal, Tumeng Hang

CHOEGYAL, L. (ed.) (1991) Nepal. Insight Guides, Hong Kong, APA Publications (HK) Ltd

CLARK, JANE (1992) Personal communication, Natural Resources Institute, Chatham Maritime, Kent, England

CLARKE, G. E. (1980) 'A Helambu history', Journal of the Nepal Research Centre, vol. 4 (Humanities), 1–38, Kathmandu, Nepal Research Centre; Wiesbaden, Kommissionsverlag F. Steiner

COLEMAN, C. (1832) The mythology of the Hindus, London, Parbury, Allen

COLLINGWOOD, PETER (1982) The techniques of tablet weaving, London, Faber & Faber

COLLINGWOOD, PETER (1987) Textile and weaving structures, London, Batsford

COOK, J. GORDON (1984) Handbook of textile fibres, 1. Natural fibres, fifth edition, Shildon (UK), Merrow Publishing

COUSIN, FRANCOISE (1974) 'Impressies de tissus au Népal', Mémorie du Musée de l'Homme, Department de Technologie no. 11, Paris

CRILL, ROSEMARY (1989) 'A new chronology about a rare group of Nepalese embroidery', HALI, Issue 44, Volume 2, Number 2, New York, HALI Publications Ltd

DAHAL, DEV MANI (coordinator) (1980) Survey report on home-made jute mats, Biratnagar (Nepal), Jute Development & Trading Corporation

DAS, SARAT CHANDRA (1902) Journey to Lhasa and Central Tibet, London, John Murray

DENWOOD, P. (1978) The Tibetan carpet, Warminster, England, Aris & Phillips, 1974, reprinted 1978

DESIDERI, FATHER IPPOLITO see Fillipi, Fillipo de (ed.)

DOHERTY, VICTOR S. (1978) 'Notes on the origins of the Newars of the Kathmandu valley of Nepal', pages 433–45 in Fisher, J. F. (ed.) q.v.

DONNER, W. (1974) Nepal: Raum, Mensch und Wirtschaft, Institut für Asienkunde in Hamburg, Schriften Bd. 32, Wiesbaden, Harrassowitz

DUNSMORE, J. R. (1988) Mountain environmental management in the Arun river basin of Nepal, Kathmandu: International Centre for Integrated Mountain Development Occasional Paper no. 9

DUNSMORE, SUSI (1981) Weaving in Nepal: dhaka topi cloth, reprinted 1983 by British Museum Publications/Overseas Development Administration, second edition 1990, Chatham, Natural Resources Institute

DUNSMORE, SUSI (1985) The nettle in Nepal: a cottage industry, London, Overseas Development Administration

DUTT, ROMESCH C. (1910) *The Mahabharatha, The Ramayana*, condensed into English verse, London, Dent, reprinted 1969

EMERY, IRENE (1966) *The primary structures of fabrics: an illustrated classification*, Washington DC, The Textile Museum

EMERY, I. and FISKE P., (eds.) (1979) *Looms and their products*, Emery Round Table on Museum Textiles 1977, Washington, The Textile Museum

EPHRAIM, H. (1905) 'Über die Entwicklung der Webetechnik', *Mitteilungen aus dem Staatlichen Museum für Völkerkunde*, Band 1, Heft 1, Leipzig

FAIRSERVIS, W. A. (1971) *Costumes of the East*, New York, American Museum of Natural History, Chatham Collection

FILLIPI, FILLIPO DE (ed.) (1937) *An account of Tibet. The travels of Ippolito Desideri of Pistoia 1712–1727*, revised edition, London, G. Routledge

FISHER, J. F. (ed.) (1978) *Himalayan Anthropology: the Indo-Tibetan interface*, The Hague, Mouton Publishing Co.

FISHER, JAMES F. (1986) *Trans-Himalayan traders. Economy, society and culture in north-west Nepal*, Berkeley, University of California Press

FORBES WATSON, J. (1866) See Watson, John Forbes

FRENCH, J. C. (1931) *Himalayan Art*, London, Oxford University Press/Humphrey Milford

FÜRER-HAIMENDORF, C. von (1956) 'Ethnographic notes on the Tamangs of Nepal', *Eastern Anthropologist* IX, 3–4, 166–77

FÜRER-HAIMENDORF, C. von (1964) *The Sherpas of Nepal, Buddhist Highlanders*, London, John Murray

FÜRER-HAIMENDORF, C. von (1966) 'Unity and diversity in the Chetri caste of Nepal', in Fürer-Haimendorf, C. von (ed.) *Caste and kin in Nepal, India and Ceylon*, London; Asia Publishing House

FÜRER-HAIMENDORF, C. von (ed.) (1974a) *The anthropology of Nepal*, proceedings of a symposium held at the School of Oriental and African Studies, University of London, Warminster, Aris & Philips

FÜRER-HAIMENDORF, C. von (1974b) 'The changing fortunes of Nepal's high altitude dwellers' in Fürer-Haimendorf, C. von (ed.) (1974) q.v., 98–113

FÜRER-HAIMENDORF, C. von (1975) *Himalayan traders: life in Highland Nepal*, London, John Murray

FÜRER-HAIMENDORF, C. von, SCHNEIDER, E., HAGEN, T. and DYRENFURTH, G. O. (1963) *The Sherpas of the Khumbu region*, Oxford, Oxford University Press

GAJUREL, C. L. and VAIDYA, K. K. (1984) *Traditional arts and crafts in Nepal*, New Delhi, S Chand & Co

GALAY, VICTOR J. (1989) *Erosion and sedimentation in the Nepal Himalaya*, Kathmandu, HM Government of Nepal, Ministry of Water Resources

GEIJER, AGNES (1982) *A history of textile art. A selective account*, reprint with corrections, first edition 1979, London, Pasold Research Fund in association with Sotheby Parke Bernet and Philip Wilson Publishers

GERARD, J. (1633) *The Herbal or general history of plants*, the complete 1633 edition as revised and enlarged by Thomas Johnson (1975), New York, Dover Publications

GIBBON, D, JOSHI, Y. R. K. C., SHARAN, KUMAR,

SCHULTZ, M. THAPA, M. B. and UPADHAY, M. P. (1988) *A study of the agricultural potential of Chheskam Panchayat*, Pakhribas Agricultural Centre (East Nepal) Technical Paper no. 95

GILLOW, J. and BARNARD, N. (1991) *Traditional Indian Textiles*, London, Thames and Hudson

GOLD, P. (1988) *Tibetan pilgrimage*, New York, Snow Lion Publications

GUISEPPI, FATHER (1807) 'The kingdom of Nepal', London, *Asiatic Researches Volume 11*, 307–22

GURUNG, G. V. (1988) *Cottage industries consultancy: feasibility survey report*, Kathmandu, report to GTZ (German Technical Cooperation)

GURUNG, HARKA B. (1965) *Pokhara valley, Nepal Himalaya*, unpublished Ph.D. thesis, Edinburgh University

GURUNG, HARKA B. (1980) *Vignettes of Nepal*, Kathmandu, Sajha Prakasan

GUY, JOHN (1992) 'New evidence of the Jagannatha cult in 17th century Nepal', *Journal of Royal Asiatic Society*, 2, Part 2, 213–30

HAGEN, T. (1980) *Nepal*. Translation by Britta M. Charleston, New Delhi, Oxford & IBH Publishing Co.

HAMILTON, FRANCIS BUCHANAN (1819) *An account of the Kingdom of Nepal and of the territories annexed to this dominion by the House of Gorkha*, Edinburgh, reprinted 1986, New Delhi, Asian Educational Service

HANSEN, H. H. (1950) *Mongol costumes*, Copenhagen, Gyidendalske Bochandel

HARDINGHAM, MARTIN (1978) *Illustrated dictionary of fabrics*, London, Studio Vista, Cassell & Collier Macmillan

HECHT, A. (1989) *The art of the loom*, London, British Museum Publications

HEUBERGER, H. (1956) 'Der weg zum Tscho Oyo. Kulture geographische Beobachtungen in Ost Nepal. Deutsche Forschung in Nepal.' *Mitteilungen der geographischen Gesellschaft*, vol. 11

HIUEN-TSIANG (629) in Beal, S. (trans.) (1906) q.v.

HODGSON, B. H. (1830–45) Unpublished papers, London, British Library, Oriental and India Office Collections

HODGSON, B. H. (1835) 'Account of a visit to the ruins of Simroun, once the capital of Mithila', *Journal of the Asiatic Society of Bengal*, Vol. IV, no. 39, 121–3

HODGSON, B. H. (1840) 'Nagakote, a cursory notice of', *Journal of the Asiatic Society of Bengal*, Vol. 9, Part 2, 1120–21

HODGSON, B. H. (1848) 'Route from Kathmandu, the capital of Nepal', *Journal of the Asiatic Society of Bengal*, Vol. 17, Part II, 634–46

HODGSON, B. H. (1857) 'Papers relative to the colonization, commerce, physical geography &c., &c. of the Himalaya mountains and Nepal', Numbers I – XI, of *Selections from the Records of the Government of Bengal* no. XXVII, Calcutta, John Gray, Calcutta Gazette Office

HODGSON, B. H. (1858) 'On the Kiranti tribe of the Central Himalaya', *Journal of the Asiatic Society of Bengal*, Vol. XXVII, no. 5, 446–56

HODGSON, B. H. (1874) *Essays on the languages, literature and religion of Nepal and Tibet, together with further papers on the geography, ethnography and commerce of those countries*, London, Trubner & Co. (reprinted New Delhi 1972 in series II of *Bibliotheca Himalayica*)

HODGSON, B. H. (1800) 'On the Kocch, Bodo and

Dhimal tribes', *Miscellaneous essays relating to Indian subjects*, Vol. 1, Section 1, Part 111, London

HOOKER, J. B. (1854) *Himalayan Journals*, London, Ward Lock (reprinted 1954, Murray)

HOOPER, LUTHER (undated) *Silk: its production and manufacture*, London, Sir Isaac Pitman and Sons Ltd

HORNE, C. (1877) 'Paper making in the Himalayas', *Indian Antiquary* Vol. 6

INNES, R. A. (1959) *Non-European looms in the collections at Bankfield Museum, Halifax*, Halifax, England, Halifax Museums

IRVIN, J. (1955) *Shawls*, London, Victoria and Albert Museum

JACKSON, J. K. (1987) *Manual of afforestation in Nepal*, Kathmandu, Department of Forestry

JEST, C. (1974) *Tarap, une vallée dans l'Himalaya*, Paris, Éditions du Seuil

JEST, C. (1975) *Dolpo. Communautés de langue Tibétaine du Népal*, Paris, Centre National de la Recherche Scientifique

JEST, C. (1984) 'Die Dolpo-pa' in Brauen, Martin (ed.) q.v.

JEST, C. (1989) *Mountain environmental management in the Trans-Himalayan region*, Kathmandu, International Centre for Integrated Mountain Development

KESARLAL (1969) 'The Tamangs', *Nepal Review*, Vol. 1, no. 3, 39–43

KHANDALAVALA, K. (1950) 'Notes on a Nepalese manuscript miniature', Bombay, *MARG*, IV, 1, 53–6

KIHARA, H. (ed.) (1957) *Peoples of Nepal Himalaya. Scientific results of the Japanese expeditions to Nepal Himalaya 1952–1953*, Vol. III, Kyoto, Fauna and Flora Research Society, Kyoto University

KING, W. A. (1958) *Warp and Weft from Tibet*, Oregon, Robin and Russ Handweavers (fourth printing 1974)

KIRKPATRICK, COLONEL (1811) *An account of the Kingdom of Nepaul*, London, Wm Miller

KOLANDER, CHERYL (1979) *A silkworker's notebook*, Myrtle Creek, Oregon, Cheryl Kolander

KRAMRISCH, S. (1933) 'Nepalese painting', *Journal of the Indian Society of Oriental Art*, Vol. 1, no. 2, 129–47

KRAMRISCH, S. (1964) *Art of Nepal*, catalogue of an exhibition, Vienna, Asia House Gallery

LANDON, P. (1928) *Nepal*, two vols, London, Constable

LANDOR, H. S. (1905) *Tibet and Nepal*, London, A & C Black

LAVIZZARI-RAEUBER, Alexandra (1984) *Thangkas. Rollbilder aus dem Himalaya. Kunst und mystiche Bedeutung*, Cologne, DuMont Buchverlag

LEONARD, R. G. (1965) *Nepal and the Gurkhas*, London, HMSO

LÉVI, SYLVAIN (1905/1908) *Le Népal. Étude historique d'un Royaume Hindou*, Paris, Ministère de l'instruction publique, Annales du Musée Guimet, Bibliothèque d'études

LIPTON, MIMI (ed.) (1988) *The tiger rugs of Tibet*, London, Hayward Gallery

LOBSIGER-DELLENBACH, M. (1954) *Népal. Catalogue de la collection d'ethnographie Népalaise du Musée d'Ethnographie de la Ville de Genève*

LOSTY, J. P. (1982) *The art of the book in India*, London, British Library Reference Division Publications

MACDONALD, A. W. (1975) 'Essays on the

ethnology of Nepal and South Asia', *Bibliotheca Himalayica Series 3*, vol. 3, Kathmandu, Ratna Pustak Bhandar

MACDONALD, A. W. and STAHL, A. V. (1979) *Newar Art*, Warminster, Aris and Phillips

McDONAUGH, CHRISTIAN (1984) 'Die Tharu' in Brauen, Martin (ed.) q.v., 99–126

McDOUGAL, CHARLES (1979) 'The Kulunge Rai', *Bibliotheca Himalayica Series 3*, vol. 14, Kathmandu, Ratna Pustak Bhandar

MACFARLANE, ALAN (1976) *Resources and population. A study of the Gurungs of Nepal*, Cambridge, Cambridge University Press

MACFARLANE, ALAN and GURUNG, INDRABAHADUR (1900) *Gurungs of Nepal (A guide to the Gurungs)*, Kathmandu, Ratna Pustak Bhandar

MAJUPURIA, T. C. (ed.) (1984–85) *Nepal: Nature's paradise*, Bangkok, White Lotus Co.

MALONEY, C. (ed.) (1974) *South Asia: seven community profiles*, New York, Holt, Rinehart & Winston Inc.

MALLA, K. P. (ed.) (1977) *Nepal. A conspectus*, Kathmandu, HM Government Press

MANANDHAR, N. P. (1980) *Medicinal plants of Nepali Himalaya*, Kathmandu, Ratna Pustak Bhandar

MANANDHAR, N. P. (1989) *Useful wild plants of Nepal*, Stuttgart, Franz Steiner Verlag Wiesbaden GMBH

MARKHAM, C. R. (1876) *Narrative of the mission of George Bogle to Tibet*, London, Trubner

MESSERSCHMIDT, DONALD A. (1976) *The Gurungs of Nepal. Conflict and change in a village society*, Warminster, Aris and Phillips

MESSERSCHMIDT, DONALD A. (1984) *Die Gurung* in Brauen, Martin (ed.) q.v., 127–45

MIEROW, DOROTHY and SHRESTHA, TIRTHA BAHADUR (1978) *Himalayan flowers and trees*, Kathmandu, Sahayogi Press

MOHANTY, B. C. (1987) *Natural dyeing processes in India*, Ahmedabad, Calico Museum of Textiles

MOORCROFT, W. (1820) Unpublished letter, London, British Library Oriental & India Office Collections MSS Eur F38/-G30/45

MOORCROFT, W. and TREBECK, G. (1841) *Travels in the Himalayan Provinces of Hindustan and the Punjab from 1819–1825*, reprinted 1979, Karachi, Oxford University Press

MULLER, CLAUDIUS C. and RAUNIG, WALTER (1982) *Der Weg zum Dach der Welt*, Innsbruck, Pinguin-Verlag; Frankfurt/Main, Umschau-Verlag

NEPALI, G. S. (1965) *The Newars*, Bombay, United Asia Publications

NEPALI, ROHIT KUMAR and SANGAM, KHAGENDRA (1990) *Status of community needs, resources and development: Sankhuwasabha District*, Kathmandu, Makalu-Barun Conservation Project Working Party Publication Series Report No. 7

NEUMANN, K. F. (1864) 'Ostasien und West Amerika nach Chinesischen Quellen', Berlin, *Zeitschrift für Allgemeine Erdkunde*, Vol. XVI, 305–30

OLDFIELD, HENRY AMBROSE (1880) *Sketches from Nipal, historical and descriptive with anecdotes of the court life and wild sports of the country in the time of Maharaja Jang Bahadur GCB*, two vols, London, W. H. Allen & Co.

OLDFIELD, H. A. and OLDFIELD, M. A. (1975) *Views of Nepal 1851–1864. (Presented to HM Birendra Bir Bikram Shah on the auspicious occasion of his Coronation by Cecilia & Hallvard Kuloy)*, Kathmandu, Tribhuvan University Press

OLI, KRISHNA B. and MOREL, A. M. (1985) 'Livestock production in the eastern hills of Nepal', in Morel, A. M. and Oli, K B. (eds) *Livestock in the hills of Nepal. Proceedings of the first seminar on livestock in the hills of Nepal*, Pakhribas Agricultural Centre, Dhankuta, Nepal

OLSCHAK, B. C., GANSSER, A., GRUSCHKE, A. and BUHRER, E. M. (1987) *Himalayas*, Fact on File Publications, New York, Oxford University Press

PAL, P. (1964) *The Art of Nepal*, New York, The Asia Society

PAL, P. (1965) 'Notes on five sculptures from Nepal', *British Museum Quarterly* XXIX, 1–2

PAL, P. (1967) *The Buddhist paintings from Nepal*, Amsterdam, Museum of Asiatic Art

PAL, P. (1968) 'The Uma Mahesvara theme in Nepali sculpture', *Bulletin of the Museum of Fine Arts*, Boston, LXVI, 345, 85–100

PAL, P. (1974a) *The Arts of Nepal*, Vol. 1, *Sculpture*, Leiden, E. J. Brill

PAL, P. (1974b) *Buddhist art in Licchavi Nepal*, Bombay, Marg Publications

PAL, P. (1975) *Nepal: where the Gods are young*, New York, Asia Society

PAL, P. (1978) *The Arts of Nepal*, Vol. 2, *Painting*, Leiden, E. J. Brill

PAL, P. (1985a) *Vaisnava iconology in Nepal*, Calcutta, The Asiatic Society

PAL, P. (1985b) *Art of Nepal: a catalogue of the Los Angeles County Museum of Art Collections*, Los Angeles, County Museum of Art in association with University of California Press

PAL, P. and BHATTACHARYYA, S. D. C. (1969) *The Astral divinities of Nepal*, Varanasi, India, Prithvi Prakashan

PETECH, L. (1958) *Mediaeval history of Nepal*, Rome, Instituto Italiano por il media ed estremo oriente

PICTON, JOHN and MACK, JOHN (1989) *African textiles*, second edition, London, British Museum Publications

PIGNEDE, B. (1966) *Les Gurungs*, Paris, Mouton

POKHAREL, R. K. (1989) *Allo in Sankhuwasabha: an appraisal report*, Khandbari, East Nepal Sankhuwasabha District Forestry Office (manuscript)

PRUSCHA, C. (Coordinator) (1975) *Kathmandu valley: the preservation of physical environment and cultural heritage. A protective inventory*. Prepared by HM Government of Nepal in collaboration with the United Nations and the United Nations Educational, Scientific and Cultural Organisation (UNESCO), Vienna, Anton Schroll

RAKESH, RAM DAYAL (1990) *Folk culture of Nepal. An analytical study*, Nirala series 6, New Delhi, Nirala Publications

RAMY, ALEXANDER and BHATTARAI, TARA DEV (1956) *Report on small village industry*, Kathmandu, Ford Foundation

RAY, AMITA (1973) *Art of Nepal*, Delhi, I.C.C.R.

READ, C. H. (1910) *Handbook to the Ethnographic Collection of the British Museum*, London, British Museum

REGMI, D. R. (1965, Part 1, 1966, Part 2) *Medieval Nepal*, four vols, Calcutta, Mukhopadhyay

REGMI, D. R. (1969) *Ancient Nepal*, third edition, Calcutta, Mukhopadhyay

REGMI, PUSKAL P. (1984–85) 'Fibre yielding plants', in Majupuria, T. C. (1984–85) q.v.

RENSBURG, L. van (1987) *The nettle and the Rai: a study of one survival strategy in the eastern hills of Nepal*, BA Hons dissertation, West Surrey College of Art and Design, England

RICCARDI, T. (1975) 'Sylvain Levi', *The History of Nepal*, Part 1, Kathmandu, Kailash 3, 5–66

RONGE, VERONIKA (1978) 'Tibetische Brettchenweberei' in *Zentralasiatische Studien: des Seminars für Sprach-und Kulturwissenschaft Zentralasiens der Universität Bonn 12*, Wiesbaden, Otto Harrassowitz

ROTH, H. LING (1977) *Studies in primitive looms*, Bedford, Ruth Bean. (Reprinted from the original Bankfield Museum Notes, Halifax, England 1950 edition.)

SANWAL, B. D. (1947–48) 'The people of Nepal', *Eastern Anthropologist*, vol. 1, no. 1, 1–7

SASTRI, B. N. (ed.) (1956) *The Wealth of India*, New Delhi, Council of Scientific and Industrial Research

SCHAEFER, G. (1938) 'The principle of the loom', Basle, *Ciba Review* 16, 542–5

SCHAEFER, G. (1941) 'The cultivation of madder', Basle, *Ciba Review* 39, 1398–1406

SCHAEFER, G. (1945) 'Hemp', Basle, *Ciba Review* 49, 1779–88

SCHMIDT-THOME, MARLIS and TSERING, T. THINGO (1975) 'Materielle Kultur und Kunst der Sherpa' in Funke, F. W. (ed.) *Materielle Kultur und Kunst*, Innsbruck, Universitäts Verlag Wagner

SEAGROT, M. (1975) *A basic textile book*, London, Herbert Press

SEDDON, D., BLAIKIE, P. M. and CAMERON, J. (1979) *Peasants and workers in Nepal*, New Delhi, Vikas Publishing House

SEELAND, KLAUS T. (1980) 'The use of bamboo in a Rai village in the Upper Arun Valley – an example of a traditional technology', *Journal of the Nepal Research Centre*, Vol. 4, 175–87, Kathmandu, Nepal Research Centre/ Wiesbaden, Kommissionsverlag Franz Steiner

SEILER-BALDINGER, ANNEMARIE (1991) 'Systematik der Textilen Techniken. Ethnologisches Seminar der Universität und Museum für Völkerkunde, *Basler Beiträge zur Ethnologie Band 32*, Basel, Wepf & Co.

SEN, K. M. (1961) *Hinduism*, London, Penguin Books

SHAH, R. K. (1991) *Biomechanical effects of the Nepalese patuka on lumbosacral spine: a pilot study*, thesis for MCh (Orth) degree, University of Liverpool, UK

SHAHA, RISHIKESH (1992) *Ancient and medieval Nepal*, New Delhi, Manohar Publications

SHAMASASTRY, R. (trans.) (1908) *Kautilya's Chamkyas's Arthasastra (the science of politics)*, Mysore, The G.T.A. Press

SHARMA, PRAYAG RAJ (1972) *Preliminary study of the art and architecture of the Karnali Basin. West Nepal*, Paris, Centre National de la Recherche Scientifique

SHRESTHA, BOM PRASAD (1989) *Forest Plants of Nepal*, Kathmandu, Educational Enterprise Pvt Ltd

SHRESTHA, T. B. (1989) *Development ecology of the*

Arun river basin in Nepal, Kathmandu, International Centre for Integrated Mountain Development

SHRESTHA, T. B. and CAMPBELL, J. G. (1990) Foreword to Nepali, R. K. and Sangam, K. (1990) q.v.

SILL, MICHAEL and KIRKBY, JOHN (1991) *The atlas of Nepal in the modern world*, London, Earthscan Publications Ltd in association with the ETC Foundation

SIMHA, TEEKA (1970) *The Royal wedding in Nepal*, Kathmandu, Mrs Teeka Simha

SINGH, M. (1968) *Himalayan Art*, UNESCO Art Book series, London, Macmillan

SINGH, S. C. and SHRESTHA, R. (1987) *Extraction and chemical analysis of Himalayan nettle fibre*, Kathmandu, (RECAST), Research and Industry 32

SLUSSER, M. (1972) 'Nepali sculptures' in Pal, P. (ed.) *Aspects of Indian art; papers presented in a symposium at the Los Angeles County Museum of Art, October 1970*, Leiden, E. J. Brill

SLUSSER, MARY SHEPHERD (1982) *Nepal Mandala: a cultural study of the Kathmandu valley*, two vols, New Jersey, Princeton University Press

SMITH, WILLIAM (1864) *Latin-English dictionary*, Second revised edition, London, John Murray

SNELLGROVE, D. (1957) *Buddhist Himalaya*, Oxford, Cassirer

SNELLGROVE, D. (1959) *The Hevajra Tantra: a critical study*. Part 1, London, Oxford University Press

SNELLGROVE, D. (1961) 'Shrines and temples of Nepal', *Arts Asiatiques* VIII (2)

SNELLGROVE, D. (1981) 'Himalayan Pilgrimage. A study of Tibetan religion by a traveller through western Nepal', Boston, *Shambala Publications Asiatiques* VIII (2)

SNELLGROVE, D. L. and RICHARDSON, H. E. (1968) *A cultural history of Tibet*, London, Weidenfeld & Nicholson

SPEISER, NOEMI (1983) *The manual of braiding*, Basel, Noemi Speiser

STILLER, L. F. (1980) *An introduction to the Hanuman Dhoka. Based on the Nepali text of Gautam Vajra Vajracharya. Second ed.'* Kathmandu, HM Government of Nepal Department of Information

STILLER, L. F. (1973) *The rise of the House of Gorkha: a study in the unification of Nepal 1768–1816*, The Patna Jesuit Society

STRAUB, M. (1977) *Handweaving and cloth design*, New York, Viking Press

THAPA, NETRA B. (1973) *A short history of Nepal*, Kathmandu, Ratna Pustak Bhandar

THOMSON, M., WARBURTON, M. and HARTLEY, T. (1986) *Uncertainty on a Himalayan scale*, London, Milton Ash Editors, Ethnographica

TOFFIN, GÉRARD (1977) 'Pyangaon. Une communauté Newar de la Vallée de Kathmandou. La vie matérielle', Paris, Centre National de la Recherche Scientifique, *Cahiers Népalais*

TOFFIN, GÉRARD (1984a) 'Die Newar im Kathmandu' in Brauen, Martin (ed.) q.v.

TOFFIN, GÉRARD (1984b) *Société et religion chez les Newar du Népal*, Paris, Centre National de la Recherche Scientifique

TUCCI, G. (1956a) *To Lhasa and beyond: diary of an expedition 1948*, Rome, Instituto Poligrafico dello Stato

TUCCI, G. (1956b) 'Preliminary report on two scientific expeditions in Nepal', Rome, *Serie Orientale Roma* XI

TUCCI, G. (1962) *Nepal. The discovery of the Malla*, translated from the Italian by Lovett Edwards, London, George Allen & Unwin

TUCCI, G. (1973) *Transhimalaya*, translated from the French by James Hogarth, London, Barrie & Jenkins

TURNER, R. L. (1931) *A comparative and etymological dictionary of the Nepali language*, London, Kegan Paul

TURNER, CAPTAIN SAMUEL (1800) *An account of an embassy to the Court of the Teshoo Lama in Tibet*, London, G. W. Nicol

UHLIG, HELMUT (1987) *Himalaya. Menschen und Kulturen in der Heimat des Schnees*, Bergisch Gladbach, Gustav Lübbe Verlag

VAIDYA, KARUNA KAR (1971) *Folk tales of Nepal* (First Series), second edition, Kathmandu, Ratna Pustak Bhandar

VEQUAND, YVES (1977) *The art of Mithila (Ceremonial paintings from an ancient kingdom)*, London, Thames & Hudson

WADDELL, L. A. (1899) *Among the Himalayas*, Westminster, Archibald Constable

WALDSCHMIDT, E. and R. L. (1967) *Nepal: art treasures from the Himalayas*, translated by D. Wilson, Calcutta, Oxford & IBH Publishing Co.

WARDLE, T. (1881) *Handbook of the collection illustrative of the wild silks of India in the Indian section of the South Kensington Museum*, London, HMSO

WATT, GEORGE (1890) *A dictionary of the economic products of India*, six vols, London, W. H. Allen

WATSON, JOHN FORBES (1866) *The textile manufactures and the costumes of the peoples of India*, London, India Office

WRIGHT, DANIEL (1877) *History of Nepal, with an introductory sketch of the country and people of Nepal*. Cambridge University Press. Reprinted New Delhi, 1990, Asian Educational Services

WULFF, H. (1974) *Textilkunst der Steppen und Bergvölker Zentralasiens*, Basel, Gewerbe Museum

ZWALF, W. (ed.) (1985) *Buddhism. Art and faith*, London, British Museum Press

GLOSSARY

Nepali words are rendered in the text as close as possible to their pronunciation. Diacritical marks have been added in the glossary where information in this complex field was available.

Allo or *hatti sisnu* (Rai): Himalyan Giant Nettle, *Girardinia diversifolia* Gurung: *Nangi.* Magar: *Pua.* Tamang: *Polo*

Angi (Sherpa): Sherpa wrap-over coat dress

Bana: Weft

Bhāng: Narcotic from leaves and flowering shoots of *Cannabis sativa*, hemp or ganja

Bhāngro: *Allo* or hemp sack-cloth. Also, *bhangria* (Hodgson 1874, 400) or *bhangara* (Campbell 1836, 225)

Bhoṭ: Tibet

Bhote or *Bhotiya*: people of Tibetan origin

Boku or *bokhu* (Gurung): Woollen hooded blanket or cover

Buṭṭā: Embroidery motif or weaving pattern. Floral motif

Carder: A pair of flat pieces of wood, 20 × 11.5 cm (Indian carder), with handles and with wire hooks set in, used to separate and align fibres

Chārā: Bird. In Nepalese weaving, a seesaw-type lifting device, usually in the shape of a bird, tied to heddle rods; in English, a heddle horse

Charkhā or *charka*: Hand-turned spinning wheel Newar: *Yaṅt, yeau* or *ya.* Rai: *Chhulang*

Chaubandi or *cholo*: Traditional, cross-over 4-tie woman's blouse

Chhipa or *chippah*: Newar dyer caste

Chitre: Plain weave in bamboo mat or woollen rug (rari). (For cotton cloth weaving the term sada is used)

Cholo: Blouse or bodice

Chuba or *Chu-pa* (Tibetan/Sherpa): Sherpa long-sleeved greatcoat

Chuk: Paste from lime juice, added as flavour to pickles and other food. Also used as mordant

Circular warp: A continuous warp used on back strap looms

Cross: The point at which the warp yarns are alternated around the posts during warping. The cross maintains the correct sequence of the warp yarns

Cross sticks: Sticks inserted in the warp to retain the cross

Dents: The spaces between the reed slats

Dharni: Measure of weight (2.4 kg)

Dhoko: Cone-shaped carrying basket

End: Single warp thread running through the length of the cloth

Felting: Interlocking or matting of fibres caused by a combination of heat, moisture and pressure or friction

Float weave: Weft or warp thread that stretches across two or more ends or picks between intersections

Fly shuttle: Shuttle set in motion mechanically

Ghùm: Bamboo rainshield

Ghùm rari: see *boku*

Gimte (Rai): Traditional diamond weaving pattern

Hāt: Periodic local market

Hāttibār: Sisal, *Agave* sp. (*hatti* meaning elephant, *bar* meaning fence)

Hātti sunr: Elephant trunk, motif in dhaka weaving

Heddle: Device for lifting warp threads (eye or loop made of strong thread through which each warp thread is passed in order to manipulate it)

Īnṭa: Stepped diamond shaped motif in dhaka weaving

Jamdani: Fine cotton pattern weaving from around Dhaka, Bangladesh, from 'Dacca Jamdane' meaning loom figured muslin (Watson 1866, 79)

Jhola: Traditional carrying bag

Jyapu: Newar farmer caste

Kachār: Dhoti or loin cloth. Possibly, towel or cotton blanket

Kamero māto: white micaceous clay soil *kamero* meaning white clay, *mato* meaning earth)

Kāmlo: Dolpo shawl/blanket

Kangiyo: Comb; in weaving, reed or beater

Kariog or *kuru* (Sherpa): Spike spindle Whorl spindle: Tibetan/Sherpa: *Phang.* Gurung (Manang): *Thong* For cotton: Newar: *Jorni* Rai: *Eng*

Keko or *kaykwo*: Hand-operated cotton gin

Kes or *khes* (Rai): Twill – diagonal patterned float weave. Newar: *Phumtu.* Tibetan: *Kha-ice*

Khādī: Handspun cotton cloth

Khamu or *Kharpan* (Newar): Newar basket carried in pairs with a yoke

Kharwa: Type of cotton cloth

Khri thags (Tibetan): Frame treadle loom (*khri* meaning seat, *thags* meaning loom)

Kiring (Rai): Small diamond or 'bird's eye' pattern Newar: *Punika* or *bhumika.* Limbu: *Parewa ankhi* (dove's eye)

Khukurī or *kukri*: Traditional Nepalese knife

Labedā: Men's traditional cross-over/ tied jacket/shirt. Part of the national costume

Lukuni (Gurung): Woollen, sleeveless jacket

Lungi (Hindi): Tubular, draped skirt

Maithili: descendants from Mithila, former kingdom, now part of Bihar and the *terai*; capital at Janakpur (from King Janak, father of Sita)

Mandala: Visual aid for concentration and meditation. (*Mandal* meaning circle)

Mandir: Temple, also motif in dhaka weaving

Mandre (Gurung): Twill in diagonally interlaced bamboo mat or woven woollen rug/rari. (For cotton cloth, the term *kes* is used)

Mandro: General term for rush or bamboo mat

Melā: Fair (for sale of goods)

Mo-gas (Dolpo): Woollen trousers for women

Mordant: A chemical substance that combines with the dye helping with the absorption of colour and to make it fast

Nambu: Tibetan/Sherpa 2/2 twill, weft-faced woollen cloth

Nāmlo: Porter's headband (Tump-line) or carrying strap

Nan-gos (Dolpo): Woollen trousers for men

Nena (Tamang): *Cannabis sativa*, hemp

Pachaura or *pachhyaura*: Shawl Newar: *Ga*

Pan-thags (Tibetan): Back-strap loom (Dolpo) (*pan* meaning breast, *thags* meaning loom)

Parbatiya: Hill or mountain people (*parbat* meaning mountain)

Patasi or *Parsi* (Newar): *Jyapu* (farmer) woman's wraparound skirt

Pati (Limbu): Wooden measure and device for heddle loops. Rai: *Pirsa* or *pelau*

Paṭuka or *padowa*: Cloth waistband

Phenga: Jacket made of allo (Rai) or hemp (Tamang)

Pick: Single weft thread woven across the width of the warp

Ply splitting or ply split darning: A method of connecting adjacent plied threads by darning a thread through their plies

Rāri or *rādi*: Woven, woollen blanket

Renga (Gurung): Carrying (cross) sling bag made from *allo* or cotton

Retting: Softening plant material by soaking, to facilitate fibre extraction

Rumāl: Covering cloth, handkerchief

Roller shuttle: Boat-shaped shuttle with two rollers set in below to allow swift passage of the shuttle through the shed

Sādā: A plain weave

S-and-Z-twist: Description of the direction of twist in a spun or plied thread, following the central part of one or the other letter

Selvage: The edge of the cloth where the weft turns around the last warp thread and back again after each pick

Shaft: A pair of sticks or a frame between which the heddles are suspended

Shemjer or *shamsha* (Sherpa): Sherpa silk or cotton blouse

Shyaku (Gurung): Gurung rainshield

Sikok: Sherpa woman's festive coat (for weddings).

Spindle: Tool for twisting fibres into a continuous thread Sherpa: *Phang*. Gurung (Manang): *Thong*. Newar: *Jorni*. Rai: *Eng*

Srog thur (Tibetan): 'Life post', in weaving, a warp lock stick

Stod-thun: (Dolpo) Vest

Stupa: Buddhist shrine

Sukul: Straw mat woven on a ground loom

Suruwāl: Nepalese trousers, part of the national costume for men

Swift: Skein or hank holder

Tān: Warp, also loom

Thaili: Nepalese draw-string purse

Thanka (Tibetan): Religious scroll

Thig ma (Tibetan): Tie-dye cross pattern

Tijang (Sherpa): Frame-treadle loom

Topi: Man's brimless cap

Tsö (Tibetan/Sherpa): Colour, also for madder (red dye). See *majitho*

Ultimate fibre: The single, indivisible unit, usually identifiable only under a microscope, of which plant fibres are composed. Quality depends particularly on length, width, strength and flexibility

Urtu or *urdo* (Tibetan/Sherpa): Sling

Vajra: Thunderbolt

Warp-faced weave/weft-faced weave: Weaving with a preponderance of warp over weft on the cloth face, and vice versa

Weft-twining: Twisting (two or more) weft strands around each other, enclosing a warp end between each half turn

INDEX